What is feminism?

Edited by

Juliet Mitchell & Ann Oakley

Basil Blackwell

This collection copyright © Juliet Mitchell and Ann Oakley 1986

First published 1986
Reprinted 1987, 1989

Basil Blackwell Ltd
108 Cowley Road, Oxford OX4 1JF, UK

British Library Cataloguing in Publication Data

What is feminism?
  1. Feminism
  I. Mitchell, Juliet   II. Oakley, Ann
  305.4'2   HQ1154

  ISBN 0–631–14841–6
  ISBN 0–631–14843–4 Pbk

Typeset in 10/11½ Plantin by Cambrian Typesetters, Frimley, Surrey
Printed in Great Britain by Billing and Sons Ltd, Worcester

Contents

The Contributors

Nancy F. Cott teaches US history and Women's Studies at Yale University, where she has been on the faculty since 1975. Her published work includes *Root of Bitterness: Documents of the Social History of American Women, Bonds of Womanhood* and *'Woman's Sphere' in New England, 1780–1835.* She is currently completing a book manuscript on feminism in the US in the early twentieth century.

Rosalind Delmar is the author of *Joris Ivens* and of *Feminisms* (forthcoming), the translator of *A Woman* by Sibilla Aleramo and has contributed to several anthologies of women's liberation. The mother of two small children, she lives in London.

Linda Gordon is Professor of History at the University of Wisconsin/Madison. She is the author of the leading history of birth control in the US (*Woman's Body, Woman's Right*) and of a forthcoming history of family violence and its control in the US.

Jane Lewis teaches in the Department of Social Administration at the London School of Economics. She is the author of *The Politics of Motherhood: Child and Maternal Welfare in England 1900–1939* and *Women in England: Sexual Divisions and Social Change, 1870–1950.* She has also edited *Women's Welfare/Women's Rights* and *Labour and Love: Women's Experience of Home and Family, 1850–1950.*

Heather Jon Maroney teaches sociology and feminist theory at Trent University, Peterborough, Ontario, Canada. Active in the women's movement since 1968, she was a founding member of the Toronto International Women's Day Committee. Co-editor with Meg Luxton of *Women's Work, Women's Struggles: Feminism and*

Political Economy (forthcoming), she is finishing a study of gender politics in Quebec.

Juliet Mitchell is a psychoanalyst who has lectured extensively throughout Europe and the English-speaking world. Her books include *Women's Estate, Psychoanalysis and Feminism* and *Women: The Longest Revolution.*

Ann Oakley is a sociologist who has researched and written extensively about gender roles, the situation of women and medical sociology. Her books include *The Sociology of Housework, Taking it Like a Woman* and *The Captured Womb.* She is currently Deputy Director of the Thomas Coram Research Unit, University of London Institute of Education.

Deborah L. Rhode is a Professor of Law at Stanford Law School, and Director of the Institute for Research on Women and Gender at Stanford. She has written extensively in the area of sex discrimination, and her book on *Feminist Theory and Legal Thought* is forthcoming from the Harvard University Press.

Hilary Rose is Professor of Social Policy at the University of Bradford and Director of the West Yorkshire Centre for Research on Women. She has researched, published and been active in the politics of science for twenty years. She is currently writing a book on feminism and the sciences.

Sheryl Burt Ruzek is Associate Professor of Health Education at Temple University, Philadelphia. She is the author of *The Women's Health Movement, Feminist Alternatives to Medical Control.* Her current research focuses on women and heart disease and she co-directs a Summer Institute for Teaching Women, Health and Healing for university faculty with Virginia Olesen at the University of California, San Francisco.

Dale Spender is an Australian researcher and writer who has lived in London for eleven years. Her books include *Man Made Language, Women of Ideas and What Men Have Done to Them* and *Mothers of the Novel, 100 Good Women Novelists Before Jane Austen.* She is the editor of *Women's Studies International Forum* and is currently involved in the research for future publications on the history of women's writing.

Judith Stacey teaches sociology and women's studies at the University of California, Davis. She is the author of *Patriarchy and Socialist Revolution in China* and a member of the editorial collective of *Feminist Studies*.

1 Introduction

Juliet Mitchell and Ann Oakley

In *The Second Sex* Simone de Beauvoir argues that the division of sexes is an irreducible, contingent fact of biology. Woman is a biological, not an historical, category, and she thus suffers from a singular oppression which knows of no historical period that precedes it. Without a different past, how can one have a concept of a different future?

In 1976, we edited a collection of essays, *The Rights and Wrongs of Women*. This volume, *What is Feminism?*, was conceived as its sequel. The contributors to both books are mostly activists, even initiators, of the women's liberation movement that started in the mid-sixties. At the outset, *The Second Sex* was the only major work of reference for most of us. Faced with de Beauvoir's analysis of women's lack of history, for some, it became a prime task to discover and create a history both for women and for their intellectual and practical struggle. *The Rights and Wrongs of Women* was a contribution to the first dimension of the task – does the concept of women or do women themselves have a history? *What is Feminism?* was conceived as a contribution to the second. E. H. Carr's *What is History?* could stand as a reference title – the source of an investigation into something that we assume we know.

At the beginning of this phase of feminism, in the sixties, there were radical feminists and women's liberationists.

Radical feminism in its beginnings was best exemplified for the public in Shulamith Firestone's *The Dialectic of Sex* (1972). The base-line of de Beauvoir's thesis of an irreducible biological category was asserted to the full – there was no history, only a biological condition outside time which nothing but a technology without circumscription by historical conditions could destroy. Thus women had a natural unity in their biology, and feminism could ally itself safely and, by definition, with all shapes and forms of validation of, and protest by, women. It was self-referring – by women for women.

Although the distinction, even for those early days, should not be maintained too rigidly between forms of feminism, most of the contributors both to this and to the earlier collection come from the liberationist tradition. Emanating in diverse ways from some type of socialist or marxist background, women's liberationists were unable to assume a common identity for women along a biological dividing line – we needed a social definition and therefore a history.

In our earlier *The Rights and Wrongs of Women* most of the essays created a concept and understanding of women through an analysis of the category within history – be it in a history of ideas or of material conditions. 'Women' became a coherent entity through their rediscovery in the interstices of literature, film, history. . . .

As women were sought and found, the nomenclature of the movement changed. The urgency of our search for a past, so that we could cohere as a unity and thus struggle for a future, is reflected in this shifting terminology of the movement. The 'women's liberation movement' became the 'women's movement', thus shedding our immediate political peers of black liberation, children's liberation and, to an extent, gay liberation, and allying ourselves firmly within our specific heritage of feminist struggle in the nineteenth and early twentieth centuries. Women's liberationists took a sideways step closer to radical feminists and became 'feminists' despite the fact that at the outset many of us shared de Beauvoir's earlier resistance to the term.

The search for this history has proved as problematic as de Beauvoir's comment warned us it would be. On the one hand, an article such as Sally Alexander's contribution in *The Rights and Wrongs of Women*, by re-examining the changing structure of manufacturing industry in London in the 1840s through the lives of women, permanently altered the social history and geography of the period. It also disturbingly unsettled all preceding notions of women's role at the time. With women there, the picture shifts; it becomes altogether denser. At the same time, the new picture changes our understanding of women.

On the other hand, as Rosalind Delmar discusses in her contribution to this volume, the search for women in history has called into question the very stability of the concept 'woman'. Feminism in the sixties and seventies has above all been distinguished from any of its earlier expressions by the deconstruction of any fixed meaning to the notion of 'woman'. If woman cannot be fixed as an identity beyond the biological female, neither can feminism have a

unified definition. In *The Rights and Wrongs of Women* we were
looking for women; in *What is Feminism?*, for feminism. In both
cases the ground changed to quicksand beneath our feet.

The final selection of articles for this volume reflects the enormous
difficulty of the question. Many more people from a wide range of
social and ethnic backgrounds were invited to participate and
accepted but got into difficulties. We feel that the essays that were
finally produced are a tribute to, not an evasion of, the difficulty.
They take different approaches to the task of examining the
quicksand that lies beneath simplistic attempts to say what feminism
is – and is not (for many of us have found it easier to define feminism
in its absence rather than its presence).

The writers of the essays inhabit different academic and intellectual settings and do not all have the same theoretical allegiances.
Despite, or even because of, these differences, we feel the final
collection of essays is able both to describe the methodology of the
search for feminism and to chart the growth thus uncovered in new,
interesting and original ways.

As Rosalind Delmar observes, the naming of the parts of modern
feminism radical feminism, socialist feminism, marxist feminism,
lesbian separatism and so on – signals a sclerosis of the movement.
The question suggested by this is whether it makes sense to assume
any necessary unity within feminism. At the start of organized
feminism, women believed they shared the same situation; yet, as
they learnt to speak about it, they fast discovered their differences
from one another. If feminists are not a collectivity, then the
question the other way round is whether collective action by women
– as in the Greenham Common peace movement – can be considered
feminist at all. Can feminism be defined simply by virtue of its object
of concern – women? Is it not feminist to profess an interest in
human welfare more generally? – and if this is the case, are men to be
allowed to dress up any variety of their concern for women in the
clothes of feminism?

In her essay, Nancy Cott explores how feminist thinking about
women's similarity to and difference from men has been implicated
in the stated goals and activities of the women's movement in its
different historical periods. All the varieties of feminism contain at
their heart a paradox – requiring gender consciousness for their
basis, their political rallying cry is the elimination of gender roles.
Cott's conclusion is that mass movements of, and on behalf of,
women are only able to emerge out of the diversity of philosophies
and practice when women have particular 'instrumental' reasons for
advancing gender interests – securing the suffrage, for instance.

Effective practical feminism is thus a strategic coalition which makes it possible to transcend theoretical difference.

Taking off from this point, Deborah Rhode's essay explores the tensions between feminist theory and the liberal legalist traditions that have shaped its development. What Rhode calls individual rights-oriented strategies have successfully overcome much sex-based discrimination, yet, by appealing to the law in its social control function, feminism defeats its own agenda by fighting for equality within a social system that cannot offer it.

The radicalization of working women pushes this fight to its limits. According to Heather Maroney, in her essay 'Feminism at Work', the rise of working-class feminism presents the women's movement with an important moment of decision: can a fusion be created between sex-based and class-based forms of opposition to the status quo?

Economically, one important and recent social change has been that in a deepening recession, when unemployment rates have taken on an epidemic character, the only people with better employment prospects are women. This redistribution of economic opportunities between the sexes isn't unique – it's happened before. In her contribution to the book Juliet Mitchell suggests that looking back, and seeing where we are now, enables us to comprehend a particular role for women in terms of acute and chronic social change – they move into the future first. Thus the relationship between social change on the one hand, and feminism on the other, is complex. Feminism may itself succeed in bringing about social change; but it finds itself being used in the process of change to construct a confrontation out of which a particular future is made that feminism did not want.

Just as we cannot know who 'women' are without looking into history, so it is meaningless to answer the question 'what is feminism?' in the abstract. One way to answer it is by exploring the personal meaning of feminism as Dale Spender does in her essay for this volume. What kind of choice does self-definition as a feminist represent and what are the implications for the individual woman of such a choice?

Feminism takes its meanings from the moment. Like all political movements, it is capable of generating and containing its own backlash; hence the 'pro-family' feminism of the 1980s, in which writers such as Betty Friedan and Germaine Greer, enormously influential in the late sixties and early seventies, appear to change their minds and tell us we got it all wrong. In so retreating from sexual politics, as Judith Stacey argues in her 'Are Feminists Afraid to Leave Home?', they inform us that the politics of revolution are the politics of rage, and of an insensible disregard for our own ahistorical vulnerability. To oppose the family, and deny men their connection with women, is to deny our own need for connectedness – which is dangerously close to the uncaring male response to the spectre of the aggrieved feminist in his midst. However, more interesting than the backlash are the reasons for it, and here the rise of conservative pro-family feminism, as Stacey shows, is closely tied to the fate of the family, an unsatisfactory but alluring institution.

Stacey also links the new conservative feminism with the personal fates of feminists who have propounded it, bemoaning in their late thirties and forties the non-achievement of a status they earlier attacked. If the first wave of this women's movement was concerned with redressing the wrongs of women, then its second wave has alighted on more positive emblems of womanhood, such as child-bearing and childrearing and well-worn capacities for emotional intimacy that once felt like oppression. The essays by Jane Lewis, Sheryl Rusek, Hilary Rose and Ann Oakley all examine the meaning of feminism within the context of women's traditional domestic labour, and point to ways in which a detailed 'inside' knowledge of this labour changes the dominant paradigm of knowledge about the condition of being human. In other words, to understand women is simply to have a different way of seeing the world.

The 'denaturalizing' of women's work in the home has enabled its dissection into both labour and love. In Hilary Rose's essay the experiential politics of time and caring oppose the language of aggression and domination which masculinist science has used to describe its relationship with nature, which must be subjugated, as women are, before real work can proceed. The question for feminists is, under what conditions is caring extracted from them? It's certainly the case, as Jane Lewis goes on to demonstrate, that the 'caring assumption' has been built into philosophies of welfare, so that women find it difficult legitimately to move beyond their roles as wives and mothers. At the personal level this is frequently reflected in uncertainty about the status of what one is doing; to care for children, to look after homes and be concerned with the welfare of men – is this labour done for oneself or is it alienated, not only because one is divorced (sometimes literally) from its product, but because one never chose to do it in the first place?

Women's choices require women to be viewed and treated as autonomous by those who make policy. This simple insight of feminism is perhaps possible because in the welfare field the equality argument seems to stand up better than in others – though being constantly limited, as we have already said, to a relatively unchanging social vision.

Sheryl Ruzek's essay on feminism and health care is somewhat different from the others in that it sets out to describe some of the ways in which the women's movement has challenged and reshaped formal health care and has led to new forms of care. It thus provides an answer to the question as to what difference feminism has made, without detailing the difference feminism is. The impact of feminism on medical practice has been uneven, and its intentions have naturally met with extreme opposition from many quarters of organized medicine. Two aspects of this are particularly interesting from the point of view of both the history of medicine and the history of women. The first is that history contains no parallel example of a clash between the interests of feminism and the interests of a profession. This suggests that feminism has something to say in general about how and why expert knowledge is constructed. As Ruzek says, feminism's dispute with medicine is not only about enabling women to take charge of their own health and health care; it is also about the status of medicine's claims to scientific status. Along with other groups interested in restoring health care to the community, feminist criticism has laid bare the uncomfortable fact that most obstetric practice is based on nothing sounder than what the obstetrician wants.

About motherhood in general, feminists have professed many different opinions and, from demanding its medicalization (in the early years of this century), they have now shifted to decrying it – though on this point their voices are by no means unanimous. Ann Oakley explores in her essay some of the symptoms of, and reasons for, the state's and the medical profession's interest in motherhood. Rather than simply reiterating the point that motherhood is a source of power for women, she proposes that the particular love of mother and child carries such revolutionary potential that, in a world where women are at least free to be citizens, this power must be controlled and turned in on itself before it has the chance to fuel a social movement.

The thesis of love possesses as its antithesis the hatred and violence generated by too much intimacy. In the case of male violence against women, the task of feminism is apparent and relatively straightforward, if difficult to accomplish. Yet where violence towards children is concerned – the theme of Linda Gordon's essay – feminism may not like what it sees. As mothers, women are both victims and victimizers; they are both dependent and depended on. To acknowledge their aggressions towards their children (which may be shown in neglect rather than direct physical violence) is problematic, since to defend women against violence requires a statement of political innocence and the more this becomes impossible, the more the abuse of power loses its gendered character.

Most of the essays in this collection end with questions. The complexity of feminism (or feminisms, as Rosalind Delmar rightly rephrases it) has drawn us into reflecting on our past and present where once we more gaily planned our future. As editors, we have had to watch the book develop into something other than what we first intended. We do not want to lose sight of the celebration behind the worries. So it is not Dutch courage if we conclude by saying that it is only through a creative use of anxiety that we can start to look forward again.

2 What is Feminism?

Rosalind Delmar

There are many, feminist and non-feminist alike, for whom the question 'what *is* feminism?' has little meaning. The content of terms like 'feminism' and 'feminist' seems self-evident, something that can be taken for granted. By now, it seems to me, the assumption that the meaning of feminism is 'obvious' needs to be challenged. It has become an obstacle to understanding feminism, in its diversity and in its differences, and in its specificity as well.[1]

It is certainly possible to construct a base-line definition of feminism and the feminist which can be shared by feminists and non-feminists. Many would agree that at the very least a feminist is someone who holds that women suffer discrimination because of their sex, that they have specific needs which remain negated and unsatisfied, and that the satisfaction of these needs would require a radical change (some would say a revolution even) in the social, economic and political order. But beyond that, things immediately become more complicated.

For example, popular approaches to feminism often contain references to a style of dress, to looks, to ways of behaving to men and women, to what used to be called 'manners'. It is, in practice, impossible to discuss feminism without discussing the image of feminism and the feminists. Feminists play and have played with a range of choices in the process of self-presentation, registering a relation both to the body and to the social meaning of womanhood. Various, sometimes competing, images of the feminist are thus produced, and these acquire their own social meanings. This is important to stress now because in contemporary feminism the construction of new images is a conscious process. There is a strand whose central concern is to investigate culture (in its widest sense) and to experiment with the means of representation. But feminism's wish that women behave differently is also an historic element: Mary

Wollstonecraft at the end of the eighteenth century called for 'a revolution in female manners'.

The diversity of representations of the feminist has undoubtedly grown since then. How difficult it would be to choose between them, to find the 'true' feminist image, the 'proper way' to be a feminist. And yet many books on feminism are written, and feminism is often spoken about, as if there were a 'true' and authentic feminism, unified and consistent over time and in any one place, even if fragmented in its origins and at specific historical moments.

Most people have heard a sentence which begins: 'As a feminist I think. . . .' It is a sentence which speaks of a wish that an agreed way of being a feminist should exist, but is not the product of any genuine agreement among feminists about what they think or how they should live their lives. In the women's movement, there is a strong desire to pin feminism down (whether as support for a series of agreed demands or as preoccupation with central concerns like sexual division or male domination) but this impulse has invariably encountered obstacles. General agreement about the situation in which women find themselves has not been accompanied by any shared understanding of why this state of affairs should exist or what could be done about it. Indeed, the history of the women's movement in the 1970s, a time of apparent unity, was marked by bitter, at times virulent, internal disputes over what it was possible or permissible for a feminist to do, say, think or feel.

The fragmentation of contemporary feminism bears ample witness to the impossibility of constructing modern feminism as a simple unity in the present or of arriving at a shared feminist definition of feminism. Such differing explanations, such a variety of emphases in practical campaigns, such widely varying interpretations of their results have emerged, that it now makes more sense to speak of a plurality of feminisms than of one.

Recently the different meanings of feminism for different feminists have manifested themselves as a sort of sclerosis of the movement, segments of which have become separated from and hardened against each other. Instead of internal dialogue there is a naming of the parts: there are radical feminists, socialist feminists, marxist feminists, lesbian separatists, women of colour, and so on, each group with its own carefully preserved sense of identity. Each for itself is the only worthwhile feminism; others are ignored except to be criticized.

How much does this matter? Is it not the case that even extreme differences in politics can often mask underlying agreement? Could it not still be that what unites feminists is greater than what divides?

Might not current fragmentation be merely an episode in an overriding history of unity?

At times it is rather attractive to think so and to let the matter rest at that. All cats look grey in the dark, and the exclusivism of feminist groups can be reminiscent of what Freud called 'the narcissism of minor differences'.[2] Even so, at a theoretical level, agreements are uncovered only by the exploration of differences – they cannot be assumed. And there is no overwhelming reason to assume an underlying feminist unity. Indeed, one unlooked-for effect of an assumed coherence of feminism can be its marginalization, as discourse or as practice.[3] In many ways it makes more sense to invert the question 'Why is there so much division between feminists?' and ask instead 'Does feminism have any necessary unity, politically, socially, or culturally?'

What is the background to current fragmentation? At the start of the contemporary women's movement in Britain it was often assumed that there was a potentially unificatory point of view on women's issues which would be able to accommodate divergencies and not be submerged by them. From the start the modern women's movement pitched its appeal at a very high level of generality, to all women, and thought of its aims and objectives in very general terms.

The unity of the movement was assumed to derive from a potential identity between women. This concept of identity rested on the idea that women share the same experiences: an external situation in which they find themselves – economic oppression, commercial exploitation, legal discrimination are examples; and an internal response – the feeling of inadequacy, a sense of narrow horizons. A shared response to shared experience was put forward as the basis for a communality of feeling between women, a shared psychology even. Women's politics and women's organizing were then seen as an expression of this community of feeling and experience.[4]

So unproblematically was potential identity between women assumed that the plural form 'we' was adopted, and it is still much used: 'we', women, can speak on behalf of all of us 'women'.[5] (In some of the first women's groups of the late sixties and early seventies every effort was made to encourage women to use this form and speak in terms of 'we' instead of what was heard as the more divisive grammar of 'you' and 'I'. It should be noted, though, that this plural form lends itself to a differently divisive grammar, that of 'us' and 'them'.)

In fact, common ground within women's politics was based on an agreed description rather than an analysis, and the absence of analysis probably enabled such a stress to be laid on what women in general could share. No-one predicted (or could predict) that uncontainable divisions would arise between and within women's groups.[6] Early optimism went together with a huge effort to create a solidarity between women (one of the meanings of 'sisterhood') which, it was thought, would arise out of shared perceptions. But in spite of the success of women's liberation in bringing to the fore and reinforcing feelings of sympathy and identity between women, political unity (another of the meanings of 'sisterhood') cannot be said to have been achieved. Analytic differences and the political differences which spring from them have regularly been causes of division in the women's movement.[7] Unity based on identity has turned out to be a very fragile thing. What has been most difficult for the women's movement to cope with has been the plethora of differences between women which have emerged in the context of feminism.

Over the past twenty years a paradox has developed at the heart of the modern women's movement: on the one hand there is the generality of its categorical appeal to all women, as potential participants in a movement; on the other hand there is the exclusivism of its current internal practice, with its emphasis on difference and division. Recognition of and commitment to hetero-geneity appear to have been lost, and with those a source of fruitful tension. A further aspect of the same paradox is that the different forms of women's politics, fragmented as they are, have been increasingly called by the same name: *feminism*. Even the term that signifies its rejection – 'post-feminism' – incorporates it.

Women's organizing was not, in general, in the late sixties and early seventies, called feminism. Feminism was a position adopted by or ascribed to particular groups. These were the groups which called themselves 'radical feminist' and those groups and individuals who represented the earlier emancipatory struggle. Both often came under fierce attack. The equation between women organizing and feminism has been implicitly adopted since then, and its usage as a blanket term to cover all women's activities urgently needs to be questioned.

Are all actions and campaigns prompted or led by women, feminist? The encampment at Greenham Common is a powerful example of a community of women in its nucleus, support groups, and the character of its demonstrations. The symbolism deployed at Greenham calls up images of the female and the feminine: the spider's web of the support network, the nurturing maternity which leaves its marks of family photographs and knitted bootees on the

boundary fence in a battle for space with the symbols of male
defence and attack: barbed wire, the nuclear missile. It is its
projection of women as those who care which allows the Greenham
camp to be represented as useful not just to women, and through
them to the species, but to the species first and foremost. Yet is this
entirely feminist? Support for Greenham does not rely in the main
on feminist groups (although it does rely on women). Greenham
actions have been *polyvalent*, capable of attracting multiple meanings
and mobilizing various ideological stances in their support: this is
part of its strength. Without a women's movement a women's peace
camp would probably not have had so much resonance; this is part of
the success of the women's movement, but does not make Greenham
necessarily feminist.

The politics of Greenham has been keenly debated among
feminists. For some, the mobilization of femininity and nurturance
is expressive of feminism, for others it represents a deference to that
social construction of woman as maternal principle which through
their feminism they attempt to challenge.[8] Not only does Greenham
represent different things to different feminists, summoning up
different meanings of feminism, it is by no means certain that those
who participate in Greenham politics, or support the camp, would
describe themselves as feminist.

Can an action be 'feminist' even if those who perform it are not?
Within contemporary feminism much emphasis has been laid on
feminism as *consciousness*. One of the most distinctive practices of
modern feminism has been the 'consciousness-raising group'. If
feminism is the result of reflection and conscious choice, how does
one place those individuals and women's groups who would, for a
variety of reasons, reject the description 'feminist' if it were applied
to them? Does it make sense to ascribe to them a feminism of which
they are unaware? What, in the framework provided by 'feminist
consciousness', is then the status of this 'unconscious' feminism?

The various ways in which such questions can be answered
connect back to the central question 'what is feminism?' If feminism
is a concern with issues affecting women, a concern to advance
women's interests, so that therefore anyone who shares this concern
is a feminist, whether they acknowledge it or not, then the range of
feminism is general and its meaning is equally diffuse. Feminism
becomes defined by its object of concern – women – in much the
same way as socialism has sometimes been defined by an object – the
poor or the working class. Social reformers can then be classified as
feminists because of the consequences of their activities, and not
because they share any particular social analysis or critical spirit.

This way of looking at feminism, as diffuse activity, makes feminism understandably hard to pin down. Feminists, being involved in so many activities, from so many different perspectives, would almost inevitably find it hard to unite, except in specific campaigns.

On the other hand there are those who claim that feminism does have a complex of ideas about women, specific to or emanating from feminists. This means that it should be possible to separate out feminism and feminists from the multiplicity of those concerned with women's issues. It is by no means absurd to suggest that you don't have to be a feminist to support women's rights to equal treatment, and that not all those supportive of women's demands are feminists. In this light feminism can claim its own history, its own practices, its own ideas, but feminists can make no claim to an exclusive interest in or copyright over problems affecting women. Feminism can thus be established as a field (and this even if scepticism is still needed in the face of claims or demands for a unified feminism), but cannot claim women as its domain.

These considerations both have political implications in the present and also underlie the way feminism's past is understood. If a history of feminism, separable from although connected with the history of changes in women's position, is to be constructed, a precondition of such a history is that feminism must be able to be specified.

In the writing of feminist history it is the broad view which predominates: feminism is usually defined as an active desire to change women's position in society.[9] Linked to this is the view that feminism is *par excellence* a social movement for change in the position of women. Its privileged form is taken to be the political movement, the self-organization of a women's politics. So unquestioningly are feminism and a women's movement assumed to be co-terminous that histories of feminism are often written as histories of the women's movement, and times of apparent quiescence of the movement are taken as symptomatic of a quiescence of feminism. This identity between feminism and a women's movement is, moreover, part of the self-image of contemporary feminism. The idea that the new movement of the 1960s was a 'second wave', a continuation of a struggle started just over a century before and interrupted for forty years (after the hiatus of the vote) pervaded the early years of the contemporary women's movement and still informs many of its debates.[10] The way feminism's past is understood and interpreted thus informs and is informed by the ways in which feminism is understood and interpreted in the present.

The problems involved in writing feminist history throw into relief some of the problems involved in specifying feminism more closely in the present. Feminist historiography highlights different versions of feminism, since it often has overt political motivations which then produce different versions of the same history. Present approaches to feminist history can themselves be historicized by comparison with the ways in which past feminists have read their own history. Even the frustrating assumption of identity between feminism and the women's movement has its advantages: it focuses attention on the area where feminism is most intimately intertwined with a generality of concern with women's issues: women's politics. The problems of separation present themselves acutely here, and this makes it a productive point of entry.

Some of the major conventions of the writing of feminist history, which are only in recent years being questioned and overturned, can be found in the classic history of the nineteenth-century movement: Ray Strachey's *The Cause*.[11] It is an important book in several ways. Not only is it still the best introduction to the subject, but it is the product of the mainstream feminism of the turn of the century. Its author was an active feminist, secretary to Mrs Fawcett and involved in the NUWSS. Her main concern was to chart the period between 1860 and 1920 during which the term feminism took on its dictionary definition, 'advocacy of the claims of women'.[12] It is also the product of a feminism which did not (unlike much contemporary feminism) define itself as 'woman-made' (it would be difficult to write a history of nineteenth-century feminism which did not include at least J. S. Mill and Richard Pankhurst). A detailed look at this work will help clarify how some of the questions raised so far relate to the writing of feminist history.

History Conventions

When Ray Strachey wrote her history the close connection between feminism and the social movement for change in women's position was redolent with meaning: the term 'feminism' was itself coined in the course of the development of the social movement. All the same, within *The Cause* distinctions are made between feminism and the social movement for change in women's position.

She starts her history by proposing two forerunners of the nineteenth-century movement. One is Mary Wollstonecraft, feminist theorist and author of *A Vindication of the Rights of Woman*. The other is Hannah More, Evangelical philanthropist and educationalist. Of the first, Ray Strachey writes that she set out in her great book 'the whole extent of the feminist ideal . . . the whole claim of equal human rights'.[13] Of the other she remarks that 'It may seem strange to maintain that Miss Hannah More and Mrs Trimmer and the other good ladies who started the Sunday-school and cottage-visiting fashions were the founders of a movement which would have shocked them profoundly; but it is clearly true.'[14]

If the nineteenth-century women's movement is looked at as a movement for increased participation by women in social and political life or as a movement which negotiated the relative and shared positions men and women were to occupy in the social, political, and economic order, it makes sense to invoke each woman as a symbolic figure. Hannah More had a part to play in the general redefinition of women's sphere; Mary Wollstonecraft articulated women's claims, needs and desires at a deeper level. By harnessing the two a neat schema can be constructed. There is theory (Mary Wollstonecraft) and practice (Hannah More), consciousness of the rights of women and lack of consciousness, Mary and Martha coinciding. One is radical, the other conservative; they responded differently to the same social phenomena, yet both had contributions to make. (This schema only works, however, because it ignores Hannah More's intellectual work.)

On the other hand, to combine the two, as Ray Strachey points out, seems 'strange' because if the purpose was to construct a history of feminism, even in Mrs Fawcett's definition of it as 'a movement for the redressal of women's grievances' it would make little sense to include Hannah More and Mary Wollstonecraft as equal partners. Hannah More was not just not a feminist, she was a rabid anti-feminist: it was she who described Mary Wollstonecraft (whose book she had not read) as 'a hyena in petticoats'. Her practice was part of overall change, but allowed women the public sphere only when domestic duties had been fulfilled. Such a position was far removed from Mary Wollstonecraft's vision, which questioned the value of women's confinement to the domestic sphere and saw increased public participation by women, up to and including political citizenship, as a good in itself.

How does Ray Strachey make her distinctions between feminism and the women's movement? Her discussion of the rise of the women's movement stresses a coincidence of factors which helped bring it into being. These include: women's shared exclusion from political, social and economic life, with a rebellion against this; middle-class women's sense of uselessness; and the formulation of common objectives, culminating in the demand for political citizenship through the vote.

But whilst the sense of uselessness or awareness of grievance might be sufficient to bring someone into the ambit of women's politics or to a lasting achievement which could benefit women in general, this in itself, in Ray Strachey's eyes, did not make someone a feminist. She does not include, for example, Caroline Norton as a feminist, nor Florence Nightingale, even though she includes Florence Nightingale's *Cassandra* as prototypical of feeling amongst middle-class women. She writes of her that 'though she was a feminist of sorts . . . Florence Nightingale had only an incomplete and easily exhausted sympathy with the organised women's movement. In her absorption in her own work she judged the men and women she lived among almost wholly by their usefulness or their uselessness to it.'[15] The inference is clear: Florence Nightingale put her own work first, women's rights were a side issue: a feminist would have put women's rights in the centre of her work. As far as Caroline Norton is concerned, Ray Strachey takes her at her own word and accepts her disavowal of feminism. This definition of a feminist as someone whose *central* concern and preoccupation lies with the position of women and their struggle for emancipation is constant throughout *The Cause*; so is feminism as conscious political choice. Together they allow a relatively objective differentiation between feminists and non-feminists. Feminists are not represented as more 'moral' than non-feminists.[16]

To define a feminist in this way still implies an intimate connection between feminism and the women's movement. The feminists are the leaders, organizers, publicists, lobbyists, of the women's movement; they come into their own and into existence on a relatively large scale in the course of development of a women's movement. The social movement, particularly in its political dimension, provides the context for feminism; feminists are its animating spirits.

This definition is valuable as one dimension of an eventually more complex definition, but cannot stand on its own. It has very little to tell, for example, of the intellectual and cultural life of feminism, of the ideas which might unite or divide feminists in their commitment to a movement or to its different aspects. In Ray Strachey's definition feminists share the same aims and the same general ideas, the same broad commitment to the great cause of female emancipation, and a capacity to put this cause in the centre of their lives. The content of their ideas merits only the briefest of sketches.

Histories of feminism which treat feminism as social movement tend to concentrate on chronicling the vicissitudes of that movement and subordinate any exploration of the intellectual content of feminism to that main purpose. *The Cause* is no exception to this rule. Divergent feminist ideas are charted according to differences in tactics and strategy, or the various issues seized upon and the consequent articulation of aims and objectives. Yet underlying unity is assumed.

Ray Strachey's account of feminism's development in *The Cause* is by now a standard one. First there is the appearance of *A Vindication of the Rights of Woman*, described as 'the text' of the later movement. Then there is a forty-year silence, preceding the emergence of the first women's organizations – the practical movement. Theory precedes practice in this narrative, and Mary Wollstonecraft is, as it were, the harbinger of the movement, a female John the Baptist, heralding what was to follow. True to the correlation between feminism and social movement, it is a narrative according to which feminism finally 'starts' and achieves itself within the form of a social movement of women for their emancipation.

What happens if this story is unpicked, if the history of ideas is allowed parity with the history of a movement?

The idea of a silent period can be compared with the results of the work done by Barbara Taylor and published in *Eve and the New Jerusalem*.[17] This shows how Mary Wollstonecraft's ideas were taken up within the Owenite socialist movement in the years which preceded the appearance of the Langham Place group.[18] The gap proposed by Ray Strachey's account is at least partially filled; rather than silence, broken only by occasional isolated utterances, there is the intermingling of feminism and socialism within utopian politics. This 'discovery' of an active feminism where none had been seen before derives from an approach which takes intellectual history seriously. It also depends on an implicit separation of the terms of the equation feminism = the social movement of women. In terms of that equation the period in question reveals nothing. A shift in emphasis unveils a hidden link in feminism's fortunes.

The exploration of feminist history is severely limited if the appearance of the social movement is assumed to be feminism's apotheosis and privileged form. For one thing, any feminism preceding the Seneca Falls Conference of 1848 in the United States or the Langham Place circle in England in the 1850s, is necessarily seen as prototypic, an early example of a later-flowering plant, a phenomenon to be understood in terms of what comes later rather than in its own terms and context.[19]

To accept, with all its implications, that feminism has not only existed in movements of and for women, but has also been able to exist as an intellectual tendency without a movement, or as a strand within very different movements, is to accept the existence of various forms of feminism. The ebb and flow of feminism's intellectual history is important here, since it enables a different perspective to be placed on the movement itself. It also points up feminists' and feminism's ability to use and to combine with diverse ways of thinking politically. A study of these various combinational forms of feminism can illuminate both the means of diffusion of feminist ideas, and the different tendencies within feminism when it does exist in conjunction with a social movement of women.

In Ray Strachey's account Mary Wollstonecraft's work gains meaning by becoming 'the text' of the later movement. But is the impression of theoretical continuity this conveys a valid one? Is Mary Wollstonecraft's philosophical radicalism shared by later feminists? The claim is made by Ray Strachey in the absence of any sustained discussion of feminism's intellectual content. Any substantiation depends on an analysis of Mary Wollstonecraft's thought and that of later feminists.

A Vindication of the Rights of Woman combines an appeal on behalf of women with a general social critique which employs key themes from the Enlightenment and uses them to illuminate women's position and needs. The demand for free individual development in a society open to talent, for example, is a demand of the French Revolution. Mary Wollstonecraft extends this idea to women, widening out criticism of hereditary rights, duties and exclusions, to include those which derive from sexual difference.

This drive to extend the field of social criticism in order to encompass women is carried forward in the name of women's basic humanity. The claim is first and foremost that women are members of the human species and therefore have the rights due to all humans. In making this claim several elements are combined. There is a Lockeian Christian argument that God has constructed the world according to the laws of reason, and that humans can reach an understanding of the laws of God by use of that reason. If women are human they have reason and have the right to develop their reason in pursuit, not least, of religious knowledge.[20] There is an argument against women's confinement to the world of artifice and their consequent exclusion from the world of natural rights. Rousseau's *Emile* is specifically pinpointed because within it women are deliberately constructed as objects of sexual desire, and by that confined to a lifetime's subordination within limits defined by male needs.[21] The main thrust of this aspect of the *Vindication* is that as members of the human species, and in the interests of their own development, women should have the same considerations applied to them as are applied to men. This is, importantly, a natural rights argument: it rests its case on the rights due to all humans as species members. Ray Strachey accurately calls it a plea for equal human rights.

This notion of *human* rights, of the Rights of Man, is not held in common between Mary Wollstonecraft and later, nineteenth-century feminists. Their debates took place in the aftermath of a major political defeat of 'natural rights' arguments, which had found their most forceful expression in the slogans of the French Revolution and which stayed alive by entering the political language of socialism.

Some did hold on to a concept of natural rights. For example, Dr Richard Pankhurst, husband of Emmeline and father of Sylvia and Christabel, pursued the following line of argument in 1867:

> The basis of political freedom is expressed in the great maxim of the equality of all men, of humanity, of all human beings, before the law. The unit of modern society is not the family but the individual. Therefore every individual is *prima facie* entitled to all the franchises and freedoms of the constitution. The political position of women ought, and finally, must be, determined by reference to that large principle. . . Any individual who enjoys the electoral right is not, in the eye of the constitution, invested with it in virtue of being of a certain rank, station or sex. Each individual receives the right to vote *in the character of human being, possessing intelligence and adequate reasoning power. To be human and to be sane are the essential conditions* . . . it is not on the grounds of any difference of sex that the electoral right is in principle either granted or denied.[22] [My emphasis]

By contrast, Helen Taylor, daughter of Harriet Taylor and step-daughter of J. S. Mill, recommended the Ladies Petition presented by Mill to the Commons in 1866, in the following terms:

> This claim, that since women are permitted to hold property they should also be permitted to exercise all the rights which, by our laws, the possession of property brings with it, is put forward in this petition on such strictly constitutional grounds, and is advanced so entirely without reference to any abstract rights, or fundamental changes in the institutions of English society, that it is impossible not to feel that the ladies who

make it have done so with a practical purpose in view, and that they conceive themselves to be asking only for the recognition of rights which flow naturally from the existing laws and institutions of the country.[23]

She invokes support for female suffrage and the suffragists on the grounds that the suffragists eschew natural rights and support the rights of property. To consider 'a *birthright* as not of *natural* but of *legal* origin is', she writes, 'in conformity with modern habits of thought in regard to civilized men, the natives of civilized societies; but *exactly as it is opposed to any a priori theories of the rights of man*, [my emphasis] it is also opposed to any attempt to give or withhold privileges for merely *natural* reasons, such as differences of sex.'[24] 'Property represented by an individual is the true political unit among us', she claims.

> By holding property women take on the rights and the duties of property. If they are not interested in politics their property is. Poor-laws and game-laws, corn-laws and malt-tax, cattle-plague-compensation bills, the manning of the navy, and the conversion of Enfield rifles into breech-loaders – all these things will make the property held by English women more or less valuable to the country at large . . . [and] it is on the supposition that property requires representation that a property qualification is fixed by the law.[25]

Richard Pankhurst and Helen Taylor were expressing an important and deep difference, between the rights of persons and the rights of property, which was at the centre of political and ideological debate in the nineteenth century and is still alive today. The affirmation of property rights over human rights and *vice versa* is sufficiently incompatible for it to be hard to see much meaning in talk of shared ideas. Mary Wollstonecraft and Richard Pankhurst share a philosophic radicalism from which Helen Taylor and others were keen to distance themselves.

It can be objected that as far as Ray Strachey is concerned, this criticism is unjust. Her claim is not, it could be said, that feminists shared a *theory* but that they shared an *ideal*. Is even this true? To the extent to which all the variety of objectives subscribed to by nineteenth-century feminists could be described as tending to produce equality for men and women alike, then it can be said that the ideal of equality was generally shared, but it is difficult to go further than this. The ideal of equal *human* rights did not stay in the centre of feminist preoccupations. The dynamics of feminist activity in the late nineteenth and early twentieth centuries moved away from it, even whilst feminists insisted on equal treatment, by developing much more than previously the concept of inescapable differences between the sexes. The term 'equal rights' became filled with different contents.

The more work that emerges on the history of the nineteenth-century movement the more difficult it is to see any one theme, campaign, or ideal as pivotal. The picture which emerges is of a fragmented movement, its aims like pebbles thrown into the stream of social, political, economic and cultural life, producing rippling circles which touch and overlap, but of which no *one* could be with any certainty called the focal point. At the turn of the century the vote took on the weight of a symbolic function, uniting the personnel of many different campaigns; and, reciprocally, support for female suffrage became the touchstone of feminism. But the vote was never in any simple way the object of feminist aspirations.

For Ray Strachey and others like her, however, suffragism was the litmus test of feminism and this is reflected in the narrative of *The Cause*: its climax is the triumph of the vote. Such an emphasis in itself marked a shift. Enfranchisement of women was not a central concern for Mary Wollstonecraft. She introduces the subject with a certain diffidence:

> I really think that women ought to have representatives, instead of being arbitrarily governed without having any direct share allowed them in the deliberations of government. But, as the whole system of representation in this country is only a convenient handle for despotism, they need not complain, for they are as well represented as a numerous class of hard working mechanics.[26]

From the 1850s onwards feminists (in Ray Strachey's definition of the animating spirits of the movement) agreed that women 'ought to have representatives', more forcefully than the idea was ever held by Mary Wollstonecraft. Not all maintained her link between women and 'mechanics': this was often jettisoned together with the concept of natural human rights which informs it. Hence the fierce debate between feminists, as well as between some feminists and non-feminists, about the relationship of women's suffrage to universal adult suffrage. What replaced the notion of 'human' rights was one of 'women's' rights which depended not so much on a concept of woman as species member, but on woman as member of a specific social group composed of herself and other women. Suffragist and suffragette alike, whatever their differences over tactics, usually agreed in constructing 'woman' as a unified category, a specifiable constituency, sufficiently different from any class of men to need their own representatives, and sufficiently similar for an enfranchised section to represent the disfranchised.

As the campaign developed and resistance to it became more articulated suffragists and suffragettes had to answer a set of questions which registered various difficulties in relation to womanhood, to the nature of representation, and to citizenship. Who could best represent women? Women or selected men? Could women's interests be distinguished from men's? If so, how and by what? What was a woman? Could women represent men? Could they represent the interests of the state? Could they take on the duties as well as the rights of the citizen?[27]

The position of married women in particular created a difficulty since in law married women were entirely represented by their husbands.[28] In the main suffragettes and suffragists alike were prepared to compromise with this state of affairs. They demanded equality on the same terms as men, even though marriage created differences between women and women as well as between women and men, and they supported bills which would exclude married women from the vote.

In the name of egalitarianism, therefore, they were prepared to accept the exclusion of a large number of women from citizenship, for a time at least. Amongst the arguments used to justify this apparent paradox was an appeal to an underlying unity between women. Mrs Fawcett for example reasoned that, because of their shared womanhood, widows and spinsters would be able to represent their married sisters. Christabel Pankhurst stressed that women were being excluded on principle, because of their sex: winning the vote for some would break the principle of exclusion for all. From this point of view it didn't matter which women were first enfranchised. Both leaders mobilized the concept of a unity of interest between women to prove that women are the best people to represent other women and that some women could wait: it is constitutive of both their feminisms and shared by them despite their differences. At the level of the concept of woman being deployed, agreement exists where it may not have been expected, and where at another level (ideas about how the British Constitution worked, for example) profound disagreement does exist.

An analysis of the shifts and changes which have taken place in the meaning and content of 'womanhood' for feminists is intrinsic to any study of feminism as a specific body of thought or practice. The study of combinational forms of feminism is also important and here the terms of general social analysis can be crucial. But overall it is even more pertinent to ask what concept of woman is being mobilized, or indeed, as far as contemporary feminism is concerned, whether a concept of woman is being employed at all.

Feminists have not always had the same concept of woman, either at any one time or over time, and those moments at which changes have taken place in dominant feminist thinking about women can be pinpointed. Taken together with an appreciation of the different alliances feminists have entered into, the concept of woman can become a means through which the influence feminists have had at a more general political, social and cultural level can be gauged. But these things can only happen if attention is shifted from continuities of feminism to the discontinuities, the breaks, in feminist discourse and practice.

One of the attractions of the history of the nineteenth-century movement for feminists is that it provides a certain reassurance in the example of women acting together in a united way. It is also possible to mould its material into a satisfying narrative. In *The Cause,* the story is one of trials, vicissitudes, but eventual success. Fifty years later, the development of a new movement led to a questioning of the terms of this 'success' and the story has been amended so that it now more often finishes in anti-climax and defeat or else in the creation of the new movement to carry the struggle further. But the underlying structure of the narrative is maintained.

Both this structure and the emotional purposes of feminist history writing relate to its political function. Combined, they can give feminist historiography an evolutionist and progressivist flavour. The present is treated as the culmination of the past and as relatively 'advanced' compared to that past. Characteristics of the modern movement (like the commitment to autonomy, separatism, or whatever) are taken as definitional of feminism and looked for in past experiences. Disjunctures and dead ends tend to be ignored. The past is thus used to authenticate the present when there is no guarantee that past feminisms have anything more in common with contemporary feminism than a name: links between them need to be established and cannot be assumed from the outset.

In my view these problems derived from an overstrict identification of feminism with a women's movement, and of the history of feminism with the history of the achievement of the aims of that movement. Such an identification depends on a definition of feminism as *activity*, whether diffuse or directed to a given end. As a perspective it generates further problems, too.

The focus on feminism as activity, as campaigns around issues, tends to underplay the nature of the general debate about women and the extent to which feminists were involved in setting its terms. Claims are often made, for example, about women's 'silence' or exclusion from public speech in the nineteenth century. It is hard to find much evidence to support this in the journals of the period.[29] A rhetoric of exclusion is taken as factual description. Although there was a good deal of thinking and writing in the politics of nineteenth-century feminism, this is rarely foregrounded. Pride of place is given to feminism's dramas.

And there is sometimes something rather suspect in this emphasis on feminism as activity, as locus of a particular campaigning spirit. In *The Tamarisk Tree* Dora Russell recalls that after the Labour Party Conference of 1926, at which her group won an endorsement of their birth control campaign, H. G. Wells sent her a postcard, part of which read 'Bertie thinks, I write, but you DO'.[30] On the face of it a compliment. Yet is it? Does it not sum up a certain position in regard to women's politics, to feminism, to its history, to women in general? Men think and write, women do; men thought and wrote, women did (the most famous novel about the New Women was called *The Woman Who Did*). Men reflect; women act out. But in their acting, what ideas were feminist women drawing on, using, transforming, creating? The answers to these questions are often occluded by the presentation of feminism as spectacle.

Present and Past

Instead of a progressive and cumulative history of feminism, it is an historical examination of the dynamics of persistence and change within feminism which is needed. Alongside those narratives which stress the success or failure of particular campaigns, some appraisal of the complicated inheritance of feminist thought and practice is required. This inheritance is not simply a part of the past but lives in the present, both as a part of the conditions of existence of contemporary feminism, and as a part of that very feminism.

When the women's liberation movement came into existence in the late 1960s, it emerged into a social order already marked by an assimilation of other feminisms. Feminism was already a part of the political and social fabric. It was not present as a dominant force: feminists were after all the representatives of a subordinate group.[31] But the logic of mainstream feminism – that there could be a politics directed towards women – had been assimilated, even if women have not normally acted as a unified political constituency, and if 'women's politics' had, by the 1960s, become stereotyped.

It had become acceptable, before the emergence of the women's liberation movement, to think about women as a separate social group with needs and interests of their own, even if this way of thinking has been unstable and not always in evidence. This does not mean that only feminists treated 'woman' as a unified category, or that anyone who does so is a feminist. Nor is it to say that all feminists share or have shared the same concept of womanhood. Although the suffrage movement effected a political shift away from exclusive considerations of women as sex to emphasize women as social group, the post-suffrage movement (after much conflict) adopted a concept of woman based on the needs of reproduction and the social value of maternity.[32]

An autonomous female subject, woman speaking in her own right, with her own voice, had also emerged. It has been part of the project of feminism in general to attempt to transform women from an object of knowledge into a subject capable of appropriating knowledge, to effect a passage from the state of subjection to subjecthood.[33] In great measure this project was realized within the feminism of the 1860s to the 1930s, albeit in literary form.[34]

Women's liberation groups formed within a context which already included a programme for women's legal and political emancipation – the unfinished business of 1928 – and pressure groups and lobbyists working for it.[35] This simultaneity of what might be called an 'old' feminism and a 'new' is perhaps one reason why broad and loose definitions of feminism have such an appeal, and why such broad definitions can be shared by feminists and non-feminists. The content of the term has not been determined by the women's liberation movement. A pre-existing content was already part of culture, and could not be negotiated or wished away.

Modern feminism is an admixture, and the boundaries between its components, between its 'past' and its 'present', are not necessarily that clear. At the start of the contemporary women's liberation movement it was common for women's liberationists to distance themselves from emancipationism, the campaign for equality between the sexes. Despite this, women's liberation has spawned campaigns for legal and financial equality, equal opportunity at work, and other demands which have an emancipationist object. 'Women's right to enter a man's world' is both demanded and criticized. The ambivalence which the issue arouses is important because it indicates areas of uncertainty and confusion about feminist aims, a confusion which might be more productive than a premature clarity.

Nor has the *image* of the feminist been the creation of women's liberation. Traces of the feminist past and its often unsolved problems persist in collective social memories and the various social meanings of feminism. What captures the public imagination about feminism is often indicative of what is both new and a survival, and a good guide to feminism's impact. It is more difficult than might at first be thought to distinguish between a feminist and a non-feminist image of feminism; often only the interpretations differ.

Feminists were, and still are, imagined as confined to the narrow world of women, the marginal world of women's issues, cut off from the general field of human endeavour (which in some vocabularies is called class politics). Fear of separation and marginalization still has a strong inhibitory power. The issue of separatism, the creation of a female culture and community, is at the heart of an unfinished debate within feminism and between feminisms.

Feminists are also imagined as the bearers of female anger, as female incendiaries. The bra-burner of 1968 merges with the *petroleuse* of the Paris Commune; the sex shop arsonist of 1978 with the pillar box arsonist of 1913. The explosive quality of feminism, its fieriness, its anger, is contained within the image of the bra-burner, as is the protest against sexual constraint.[36]

There were in effect various concepts from feminist discourses (and various responses to them) already in circulation when the first new women's groups began to meet in the 1960s. It is possible to look at the three already mentioned (the idea of women as a social group with an underlying unity of interest, the realization of a feminine subject distinguishable from the male, the possibility of a politics which could focus exclusively on women) and mark, after twenty years, the changes each has gone through, if only in a schematic way.

One of the most striking features of women's liberation and radical feminism was their recourse to a new language – the language of liberation rather than emancipation, of collectivism rather than individualism. Radical sociology and marxism were placed in the foreground of attempts to analyse women's position. There were new forms of practice too – the consciousness-raising group, the refusal of formal, delegated structures of political organization, a stress on participation rather than representation – and a new concept: that of 'sexual politics'.

'Sexual politics' held together the idea of women as social group dominated by men as social group (male domination/female oppression), at the same time as turning back to the issue of women as sex *outside* of the bounds of reproduction. It threw political focus onto the most intimate transactions of the bedroom: this became one of the meanings of 'the personal is political'. These two aspects have not always stayed held together: some feminists have attached most value to the study of 'women' as social group and object of political concern. It is, however, the pursuit of questions about the female body and its sexual needs which has become distinctive of contemporary feminism.

For past feminisms it was male sexuality that was at issue: the need was as much to constrain male sexuality as to liberate women from the work of paying the costs of male desire. There are feminists today for whom women's problem is still male desire. But alongside the challenge to male sexuality there goes a curiosity about female desire, female sexuality, and the problems of relations between women.

At the same time the autonomous female subject has become, in a much more pronounced way, the subject of feminism. In 1866, J. S. Mill could be welcomed as an adequate representative of women's aspirations by the first women's suffrage societies. As recently as 1972 Simone de Beauvoir could refer to feminists as 'those women or even men who fight to change the position of women, in liaison with and yet outside the class struggle, without totally subordinating that change to a change in society.'[37] Now, in the mid-eighties, it is practically impossible to speak of 'male feminism'. Feminism is increasingly understood by feminists as a way of thinking created by, for, and on behalf of women, as 'gender-specific'. Women are its subjects, its enunciators, the creators of its theory, of its practice and of its language.[38]

When this intensification of emphasis on women as the subject of feminism coincides with an emphasis on women as feminism's object and focus of attention (women's experience, literature, history, psyche, and so on) certain risks are run. The doubling-up of women, as subject and object, can produce a circular, self-confirming rhetoric and a hermetic closure of thought. The feminine subject becomes trapped by the dynamics of self-reflectivity within the narcissism of the mirror-image.[39]

Feminism's fascination with women is also the condition of the easy slippage from 'feminist' to 'woman' and back: the feminist becomes the representative of 'woman', just as 'feminist history' becomes the same as 'women's history' and so on.

This intensification of the use of concepts already in circulation has produced not so much a continuity of feminisms as a set of crises. It is, for example, one of women's liberation's paradoxes that although it started on the terrain of sexual antagonism between men and women, it moved quickly to a state in which relations between women caused the most internal stress. Women, in a sense, are feminism's greatest problem. The assumption of a potential identity between women, rather than solving the problem, became a condition of increasing tensions.

Of these tensions, not the least important is the intellectual tension generated by a crisis of the concept 'woman' within feminist thought. As a concept, 'woman' is too fragile to bear the weight of all the contents and meanings now ascribed to it. The end of much research by feminists has been to show the tremendous diversity of the meaning of womanhood, across cultures and over time. This result serves feminist purposes by providing evidence that change is possible because the social meaning of womanhood is malleable. But to demonstrate the elusiveness of 'woman' as a category can also subvert feminists' assumption that women can be approached as a unity. It points up the extent to which the concept of womanhood employed by feminists is always partial.

One indication of this crisis is the way in which 'sexual division' and 'sexual difference' are named with increasing frequency as the objects of feminist enquiry. Where this happens there is a shift away from the treatment of 'men' and 'women' as discrete groups and a stress on the relationships between the two. Of particular significance here have been the uses of psychoanalytic and critical theory in the attempt to understand the 'sexed subject', with a consequent movement from the unsatisfactory terms 'man' and 'woman' to the differently unsatisfactory terms 'masculinity' and 'femininity'.

This work is often criticized as 'non-political', but in my view its political implications are what raise alarm. The employment of psychoanalysis and critical theory to question the unity of the subject, to emphasize the fragmented subject, is potentially subversive of any view which asserts a 'central' organizing principle of social conflict. Radical feminism, for example, has depended as much as some marxist political theories on such an assertion: sex war replaces class war as the 'truth' of history, and in its enactment the sexes are given a coherent identity. To deconstruct the subject 'woman', to question whether 'woman' is a coherent identity, is also to imply the question of whether 'woman' is a coherent political identity, and therefore whether women can unite politically, culturally, and socially as 'women' for other than very specific reasons. It raises questions about the feminist project at a very fundamental level.

Such questions are open ones and need to remain so. How far the practico-theoretical fragmentation of what calls itself the women's movement can be related to the lack of cohesiveness of the concept 'woman' is a matter of speculation. The nineteenth-century social movement was also fragmented, and spoke, as do feminisms today, to a general political crisis of representation. This crisis is not restricted to feminists, nor to the political institutions and political languages which they have had a part in making. In what form, forms or combinations feminism will survive is not a question which can yet be answered.

Notes

1 Parts of this article were included in a paper given to the London History Workshop Seminar in April 1983. I would like to thank all those who participated in the discussion which followed and all those friends and colleagues who have discussed the various themes of this article with me. Special thanks are due to Beatrix Campbell, Catherine Hall, Juliet Mitchell, Mike and Ines Newman, Geoffrey Nowell-Smith and Brenda Storey.

2 'Of two neighbouring towns each is the other's most jealous rival; every little canton looks down on the others with contempt. Closely related races keep one another at arm's length; the South German cannot endure the North German, the Englishman casts every kind of aspersion upon the Scot, the Spaniard despises the Portuguese.' Sigmund Freud, *Group Psychology and the Analysis of the Ego*, (Standard Edition, Vol 18, Hogarth, London, 1958), 101 See also *Civilisation and its Discontents*, ch. V (Vol 21 of the same edition).

3 This can happen in both politics and culture. One example is the creation of 'feminist art' as a category within art criticism into which the work of many women artists is conveniently slotted. Far from focusing attention on the work of those artists who are feminists, such a label removes their art practice to the margins, and forecloses the question of whether such a thing as 'feminist art' exists. For a discussion of feminist art practice see Mary Kelly, 'Desiring Images/Imaging Desire' in *Wedge*, 6 (New York, 1984).

4 This point of view was expressed, for example, in the London Women's Liberation Workshop Manifesto, drafted in 1970 by a group of London women as the basis of their work together. Part of it read: 'Women's Liberation Workshop believes that women in our society are oppressed. We are economically oppressed; in jobs we do full work for half pay, at home we do unpaid work full time. We are commercially exploited by advertisements, television and the press. Legally women are discriminated against. We are brought up to feel inadequate, educated to narrower horizons than men. It is as women therefore that we are organizing.' The manifesto was circulated as a cyclostyled sheet to all those interested in the Workshop and was published monthly in its magazine *Shrew*. All those who shared its perception of what it meant to be a woman could take part in workshop activities and thus become participants in the women's movement.

5 This 'we' is reminiscent of what Benveniste calls the 'dilated I', a 'we' which 'annexes to the "I" an indistinct globality of other persons', Emile Benveniste, *Problèmes de Linguistique Générale* (Gallimard, Paris 1966), 235.

6 Indeed, the Workshop manifesto stressed heterogeneity: 'Women's Liberation Workshop is essentially heterogeneous, incorporating within it a wide range of opinions and plans for action. The assumption was that these opinions and plans could harmonize because in the context of a movement women could find a new way of working together.

7 For example, the statement that women in the home 'do unpaid work full time' is one that could be agreed by all supporters of the Manifesto. The analysis that this hidden labour (hidden from the point of view of capital) is the secret of capital's exploitation of women and that therefore there should be a campaign for wages for housework in order to reclaim its value was highly contentious and never gained more than minority backing.

8 For discussions of Greenham Common see Caroline Blackwood, *On the Perimeter* (Heinemann, London/Viking, NY, 1984; Alice Cook and Gwyn Kirk, *Greenham Women Everywhere* (Pluto Press, London/The South End Press, Boston, 1983); Lynne Jones (ed.), *Keeping the Peace* (The Women's Press, London 1983); and *Breaching the Peace* conference papers by a group of radical feminists (Onlywomen Press, London, 1983).

9 Professor Olive Banks, for example, employs this broad definition: 'Any groups that have tried to *change* the position of women, or ideas about women, have been granted the title feminist' in her *Faces of Feminism* (Martin Robertson, Oxford 1981), 3.

10 'In the radical feminist view, the new feminism is not just the revival of a serious political movement for social equality. It is the second wave of the most popular revolution in history', Shulamith Firestone, *The Dialectic of Sex* (Cape, London, 1971), 16. *The Second Wave* was also the name of a US radical feminist journal. It is a phrase which is still used.

11 Ray Strachey, *The Cause* (Bell, London 1928; reprinted Virago, London 1978).

12 *Shorter Oxford English Dictionary*, 1933.

13 Strachey, *The Cause*, 12.

14 Ibid., 13.

15 Ibid., 24.

16 At least, so it seems to me. Margaret Forster writes that feminists like Harriet Martineau regarded Caroline Norton with 'contempt' for her disavowal of feminism, and claims that Caroline Norton's insights were 'more truly feminist than any of the openly feminist tracts of her day', *Significant Sisters* (Secker & Warburg, London, 1984), 50. This argument begs the question of the content of feminist ideas.

17 Barbara Taylor, *Eve and the New Jerusalem* (Virago, London, 1984).

18 For a further account of this period, see Jane Rendall, *The Origins of Modern Feminism* (Macmillan, London, 1985).

19 Cf. Joan Kelly, 'Early Feminist Theory and the *Querelle de Femmes*' in *Signs*, 11, Vol 8, 1982: 'Most histories of the Anglo-American women's movement acknowledge feminist "forerunners" in individual figures

such as Anne Hutchinson, and in women inspired by the English and French revolutions, but only with the women's rights conference at Seneca Falls in 1848 do they recognise the beginnings of a continuously developing body of feminist thought.'

20 In *The Reasonableness of Christianity* Locke includes women amongst those 'who cannot know and therefore must believe'; as such they could be excluded from considerations of equality. In his own lifetime Mary Astell and the unknown author of *An Essay in Defence of the Female Sex* used his work on human understanding to stake the claim that 'mind has no sex' and that women, as members of the human species, had rights to equal mental development with men.

21 Both Locke and Rousseau are used against themselves. Their categories of the individual as property owner and *paterfamilias* are subverted by the claim that women have the right to be considered thinking and reasoning subjects (after Locke) and feeling subjects (after Rousseau). This is not a rejection of their arguments, but an incorporation of them. In particular, Rousseau is not, as is sometimes claimed, rejected by Mary Wollstonecraft but is used and assimilated within her work.

22 Dr Richard Pankhurst, 'The Right of Women to Vote under the Reform Act, 1867' in *Fortnightly Review*, Vol 10 (September 1868), 250–4.

23 Helen Taylor, 'The Ladies Petition' in *Westminster Review* (January 1867), 63–79.

24 Ibid., 63–4.

25 Ibid., 70.

26 Mary Wollstonecraft, *A Vindication of the Rights of Woman* (Norton, NY, 1967), 220.

27 There was much discussion, for example, of whether women could take on the duties of the armed citizen. It was several years before suffragists began to say that women in childbirth risked their lives as much as did the soldier. The Conservative politician, Goldwyn Smith, expostulated, 'we have only to imagine the foreign policy of England determined by women, while that of other countries is determined by the men; and this in the age of Bismark'. ('Female Suffrage', *Macmillan's Magazine*, Vol 30 (June 1874), 139–50.) The concept of woman implicit in this vision was shared by many feminists who asserted that women's gentler nature would attenuate the violence of male politics.

28 The most famous definition of this principle came from Blackwood's *Commentaries*: 'By marriage the very being or legal existence of a woman is suspended, or at least it is incorporated or consolidated into that of the husband, under whose wing, protection, and cover she performs everything and she is therefore called in our law a feme covert' (*femme couverte*). The principle of *coverture* meant that generally speaking the married woman did not exist as legal subject or as property owner.

29 Apart from a stream of articles from various hands published in the *Fortnightly Review* and the *Westminster Review*, the *Edinburgh Review*, *Contemporary Review*, *Fraser's Magazine*, *Macmillan's Magazine*, the *Nineteenth Century*, the *New Review*, the *National Review*, and the *Theological Review*, all carried a range of articles written by women who would have described themselves as feminists.

30 Dora Russell, *The Tamarisk Tree* (Virago, London 1977), Vol 1, 189.

31 Participants in nineteenth-century campaigns included the daughters of British radicalism, of fathers active in the Anti-Corn Law League, the movement to abolish slavery, the agitation for the 1832 Reform Bill. Their aim was to be incorporated into the ruling group, to have their rights recognized and their ideas re-represented within a liberal consensus. *The Cause* gives a good portrait of this aspect of the suffrage movement. Paul McHugh, in *Prostitution and Victorian Social Reform* (Croom Helm, London, 1980), includes an account of the personnel involved in the Ladies National Association for the Abolition of the Contagious Diseases Act.

32 The years following the suffrage witnessed fierce debates between 'old' feminists and 'new'. The platform of the 'new' feminists, adopted by the National Union of Societies for Equal Citizenship (the new name of the National Union of Women's Suffrage Societies) in 1925, was that feminists should turn away from demands for equality with men, and concentrate on those issues specific to women as women. They linked women's special needs to those concerned with maternity and reproduction, and feminism to issues like birth control and family allowances. See Mary Stocks, *Eleanor Rathbone* (Gollancz, London, 1949) and Rosalind Delmar, 'Afterword' to Vera Brittain, *Testament of Friendship* (Virago and Fontana, London 1980).

33 One can trace elements of this project in the combination of Mary Wollstonecraft's political and fictional writings. Alexandra Kollontai picks out the theme in the conclusion to her essay 'The New Woman', when she writes that 'Woman, by degrees, is being transformed from an object of tragedy of the male soul into the subject of an independent tragedy', *Autobiography of a Sexually Emancipated Woman* (Orbach and Chambers, London, 1972), 103.

34 This is not so true of cinema and television and is perhaps why feminists have made such a distinctive contribution to the analysis of cinematic representation. See Constance Penley (ed.), *Feminism and Film Theory* (BFI Publishing, London, forthcoming).

35 The Sex Discrimination Act went through Parliament in 1975 after a campaign in which the new women's groups took very little interest; there were other women's organizations carrying that particular torch. Mary Stott evokes the encounter between these 'old' and 'new' feminists in *Before I Go* (Virago, London, 1985).

36 Although the 'real event' of bra burning is often fiercely denied, and Edith Thomas has questioned the existence of the *petroleuses*, it is interesting that Josephine Butler believed in their existence and justified their actions, assuming them to be women forced into prostitution and released from brothels by the Commune. See her *Some Lessons from Contemporary History* (The Friends Association for the Abolition of State Regulation of Vice, London 1898). Martha Vicinus explores the recurrent imagery of fire in suffragette writing in her *Independent Women* (Virago, London and University of Chicago Press, 1985).

37 Simone de Beauvoir, interview with Alice Schwartzer; translation published in *7 Days*, London, 8 March 1972.

38 I am grateful to Stephen Heath, whose unpublished paper, 'Male Feminism' helped clarify this point for me. The changes indicated here

are expressive of a general shift in relations between men and women *within* feminism.

39 This dimension of feminism is absorbingly represented in the film *Riddles of the Sphinx* by Laura Mulvey and Peter Wollen (BFI, London 1977). See especially episode 12, 'Maxine's room', described in the script as 'space fragmented by reflections and reflections within reflections' (*Screen*, Vol 18, Summer 1977, 2).

3 Reflections on Twenty Years of Feminism

Juliet Mitchell

It is twenty-one years since the publication of Betty Friedan's *The Feminine Mystique*. It seems a good time to look back – admittedly with nostalgia, but more importantly with some critical reflections on the history of feminism in our times.

The Women's Liberation Movement started in the mid sixties; its initiating literature preceded it by about a year. Looking back from the eighties, Umberto Eco, at the opening of *The Name of the Rose*, writes of the late nineteen-sixties when he discovered his fictional manuscript: 'In the years when I discovered the Abbé Vallet volume, there was a widespread conviction that one should write only out of commitment to the present, in order to change the world. Now, after ten years or more, the man of letters . . . can happily write out of pure love of writing . . . [a story] gloriously lacking in any relevance for our day, atemporally alien to our hopes and our certainties.'[1]

The heady days of sixties radical protest – Blacks, Students, Women – are over. I believe that the transition to the relative inactivity of the eighties indicates more than the fact that our movement has come of age, more too – though this is true – than that those of us who were active at the outset are now looking back from the seeming quietude of middle age. If we must recollect in tranquillity, perhaps we should try to understand why this is so.

Feminism as a body of thought and as a political movement marches on, but has it developed? What Eco points to as a generality suggests something disturbing in the specifics of feminism. In order to reflect on the significance for feminism of this transition of spirit, I shall focus on two questions: What large-scale changes have there been in the position of women in the last two decades? And what is the relationship of feminism of these changes?

By way of an apology for the crudities of my use of history and economics in this essay, I would emphasize that I am neither a historian nor an economist. From the standpoints of these disciplines, mine is very much an outsider's curiosity. My questions come from an attempt to understand the position of women as a feminist and a psychoanalyst.

I shall use England as my source material for the obvious reason that it is the country with which I am most familiar. But also because, in the past, its development has been, in some ways, exemplary and it can thus be used not for its particularities but for its generalities. In this way what I am aiming at is not a history, but a case-history – an instance that can stand in for others.

Feminism in England and North America has interacted extensively, reflecting in this, the general political and economic involvement of the two countries. But I shall use what little I know about the United States only to ask some questions about England; not to examine American processes but to use American results to question our experiences. America often appears to be ten or even twenty years ahead of us. Does American society prefigure a general historical change? Perhaps change is now retarded in England? Can we use America and England against each other to show up more widespread changes in Western capitalism?

The most dramatic change affecting women in England – indeed, in Europe – is the steep rise in unemployment. Within the growing unemployment, the most significant factor for feminism is that women form the only sector of the community with increased employment prospects. Women, usually in early middle age, are getting the jobs. As a well-known British economist recently told a group of high-school leavers: 'it is not you who will find jobs, but your mothers'. Of course, while such polemic is true, it is also misleading.

The situation is not as in wartime when women literally took over jobs that were, and would again be, done by men. Today women are doing the type of service jobs that men have never done and that young people, starting adult life, would probably not consider doing.

In the twenty odd years of feminism in Britain, women have increased as a percentage of the labour-force from 33 per cent to 40 per cent (a figure reached twenty years ago in the United States). In an overall way, relative to men's, women's work is increasing so that it is predicted that by 1990 women will take up two-thirds of the net increases in jobs. What are we witnessing in the increased employment of women?

The entry of women into jobs at a time of male unemployment has happened before. It is not a unique phenomenon – there have been other moments in history when a comparable switch in the economic distribution of the sexes has occured. Do these periods have something in common, do these repeated occurrences suggest that women serve a particular function at certain given historical junctures?

In Europe today, are we experiencing a crisis, a period of prolonged transition, some adaption to a new form of capitalism, or are our apocalyptic nightmares of nuclear destruction an ideological reflection of the fact that we are in the very late stages of the decline and fall of a way of life, a major mode of production?

I want to suggest tentatively that by many and complex comparisons of the position of women at various historical con-junctures, we could gain some insight into the type of process in which we are presently caught up. Several political thinkers have, in different ways, argued that the position of women in society indicates the general level of social advance; I am wondering whether we could not produce a more specific analysis that would help us to see where we are.

Our situation as women at any given time may not only be a general index of social advance towards a humane and equitable society, but a more sensitive (and problematic) indication of the stage of the process of social change. Thus I do not entirely agree, for instance, with either Fourier or Marx, that the position of women signals the level of civilization, so that the better our position, the higher the values of the society. The history of women's status is a more stop-go affair – a reflection not only, or not so much, of general social improvement, as of the unevenness of social change.

My tentative hypothesis is that women are used within the economy as a temporary advance guard or, perhaps, as a toe in the water of an unknown sea. I suggest that women are the first, temporary inhabitants of the future. That, contrary to myth, within history, it may well be that women are there first and that then men are made in the image of women. If this is so, it may well be true only of capitalist or only of industrial countries. It may be true more generally; I do not know.

I shall single out one striking instance from the past of the increasing employment of women in the context of rising male unemployment – an instance whose documentation by Friedrich Engels has become part of the fabric of contemporary feminist thought.

Engels's *The Condition of the Working Class in Britain in 1844* is a superb work of social history in the tradition of Mayhew and other classical nineteenth-century observers. The shift from small-scale manufacturing to the vast industrial factories was taking place – machinery that could replace human labour threw men out of work. But it was women and children who first went in to undertake the new work of running and servicing the machinery. By a close survey of conditions in major new industrial centres, particularly Manchester, Engels breaks down the general observation that the introduction of new machinery is responsible for the widespread unemployment:

> Let us examine somewhat more closely the fact that machinery more and more supersedes the work of men. The human labour, involved in both spinning and weaving, consists chiefly in piecing broken threads, as the machine does all the rest. This work requires no muscular strength, but only flexibility of finger. Men are, therefore, not only not needed for it, but actually, by reason of the greater muscular development of the hand, less fit for it than women and children, and are, therefore, naturally almost superseded by them. Hence, the more the use of the arms, the expenditure of strength, can be transferred to steam or water-power, the fewer men need be employed and as women and children work more cheaply, and in these branches better than men, they take their places. In the spinning mills women and girls are to be found in almost exclusive possession of the throstles; among the mules one man adult spinner (with self-actors, he, too, becomes superfluous), and several piecers for tying the threads, usually women and children, sometimes young men of from eighteen to twenty years, here and there an old spinner thrown out of other employment. At the power-looms women, from fifteen to twenty years, are chiefly employed, and a few men; these however, rarely remain at this trade after their twenty-first year. Among the preparatory machinery, too, women alone are to be found, with here and there a man to clean and sharpen the carding-frames . . . the actual work of the mills is done by women and children.[2]

What Engels, of course, could not foresee in 1844 was that once the transition was effected, men would take over as the main industrial work-force.

Are there any meaningful resemblances to our own epoch? At first it would seem that the global comparisons are only of increased general unemployment and, within this, a relative increase in women's employment. To compare our inner cities, and child poverty and abuse with Dickensian England, seems at first sight preposterous and vulgarly polemical. There are, of course, important differences – but I suggest that there are important similarities too.

What were the social effects of women's vanguard entry into industrial production? Engels commented on the early sexual maturity of mill-girls (thought to be the effects of over-heating as in the tropics), the promiscuity, the illegitimacy, the rate of abortions, the amenorrhea and the infertility. New and more virulent sex-based diseases appeared. He observed how adolescents came to use their homes as bed-and-breakfast lodging houses; often the family bread-winners, they appeared more like the adults to their unemployed and hence infantilized fathers. To illustrate the effects on the previously established sexual division of labour, Engels reports a conversation between his working-class friend Joe, and Joe's mate, Jack:

'. . . my poor missus is i' th' factory; she has to leave at half-past five and works till eight at night, and then she is so knocked up that she cannot do aught when she gets home, so I have to do everything for her what I can, for I have no work, nor had any for more nor three years, and I shall never have any more work while I live;' and then he wept a big tear. Jack again said: 'There is work enough for women folks and childer here abouts, but none for men; thou mayest sooner find a hundred pound on the road than work for men – but I should never have believed that thou or anyone else would have seen me mending my wife's stocking, for it is bad work. But she can hardly stand on her own two feet; I am afraid she will be laid up, and then I don't know what is to become of us, for it's a good bit she has been the man in the house and I the woman; it is bad work, Joe;' and he cried bitterly, and said 'It has not been always so . . . thou knowest when I got married I had work plenty. . . . And we had a good furnished house, and Mary need not go to work. I could work for the two of us; but now the world is upside down. Mary has to go to work and I have to stop at home and mind the childer, sweep and wash, bake and mend; and, when the poor woman comes home at night, she is knocked up. Thou knows, Joe, it's hard for one that was used different.'[3]

In his commentary, Engels fairmindedly reminds us that this family-turned-upside-down should act as evidence of the pristine inhumanity of male rule in a family 'the right way up'. The restoration of the traditional patriarchal structure is no solution to this 'insane state of things'.

Today, we are not going through a transition from smaller-scale home or community based work to industrial manufacture with its massive institutions of factories and schools, nor are we coming directly out of such an industrialized, urban world into something else. Many changes have intervened between 1844 and 1984. My point here is merely a comparison of two moments of transition in the same country in the advanced world.

There may be historical moments when the normal processes of change are speeded up. A major economic shift, at certain times, may demand a social change which amounts to a trauma. Old lines of class opposition are redrawn, the meanings of masculinity and femininity nudge each other and jostle for new places. In Engels's words, at a point of transition, the crisis 'unsexes the man and takes from the woman all womanliness without being able to bestow on the man true womanliness or on the woman true manliness. . .'.[4] Today, maybe, a new dominant class opposition and a new content to the definition of sexual difference are in their birth-throes. Maybe this shift is being effected through employed women and unemployed men.

The sexual revolution of the nineteen sixties had its revolutionary moment repressed and succeeded by drugs, disease and the desperate crime and violence of the urban dispossessed. In England we now have the curtailment of social welfare, of education, of medical care – the sending into the community, as in the early nineteenth century, of the newly and obnoxiously designated 'unemployable'. And in the home – for the working class – once more, the family turned upside down. While this crisis and chaos continues, can we glimpse aspects of the social change it indicates?

Using the United States as our retrospective forecast we can see that, in this area, what has been achieved is an acceptance of fairly high full-time unemployment, low social services and a highly mobile and relatively flexible work-force.

The change that is taking place in England is towards a similar level of unemployment screened by an ideology of a leisure society, a shift from full-time to part-time employment and from manu-facturing to service industries. The very words – part-time work, leisure, service – sum up our image of women. But then so did other features, such as nimble fingers, characterize women for factory owners and their critics alike, 140 years ago. Our idiom, as is typical in other fields as well, has changed from the physiological psychology of the nineteenth century to the sociological psychology of the twentieth.

In England today, we have a situation in which male industrial workers are thrown out of jobs because of the closure or near complete computerization of heavy industries – steel, coal, shipping, and middle-aged women are employed part-time in the service industries. Overall the only increase in employment is among the self-employed for men and the part-time for women. The self-employed men are small-time entrepreneurs, often encouraged initially by small government grants, the part-time women are in cleaning, catering, hairdressing and other personal services, if they are working class, and in the professional and scientific services, if they are middle class. The largest categories of unemployed are the old and the young, creating on the one hand a sector needing services, and on the other, a severe degree of demoralization manifested not in radical politics but in urban decay, vandalism and rioting.

When they leave school at sixteen and for the next few years, the distinction between boys and girls is apparently obliterated; they share the same fate: unemployment. They cannot become coal-miners or coal-miners' wives. We cannot know what they will become. Perhaps we will have to wait a generation or more to see if the lack of sexual differentiation at the level of employment and occupation remains. Somehow I doubt it, despite the tendency towards this at the moment. Already in America, in the mid-eighties, there is an increase in sex-based segregation at work despite earlier countervailing impressions.

Even within the period of critical change, its crisis marked by the entry of women into employment, a glance at education and training suggests that future sex differentiation may be lying in wait to be redeployed in a period of stabilization.

Both sexes of school-leavers are characterized by unemployment; they differ in that boys fare worse. Boys are more unemployed. At eighteen, 23 per cent of boys and 18 per cent of girls are without jobs. But there is a further difference between those who are not in paid employment but who are occupied: there are more boys in some sort of training scheme and more girls in some sort of education beyond the age at which it is compulsory. (Of girls who are in training schemes, by far the higher proportion are in ones run by employers in a fashion somewhat analogous to those run by benevolent factory-owners in the nineteenth century.) I believe that once men and women become identical as a new social class or occupy new positions together within the same re-defined social class, a sexual division – drawn along new lines of connotation – will operate within this.

When children went into the factories 150 and more years ago, they did so regardless of sex – but within the overall similarities, there were specific occupational differences. A few decades later, compulsory education was established to 'teach the orphan boy to read' for the new technology, the 'orphan girl to sew' for the services needed. If today boys are getting more training and girls more education, is it so that the boy orphaned from the traditional working class will be able to man the computers, and the orphan girl, with her education, to care for the aged, the sick and the needs of the leisured, the child and the 'unemployable'? Probably that is too simple a division. But at least while we wait and see in what ways or whether the present distinction in today's unemployed youth is significant, we can observe that a training is immediately geared to future employment (as reading was in the nineteenth century), whereas, like sewing, a general education at a time when, in England, education is being massively down-graded, will keep. We should note too, the surely significant fact that, while girls have made a shift from their almost exclusive occupation with languages and the arts into the sciences, it is particularly into the non-applied, above all the biological, sciences, that they have gone. The one science into which girls have made no important increase in their entry in the last decade is computer science (indeed, the number of girls entering it have slightly declined).

In this period of intensified change, as a general tendency, it seems that older women are taking on new jobs. Both middle- and working-class women take on these jobs, which, I believe, will be the jobs of the future working class – male and female. Men, at this point, become unemployed. However, from within the ranks of the unemployed men and possibly from among the newly employed middle-class women, a new group of the self-employed and of entrepreneurs emerges. It is this 'self-employment', then, that produces the necessary dominant ideology of 'classlessness' mandatory for any transition. It has happened before.

What has been the relationship of feminism to the processes of social change, those processes that have so dubiously focused on the advancement of women into the workforce?

If women are put into a temporary vanguard position in relation to economic and social change, this cannot be the result of an overnight directive; something must facilitate this shift. In looking at this question of the role of ideology in relation to changes in production, it is important to bear in mind differences of social class.

In this context, what has been the conscious role and unconscious function of the women's movement and its dominant concepts in the last two decades?

I believe that our feminist attacks on the system, despite our intentions, were highly complicit with the present changes. This is not to castigate ourselves (though certainly self-criticism is involved), but rather to demonstrate once more that a radical politics, indeed any radical thought, must bear the marks of its origin which may not be perceived until it is too late.

Looking back, for the sake of an organizing schema, we can divide our recent feminist history into two stages. To characterize the two stages I would invert the title of a preceding anthology of essays which I edited with Ann Oakley in 1976. It was called *The Rights and Wrongs of Women*, itself the title of a seminal essay by Margaret Walters on, among others, Mary Wollstonecraft who, as well as writing *The Vindication of the Rights of Woman*, wrote a novel called *Maria, or The Wrongs of Woman*.

The first stage of our movement was directed to putting right the wrongs of women, the second to an emphasis on the values, the importance of the qualities of womanhood and femininity – peace, caring, nurturance. (We should note the further turn of the screw about the rights of women – again the predictable discovery in recent feminist literature that we are all wrong (in another way) after all. Now we are full of masochism, the desire to be abused or raped, our own worst enemies – thus we help prepare the way for the redenigration of women as the time fast approaches when we will step back from the front lines into our marginality. But by this point I think what we can call our wave of feminism has heard its death knell – the term feminism loses all meaning at this stage of self-flagellation.) Such a schema is too simple, but it will do for the purpose of organizing our recent history.

First the wrongs. In England, our demands were two-pronged: on the one hand, for equal pay and work opportunities and, on the other, for a change in the sexual image and status of women. Both were badly needed.

If we examine critically our struggle for equal pay and work opportunities (again, within the ethics of our society, perfectly proper aims in themselves), the nominal achievement of these facilitated future male unemployment and the debasement – temporarily – of the condition of workers in general. To go back once more to 1844, Engels had commented on the role of the cheap labour of women and children: its task was to introduce a lower standard of living and lower wages for men. In the intervening period the trade union movement to protect the rights of workers had been established and the threat to the male worker's wage of women's cheaper labour had been recognized. Once, in the late sixties, women had been awarded the right to equal pay (in fact only achieved today in Britain, nearly eighteen years later, in the police force and among butchers), there could no longer be any union opposition to their employment. However, women's real pay is always lower and women predominantly work part-time and hence are largely unprotected. Women are poorly unionized at a time when union strength was to be assailed from all sides; lacking job security and health and old-age benefits, women have no reason, therefore, not to move jobs or move out of jobs should the need arise. Our aim was equal pay; a tragic effect of our achievement was to remove pay as an obstacle and then to erode the conditions of employment, to help lower the expectation of social security, state benefits, trade union support . . . workers' solidarity . . . to make way for a mobile, flexible worker and the self-employed. In fighting for equal pay, in no way was this our intention, but the passing of the law did facilitate the change.

Consciously we were attacking a consumer society and the place of women within it. We slapped stickers over the Underground – 'this ad. insults women', attacked 'Miss World' contests and challenged the treatment of women as sex objects. In America the epiphany, whether truth or fiction, was the bra-burning in Washington.

Twenty years ago in Europe, women were used as sexual objects in advertising and in the media in a far more blatant way than was the case in the USA. I can remember how appalled American feminists were by our bill-boards. I have done no statistical survey but, as a lay observer, I believe we have far fewer advertisements using women as their sales object today in Britain; instead there is a proportionate increase in appeals to minority groups such as Blacks and above all to children (again America was far ahead of us in this). The child, not the housewife, is today's consumer. Is this removal of women from advertising to be chalked up as a success for feminist campaigns, or as something more complex over which we had no control?

I wonder, though this does not invalidate the protests, whether in fact we are not attacking something already on the way out. Were we giving a helpful shove to an ideology that was already inappropriate? In the late sixties and early seventies we were attacking women as objects of consumer campaigns at exactly the time when women were wanted back into the workforce. It was precisely the housewives who a decade earlier had had to vie for the whitest wash of all who were now wanted for the part-time labour force – their children could be compensated by more and more toys. Women were not to be sex objects but service workers. In attacking the place of women in consumer society and in simultaneously promoting the employment of women, unwittingly, we were perhaps assisting a change already taking place.

In the second phase of our movement we attacked the idealization of women by men in territories occupied by women only: the home, reproduction and caring for others. This 'pedestal' treatment, like all idealizations, was rightly seen to contain its negative, denigratory side.

It is interesting that after attacking the pedestal treatment of women as earth-mothers, after fighting and showing that we could do what men could do, we then discovered that for our vision of equality, we needed them to do what we could do. Motherhood and domesticity having been negatively appraised, we re-valued them. And so with the wrongs nominally righted, the way was open for the positive aspects of womanhood to be rediscovered. In discovering our values, we made the social and the psychological areas traditionally occupied by women fit for occupation by men – the home was a place for men to inhabit while the women went out into the world of work – for the time being. We facilitated a social shift: if women were to become more like men, men were also to be more like women: 'Men and women cannot be equal partners outside the home, if they are not equal partners inside it', wrote Ann Oakley. For the middle classes this was, and is, very acceptable; a four day week for the professional man with paternity leave and the real pleasures of comfortably off child-care and domesticity; for the woman, a part-time job in which the lack of security presents no hazards. For the working-class couple it is another story: an unemployed coal-miner and his wife bringing in the earned income from cleaning or clerical work. In theory, women, unified as a group, could do similar service jobs, whatever their class, but with very different effects.

However, something yet more important than our facilitation of women into the work-force and out of an old-style, consumer-oriented femininity seems to have been going on.

Challenging the wrongs of women – at work, as sex objects, in education – we were comparing ourselves with men. We could then assert our discrete and independent value. To do this we created or recreated a new unity: women. With tortuous arguing in the early days, we tried to see whether we could call ourselves a class, a caste, a social group and so on. The point is that, calling ourselves 'sisters', we created ourselves once more as a category.

When I started working on the topic of women in 1962, it was virtually impossible to get the differential information on the sexes –

I remember how particularly hard it was in the field of education. Everything was broken down into socio-economic groups. Today I find the reverse: it is easy to obtain information on male/female differences but not on social class achievements and positions.

In forging a concept of women as a unity, we promoted a situation in which old class antagonisms would shift through a period of chaos into something new. In recognizing on paper the class and race distinctions of women but being unable, by definition, to make them the focal thrust of our movement, we contributed to an ideology that temporarily homogenized social classes and created a polarity that disguised other distinctions by the comprehensive, all-embracing opposition – men/women.

We aimed to erode, and indeed did in part erode, the old distinctions between men and women, yet to do so we helped create a major opposition between the sexes. The paradox is only apparent.

By setting up the opposition of the sexes as dominant, we helped to produce the ideological notion of a 'classless' society by which, in this instance, one may mean a society in which the transition to new class lines, or a new class composition, has not yet solidified.

I am left with the two questions with which I started out. What is the meaning of the changed position of women in the last two decades? And, what is the relationship of feminism to this change?

If it is true, as the statistics assert, that women's employment has increased in the wake of male unemployment, what is the cause and what is the effect of this? In the first instance, it would seem that women at work serve to debase the standard of living, to create a new poor from the conditions of the industrial working-class family. Despite 'equal' pay acts, women are used to lower pay and lower conditions of work, to lower expectations; when men, in the future, take over the new jobs from women, the snail of progress will have slithered a foot back down the well. With men's future re-employment firmly established, the snail will struggle up again until the next crisis. But is there something less cyclical going on? Is there more of a linear progression in process, with less backwards slides? Through women's marginality and hence through our flexibility can humankind as a social being move for ever upwards? Do women put the future on trial? The one possibility does not exclude the other.

Both the forward-looking and the complicit aspects of feminism would seem to echo these two possibilities. But first the statistics of change must be looked at more closely. Feminist historians are starting to question Engels's portrait of the increased employment of women in 1844 and, today, even as in this essay I try to construct a picture, its prime colours start to decompose. The very statistics of women's entry into production are subject to both class and sex bias.

There is a massive labour force of working-class and immigrant women which is hidden – I am not here referring to the vexed issue of unpaid labour of childcare and housework – but to the paid, undeclared 'casual' labour and to the home-based production in the myriad forms of 'outwork'. Most women in England always work for wages of some sort. Is the claimed increase of women into production a largely middle-class phenomenon that casts its hegemonic mantle over other women's invisibility? Has one of feminism's unconscious tasks in getting woman out of history's hiding places been to turn her, for the time being, into a legitimate wage-earner for a family with an unemployed man? Does the creation of an umbrella category, 'woman', falsely suggest that middle-class entry into and exit from production which is sporadic, applies to all classes? Is my very argument in this essay trapped in the trammels of the class and sexist assumptions that it is trying to analyse?

In one women's liberation group in which I participated around 1970, we set ourselves the task of charting the amount and nature of the work and the conditions of women 'outworkers' in the area of London where we lived. The result of our enquiry was to uncover an extensive mycelium which only occasionally mushroomed above ground into legality and hence statistics. Today, we have national statistics on 'outwork'. As a further ironic twist of our type of enquiry, a family is less eligible for state benefits where the woman is known to be working.

What we can probably say with some confidence is that, overall, there is a large increase in the number of women seen to be working both in absolute terms and in relation to men. I think also that it is quite likely that women who worked in invisible jobs have for the time shifted into recognized work; maybe this is in addition to their previous work becoming recognized. Certainly it would seem that there is a real increase in middle-class, middle-aged women working for the first time since motherhood.

If we look back at the history of feminism, to its fits and starts, its uneven development over the past 300 years, do its times of efflorescence coincide with a particular type of social and economic transition that temporally places women in a vanguard position either through their new entry or newly acknowledged entry into production? This possibility makes sense to me. It was the eminent feminist Elizabeth Cady-Stanton who encouraged the advance of women, not into production but into a new relationship to circulation, that of consumption, with these words, to an imaginary congressman's wife:

Go and buy a new stove! Buy what you need! Buy while he's in
Washington! When he returns and flies into a rage, you sit in a
corner and weep. That will soften him! Then when he tastes
his food from the new stove, he will know you did the wise
thing. When he sees you so much fresher, happier in your new
kitchen, he will be delighted and its bills will be paid. I repeat
– GO OUT AND BUY.[5]

Feminism does emanate from the bourgeoisie or the petit-
bourgeoisie, the social class which, in capitalist society, where it is
dominant, gives its values to the society as a whole. It represents its
particular interest as universal interest, its women as 'woman'. To
see this is not to turn aside from feminism, but to note that as yet it
has not transcended the limitations of its origins. We should use any
radical movement or thought as an early warning system to make us
aware of changes already in process.

In arguing as feminists for an end to the sexual division of labour,
for social bisexuality, were we promoting an ongoing process of
capitalism, a process whose triumph could only be enjoyed under
socialism?

Many have argued that the process of capitalism (leading, indeed,
to the communism envisaged by Marx and Engels) reduces the
distinction between the sexes to the point of disappearance. Lyotard,
for instance, suggests that the creation of a social-psychological
androgyne (again an ideological contribution from, among others,
the women's movement) is the ultimate goal of an economy driven
towards a final point which is organized solely around the circulation
of exchange objects.

Certainly the thrust of our movement's intention was to overcome
the opposition we had perceived and highlighted – to make men and
women more alike. Whatever our positions, whether as socialist-
feminists coming with marxist traditions (more typical of England)
or as radical feminists (more typical of the United States) our visions
of the future eroded the division of labour within the family, de-
structured generational divisions and dispersed the family tasks of
reproduction and nurturance into myriad alternatives.

However, I do not believe we are simply involved in a straightforward and inevitable progression to an ultimately androgynous
society. If women are the vanguard troops of change, it is not only
because the whole society is becoming feminized or androgynized –
though that is partly true. It is also because, as women, we occupy a
socially marginal and hence shiftable position.

At each crisis of change, I believe, we imagine this androgyne and this endless circulation and free play of multifarious differences; with each period of stabilization, something has to occupy the new point of opposition. In periods of intensified social change, men and women, the masculine and the feminine, come closer together; a new unity is created, a new man, and something different has to confront him. For the time being, we should note that, between the sexes, this new point of difference is called 'woman'.

I would suggest, then, that feminism is an ideological offspring of certain economic and social conditions. Its radicalism reflects the fact that it comes to prominence at points of critical change. It both abets this change and envisages it with an imagination that goes beyond it.

There was nothing wrong with our visions; they just reflected a shift already in process – as indeed they must, but we should have been conscious of this and (a matter for self-criticism) we were not. Again we can return to 1844. Like the machinery that replaced the gruelling labour, the leisure that could replace a long work week, the new technology and a sexual equality that was freed from the conditions of a class society would all be positive changes. This was our vision. As feminists we conceived yesterday's future.

Notes

I would like to thank Margaret Walters, Jennie Popay and the audiences of the Gauss seminars, Princeton, and of Barnard College, New York (1985) where earlier versions of this paper were presented.

1 Umberto Eco, *The Name of the Rose* (Secker & Warburg, London 1983), 5.

2 Frederick Engels, *The Condition of the Working Class in England in 1844* (London 1952), 141.

3 Ibid., 145.

4 Ibid., 146.

5 Elizabeth Cady-Stanton, quoted in Rachel Bowlby, *Just Looking: Consumer Culture in Dreiser, Gissing and Zola* (Methuen, London 1985), 20.

4 Feminist Theory and Feminist Movements: the Past Before Us

Nancy F. Cott

Feminism is nothing if not paradoxical. It aims for individual freedoms by mobilizing sex solidarity. It acknowledges diversity among women while positing that women recognize their unity. It requires gender consciousness for its basis, yet calls for the elimination of prescribed gender roles. These paradoxes of feminism are rooted in women's actual situation, being the same (in a species sense) as men; being different, with respect to reproductive biology and gender construction, from men. In another complication, all women may be said to be 'the same', as distinct from all men with respect to reproductive biology, and yet 'not the same', with respect to the variance of gender construction. Both theory and practice in feminism historically have had to deal with the fact that women are the same as and different from men, and the fact that women's gender identity is not separable from the other factors that make up our selves: race, region, culture, class, age. How have past women's movements accommodated these realities? In both England and the United States from the mid-nineteenth century on, it can be seen that women's rights ideology has taken different forms and emphases depending on whether women's 'equality' or 'difference' comes to the fore; conflict or convergence between these themes has had bearing on the qualities and mass appeal of the women's movement. Until the 1960s and 1970s, feminist ideology did not take much cognizance of women's self-identification besides gender, but it has not been possible to marshal movements of women, in a practical sense, without attention to those factors. A look at the history of the greatest mobilization of women on their own political behalf before the 1960s – that is, in the woman suffrage movement – and its aftermath, provides a case in point. The following discussion focuses on the United States, though one need not go far to find parallels between the United States and England, despite differences in class and political structures between the two countries, as Olive Banks's overview has recently made clear.[1]

Women's rights advocates in the nineteenth and early twentieth centuries pursued long, often passionate struggles for individual autonomy and for women's access to all men's prerogatives in higher education, paid employment, the professions, and citizenship (meaning, of course, the ballot). Their arguments for women's advancement were grouped around two poles – two logically opposing poles, which I am going to call, for the sake of convenience, the 'sameness' and 'difference' arguments. That is, on the one hand women claimed that they had the same intellectual and spiritual endowment as men – were human beings equally with men – and therefore deserved equal or the same opportunities men had, to advance and develop themselves. On the other hand women argued that their sex differed from the male – that whether through natural endowment, environment or training, human females were moral, nurturant, pacific and philosophically disinterested, where males were competitive, aggrandizing, belligerent and self-interested; and that it therefore served the best interests of both sexes for women to have equal access to education, work and citizenship in order to represent themselves and to balance society with their characteristic contribution. For instance, one mid-nineteenth-century United States reformer and suffragist wrote in *The Agitator*, a paper she edited herself, 'Nothing less than admission in law, and in fact, to equality in all rights, political, civil and social, with the male citizens of the community, will answer the demands now being made for American women'; while a contemporary wrote in another journal, *The Lily*, 'It is woman's womanhood, her instinctive femininity, her highest morality that society now needs to counter-act the excess of masculinity that is everywhere to be found in our unjust and unequal laws.' What is even more interesting, women could voice these two arguments almost in the same breath.[2]

Taking a slightly different slant on it, Aileen S. Kraditor, in her 1965 book *The Ideas of the Woman Suffrage Movement*, characterized these two approaches in the United States suffrage movement as the natural rights or 'justice' argument, and the argument from 'expediency'. She claimed that the former dominated among nineteenth-century women's rights advocates, and the latter after the turn of the century. Kraditor acknowledged the coexistence of both arguments all along the way, however, and recent historians of woman's rights and woman suffrage ideology, including William Leach, Carole Nichols, Steven Buechler, and the contributors to the volume on feminist theory edited by Dale Spender, have made clear that both kinds of arguments flourished during the whole long span between Mary Wollstonecraft's *Vindication* and the attainment of woman suffrage after World War I.[3]

Whether women framed their arguments principally around 'justice' (or, to put it another way, 'sameness', or, to put it yet another way, 'equal rights') or did not, it was clear both before and after 1900 that they were impelled by a strong sense of the *in*justice of existing circumstances for women. In reminiscences of women born in the 1850s to 1880s (whose energies fuelled the woman suffrage movement), one finds the genesis of their views in uncomplicated rage at male dominance and the arbitrariness of male privilege, and jealousy of male prerogatives, even when – perhaps because – one finds affirmation of female character. Writer Mary Austin's retrospect on small-town America's expectations in the 1880s suggests women's motivation to argue on grounds of *both* common humanity and sexual difference, to adopt (lawyer-like) every possible defence to meet resistance: as she experienced it, 'there was a human norm, and it was the average man. Whatever in woman differed from this norm was a *female weakness*, of intelligence, of character, of physique.'[4] The coexistent (logically contradictory) emphases, on women's full and equal human capacity, and yet on women's unique strengths and potential, reflected the fact that 'woman's sphere' was both the point of oppression and the point of departure for nineteenth-century feminists. 'Womanhood' was their hallmark and they insisted it should be a 'human norm' too.

Furthermore, woman's rights advocacy was always in dialogue with those hostile to its aims; if the 'antis' protested that woman were 'unsexing' themselves and seeking identity with men, one kind of argument was called for; if the 'antis' said women were less competent than men in the public arena, another kind; if the antis said 'strong-minded' women sought to rule over men, another response – and so on. Through the long history of the woman's rights movement the two strands of argument, 'sameness' and 'difference', 'justice' and 'expediency', were not seen as mutually exclusive, but as juxtaposable. I do not mean to accord one side of these sets of terms greater value than another. Kraditor's term 'expediency' has a negative ring, especially in contrast to 'justice', but I mean it to be understood in its most neutral sense. The term should encompass all interpretations of the instrumentality of social rights to women, including social justice and self-protection as well as social control. American suffragist Harriet Burton Laidlaw captured the dual message most succinctly in her 1912 assertion that insofar as women were like men they deserved the same rights, and insofar as they differed they ought to represent themselves.[5]

At the time Laidlaw staked that two-pronged claim, a mass women's movement, which would at its height involve two million women, was cohering around the issue of woman suffrage in the United States. By the decade beginning in 1910 the demand for woman suffrage was a capacious umbrella under which a large diversity of beliefs and organizations could shelter, or (to use a more appropriate metaphor), an expansive platform on which they could all comfortably, if temporarily, stand. The nineteenth-century view of the ballot as symbol of the self-possessed individual's relation to the state was joined and to an extent superseded, in the early twentieth century, by new emphasis on the ballot as tool of group interests. Population growth, in-migration, industrialization and the rise of great cities were re-working the implications of the ballot, and compelling progressive reformers to re-envision the state as the arena in which group particularity and potential cooperation might be worked out. City and state 'machine' politics, though often deplored by suffragists, made one message especially clear: votes were a principal means for self-identified groups to have immediate needs answered, and/or to be manipulated. (The woman who would later become the victorious general of the campaign for the Nineteenth Amendment, which gave women the vote, Carrie Chapman Catt, in 1908 first successfully instituted in New York City so-called 'machine' methods of canvassing and recording of electoral districts in woman suffrage work.)

Several historians have given us the impression that American suffragists moved towards victory in the decade from 1910 only by relying on 'expedient' arguments (in Kraditor's words), by stressing what I have called 'difference' arguments, by accommodating their aims to the image of the maternal, nurturant, altruistic woman, and therefore becoming more 'conservative'.[6] Such emphases *were* visible in the decade after 1910, but it should not be assumed that because arguments from 'difference' or 'expedience' *could* be conservative, they necessarily were. On the contrary, claims for women's 'difference' could be turned to radical social goals. Mary Heaton Vorse, for instance, a labour agitator and partisan of the Industrial Workers of the World, socialist, suffragist, feminist, and editor of *The Masses*, believed that women as a group were best suited to work for the end of class exploitation and achievement of social justice.[7]

In the decade beginning in 1910 women from never-before-mobilized groups – blacks, new immigrants, political radicals, college students – joined the American woman suffrage movement, multiplying grass-roots organizations; women influenced by British suffragettes instigated 'militant' tactics. This was the first time that the word 'feminism' came into use, to denote, in Charlotte Perkins Gilman's words, 'the social awakening of the women of all the world', or, in Inez Milholland's, the 'significant' and 'profound' 'movement to readjust the social position of woman . . . in its largest general aspects'. Socialists moved in force into the movement for woman suffrage. As never before, men and women in discrete ethnic or racial or ideological groups saw the advantage of doubling their voting numbers if women obtained suffrage. Black suffragists, for example, whose numbers swelled in the decade following 1910, felt that the enfranchisement of black women would address, and help to redress, the forcible disfranchisement of black men in the South; they mobilized not only as a matter of gender justice but of race progress, despite their awareness that white racist arguments were simultaneously being raised on behalf of woman suffrage. The mass movement that gathered at this point was not, on the whole, conservative and accommodationist but, rather, encompassed the broadest spectrum of opinion in its history, from conservative to radical, from accommodationist to revolutionary.[8] At the same time, the extent to which reformers, men and women (although voteless), had worked to incorporate social welfare into the purview of government – the extent to which the modern state had assumed health, safety and welfare functions – domesticated the content of politics, helping to make votes for women more acceptable. What had been a radical threat to conventional ideology of 'woman's sphere' in the mid-nineteenth century came more into accord with conventional notions of woman's appropriate realm.[9] Just as important, the grass-roots activity building toward coalition in favour of woman suffrage was part and parcel, in the decade from 1910, of flux and creativity in American politics and society – these being years when urban politics elicited coalitions among members of the middle class, working class, and organized labour, when national politics brought forth a 'Progressive' third party, a 'New Freedom' among the Democrats, and the greatest-ever electoral success of socialists; years when cultural and social rebellion swirled and eddied along with the political.

The vote was not only a goal shared by women of divergent political leanings, it was a goal that, as understood by early twentieth-century suffragists in the United States, harmonized the two strands in foregoing women's rights advocacy: it was an equal rights goal that enabled women to make special contributions; it sought to give women the same capacity as men so they could express their differences; it was a just end in itself but it was also an expedient means to other ends. Suffragists in the decade from 1910 were as likely to argue that women deserved the vote because of their sex – because women as a group had relevant benefits to bring and values to defend in the polity – as to argue that women deserved the vote *despite* their sex. The demand for equal suffrage for women could be brought into accord with the notion that women differed from men, because the vote was recognized as a tool of group interests as well as a symbol of equal access of citizens to self-government. Indeed, the more that women's particular interests were stressed, while the premise of equal access was sustained, the better the argument for woman suffrage. Analogous arguments could be, and were, used about the particular interests of any self-identified sub-group of women – for instance, women industrial workers, who argued for reasons of class and sex their warrant for the ballot. Thus Mollie Schepps, a New York City garment maker, reasoned in the wake of the disastrous Triangle factory fire that killed over 140 women employed there, 'working women must use the ballot in order to abolish the burning and crushing of our bodies for the profit of a very few.'[10]

The mass movement assembled by a coalition of women of diverse racial, ethnic and political identities was successfully ambiguous, or inclusive, on the point whether women were most significantly the same as, or different from, men. Both 'sameness' and 'difference' arguments, both 'equal rights' and 'special contributions' arguments, both 'justice' and 'expediency' arguments existed side by side. Although the sexual 'differences' that were highlighted drew on traditional notions of women as nurturers and mothers, the implicit constraints of conventional stereotypes were minimized by turning stereotypes to serve goals of equal access and equal rights. Activists had a workable (if not logically coherent) understanding of the social construction of womanhood. True, they did not wholly repudiate biological or God-given grounding for what women had in common (i.e. motherhood and its said-to-be-attendant qualities). Many women activists, however, in the train of Darwin, and especially in the train of Charlotte Perkins Gilman's analysis of the 'sexuo-economic' relation between woman and man, had a social/evolutionary analysis of their 'differentness' from men (of their 'group'-ness), that led toward change even when it lent itself to conventional sentimentalization.

I assume here that feminism requires some extent of conceptualization of sexual difference, to generate identification with the group 'women'; and that such a conceptualization must build around the belief that gender – or, let us say, 'woman's condition' – is socially constructed and thus can be dismantled or changed. Until the national victory of woman suffrage, women had (if they looked for it) a convenient, reliable and in fact *profound* index and emblem of their socially constructed, humanly constructed gender difference: their common disfranchisement. Shared votelessness was a powerful reason why, despite all the social diversities among women, 'the cause of woman' could seem a reasonable cause, a spur to, rather than a rein on, whatever other identity or goals a woman might have. Just as Mary Ritter Beard, a municipal activist and early adherent to Alice Paul's militant Congressional Union (and later a historian of women), said in 1914 that she could not rank her commitment to suffrage and labour reform because the two were 'inseparable' in her interest, suffrage became for many women in the decade from 1910 inseparable from other, possibly divergent goals.[11]

The feminist conceptualization of women's solidarity, and motivation toward coalition of 'all women', lasted little beyond the goal of the ballot. Just a few years after the Nineteenth Amendment to the United States constitution was ratified, commentators observed, 'the American women's movement . . . is splintered into a hundred fragments under as many warring leaders'; 'the woman "bloc" does not tend to become more and more solidified but tends to become more and more disintegrated.'[12] The most palpable evidence of lack of a ruling consensus among women activists was division of opinion over the Equal Rights Amendment. The renewed National Woman's Party, born of the militant suffrage activists, developed that new proposal to bring full legal equality by constitutional amendment in the period immediately following the gain of suffrage; the amendment was first introduced into Congress in December 1923. Just as the Woman's Party, with its sole focus on the United States constitution, its efforts to create women's voting blocs, its constant lobbying of national political leaders, and its direct action techniques of picketing, demonstrating, and going to jail, had comprised a small and controversial, but highly effective minority within the suffrage movement, so it marshalled only a tiny minority of active women when it adopted the programme of the ERA. Once the National Woman's Party declared its policy of 'blanket' legislation for equal rights, its former allies for the ballot, the major women's voluntary organizations and the Women's Bureau of the United States Department of Labor, were arrayed against it. Differences between the 'militant' minority and other groups that had been tolerable in the suffrage coalition were tolerable no longer.

In the NWP's view the Equal Rights Amendment was the logical sequel to woman suffrage, the fulfilment of Susan B. Anthony's vision. The many differences in state codes and practices in sex discriminations made a constitutional amendment the most direct route to equal rights. Even so-called 'protective' legislation, if sex-based, the NWP claimed, kept women from equal opportunity: the laws, for instance, regulating hours, wages and conditions of work for women and minors, while none regulated men's, kept women classed with children as the industrial 'wards' of the state. Opponents of the ERA (among women who considered themselves feminists) were mainly concerned with keeping sex-based protective labour and welfare legislation in force. They were opposed to other sex discriminations in law, such as those affecting women's nationality, or jury service, but argued that those would be removed more appropriately and efficiently by attacking each specific case. They assumed that an ERA would invalidate protective labour legislation – the result of decades of women reformers' efforts – or at least throw it into the courts for protracted argument. Most women workers, they argued (with basis), appreciated protective legislation as a hedge against exploitation by employers. If protective laws hampered job opportunities for some small minority of working women, they reasoned, then the proper tactic was to exempt some occupations, not to undermine such laws altogether, in the way a constitutional amendment would.[13]

The ERA controversy was symptom rather than cause of divisions in the 1920s among a former united front of women. The National Woman's Party, supporters of the ERA, stressed the capacities women shared with men, as individuals in society, rather than how the two sexes differed by virtue of their reproductive or familial roles. They looked out on the social landscape and saw women who were (like themselves) vigorous and capable. They wanted to premise social policy on the equality of the sexes, since they saw sex equality as both possible and desirable. Opponents of the ERA (the great majority of politically active women) stressed instead women's biological and socially induced differences from men. They focused on the roles and identities of women as members of families more than as individuals. They premised *their* social policy on the observation that women were weak, or vulnerable; they believed one had to treat the world as it *was*, a world of sex inequality. 'So long as men cannot be mothers,' Florence Kelley wrote eloquently in this vein in 1921, 'so long legislation adequate for them can never be adequate for wage-earning women; and the cry Equality, Equality, where Nature has created Inequality, is as stupid and deadly as the cry Peace, Peace, where there is no Peace.'[14]

The division between advocates of 'equal rights' and 'special protections' for women in the United States was paralleled in England, though the legislative question was not precisely the same.[15] Individuals' positions on this issue depended on their priorities for social justice and social change, their political and class loyalties, and, just as clearly, on their views of woman's nature and purpose. The salutary ambiguity sustained by the suffrage coalition on the question of likening women to or distinguishing them from men was put under severe stress by the ERA debate; at the same time the ruling consensus on what women shared – on the social construction of womanhood – was shattered. The themes of 'sameness' and 'difference' were lodged on opposite sides of the controversy. The logical contradictions between the two poles of argument came to the fore. Women in the uneasy position of opposing 'equal rights' stressed how their sex differed from men to the extent of sounding anti-feminist. Those supporting 'equal rights' so bypassed the issue of difference that their clarion call to solidarity rang hollow in most women's ears.

The demobilization of the women's movement in the 1920s was a complex process, for the partisan differences that occurred among feminists were socially and ideologically situated in an era of exhaustion of optimism after World War I, an era of reaction against the Bolshevik Revolution and militant labour, an era of mass consumerism, and mass commercialization of sexual and family values. In such a situation, women's politics in the United States diverged on many different axes besides the question of 'equal rights' versus 'protection': women as individuals and in groups differed on questions such as public ownership, disarmament, Prohibition, women's role in political parties; they differed in increasingly noticeable ways on the political spectrum from left to right. There were also issues on which women's groups were able to work in concert: for instance, to eliminate discrimination in the laws governing married women's nationality, or to protect married women's employment (as the Depression set in). There were some new coalitions: an amalgam of peace groups in the mid-1920s, for instance, and an unprecedented, if tenuous, alliance between black women's and white women's groups in the South, both striving to end lynch law.[16] What one does not find in the 1920s is any overall shared conception of 'the woman question' – of what needed to be changed in the sexual structure and what equipped women together to create change – that could mobilize divergent groups of women as the goal of the ballot had.

In trying to understand and explain the disaggregation of the women's movement in the 1920s, or, for that matter, the different situation we face today as compared to the period 1967–74, it is too easy and mistaken to expect that women's interests are 'normally' a unity. One cannot take an extraordinary period of coalition building and common-ground sharing among women of differing needs and politics – for instance, 1912–19 and 1967–74 – as the ordinary, the 'norm' from which the sequel is grievous decline. There is an element of inevitability or predictability in any fragmentation that follows a united front of women, for as much as women have common cause in gender issues, they are differentiated by political and cultural and sexual loyalties, and by racial, class and ethnic identities, which inform their experience of gender itself. Only women holding culturally hegemonic values and positions – that is, in the United States, women who are white, heterosexual, middle class, politically midstream – have the privilege (or deception) of seeing their condition as that of 'woman', glossing over their other characteristics. Such hegemonic understanding of womanhood has, historically, an essential strategic function in creating sex solidarity among women and in consciousness raising. Thus, at the turn of the century black women, or Jewish immigrants, or industrial workers, or socialists, shared in the galvanizing, malleable notion of women's social identity as mothers and caretakers of humanity, and yet also distinguished particular aspects of its relevance or irrelevance to them. The same dynamic that mobilizes women who see their lives as women as socially constructed leads them to name and particularize the attendant characteristics of their gender identity. What is crucial, of course, in developing or constricting a mass movement, is whether women's particular loyalties and gender identity work in tandem or against each other. That depends on the persuasiveness of prevailing notion(s) of feminism and who are its standardbearers. It depends in important ways on the political climate in general, too: political and cultural rebellion on many fronts characterized both the periods 1912–19 and 1967–74, in which there were mass movements of women.

The analogy between the decade following 1910 and the height of the women's liberation movement in our lifetimes is certainly not perfect. The overriding goal of the suffrage imposed a unity (even if specious) on the earlier decade that is not replicated even in the overlapping goals of many sectors of the recent women's movement – reproductive rights, for instance, or the ERA. The range of theories and of constituencies in recent feminism is wider and more differentiated than in the decade from 1910, and one must also consider new factors such as mass audiovisual media in the spread and impact of the movement. The political parallels can be instructive, nonetheless, especially now that divisions within the movement, younger women's 'postfeminist' attitudes, and rightwing backlash echo problems of the 1920s, and make the pattern of mobilization and demobilization around and after suffrage more understandable to us than it might have been ten years ago.

If there is a model here, looking back on two extraordinary periods of mass movement by women, it would have two conditions. One would be a conceptualization of the social construction of womanhood that does not bar simultaneity of feminist arguments for women's difference from and equality to men – a conceptualization with sufficient relevance and malleability to sustain coalition. If we look closely at even the extraordinary periods of 1912–19 and 1967–74, they exhibit not 'unity' but strategic coalition. Whether we see this as heroic, or lamentable, or merely human nature, it seems that mass movements of women have only been possible when women have instrumental or 'expedient' reasons for advancing gender interests – when, in other words, characteristics or aims besides gender grievances also motivate them. The vote, for instance, was pursued for different reasons by socialists and by members of the Daughters of the American Revolution, by black women and white racists; 'sexual politics' has been differently understood by, though equally central to, radical lesbians and middle-class wives.

In the recent women's movement there has never been one ruling version of woman's place, but a spectrum of conceptualizations from 'socialization' to 'oppression' to 'patriarchy'. There has been a constant tension between the claim for the power of sisterhood – the viability of an analysis of 'all women' – and the voices of women of non-hegemonic groups, especially women of colour and lesbians. The definition of women as a sex/class, which is a major, perhaps the major, contribution of recent feminist theory, has been pulled in two directions: towards the elimination of gender roles ('sameness' argument) and toward the valorization of female being ('difference' argument).

The past eight to ten years have been characterized by what seem to be especially contradictory developments. The value accorded to 'sexual difference' in feminist theory has increased at the same time that the universality of the claim for sisterhood has been debunked. Ethnic, racial, and sexual diversity among women is stressed more than ever before in feminist theory, but so is the emphasis on how women (as a whole) differ from men (as a whole). Perhaps, though, these are not contradictory developments, nor even ironically related. Feminist stress on women's socially constructed 'difference' from men can go along with recognition of diversity among women themselves, if we acknowledge the multifaceted entity – the patchwork quilt, so to speak – that is the group called women. That acknowledgement allows coalition building, the only realistic political 'unity' women have had or will have.

The second condition in this hypothetical model is the fertile ground provided by an era of political and cultural rebellion. 'There has always been a women's movement in this century' – agreed; but whether there will be mass movement or not, whether feminism will be a self-propagating or a sectarian ideology, has much to do with the predisposing ground. Feminism does not have a story discrete from the rest of historical process. As Ray Strachey, a leading British suffragist, wrote with regard to the rise of the women's movement in the nineteenth century, 'Nothing which occurred in those years could be irrelevant to the great social change which was going on, and nothing was without its share of influence upon it.'[17] Just as women are part of humanity, and yet have their own recognizable identity within any society's cultural construction of gender, feminism takes part in – comprises part of – the general cultural order, while it has its own tradition, logic and trajectory. Sole concentration on the internal evolution of feminist ideology and leadership will not read the past accurately, nor, alone, will the placement of feminist movements in overall political or cultural change, but the two together have something to teach us.

Notes

1 Olive Banks, *Faces of Feminism* (Oxford, 1981).
2 Mary Livermore in *Agitator* 1 (13 March 1869), 4; Jane Frohock in *Lily* 8:23 (1 December 1856).
3 Aileen S. Kraditor, *The Ideas of the Woman Suffrage Movement, 1890–1900* (New York, 1965), 38–43, 87–91; William Leach, *True Love and Perfect Union* (New York, 1980), esp. 8, 276–87; Carole Nichols, 'A New Force in Politics: The Suffragists' Experience in Connecticut' (MA essay, Sarah Lawrence College, Bronxville, NY, 1979), 15–16, 26–30, and 'Votes and More for Women: Suffrage and After in Connecticut', *Women and History*, 5 (Spring 1983), 29–30; Dale Spender (ed.), *Feminist Theorists* (New York, 1984), esp. Jenny Uglow, 'Josephine Butler: From Sympathy to Theory'; Steven M. Buechler, *The Transformation of the Woman Suffrage Movement: the Case of Illinois, 1850–1920* (New Brunswick, NJ, 1986).
4 Mary Austin, *Earth Horizon: Autobiography* (Boston, 1932), 156, 91–2, 128. See also E. S. Dummer, *Why I Think So* (Chicago, 1937), 10; Miriam Allen de Ford, 'Feminism, Cause or Effect?', typescript, 5pp., de Ford Papers, Box 573, San Francisco Historical Society; C. C. Catt,

'Why I have Found Life Worth Living.' 29 Mar 1928, Catt Papers microfilm, Reel 9 (from Library of Congress, Washington DC); Lorinne Pruette, 'The Evolution of Disenchantment' and Inez Haynes Irwin, 'The Making of a Militant' in Elaine Showalter, ed., *These Modern Women*, (Old Westbury, NY, 1978), 71–2, 39; Rheta Childe Dorr, *A Woman of Fifty* (New York, 1924), 13.

5 Quoted in Kraditor, *Ideas*, 91.

6 E.g., Kraditor, *Ideas*; Richard Evans, *The Feminists: Women's Emancipation Movements in Europe, America, and Australasia, 1840–1920* (New York, 1977), 214–27; Carl N. Degler, *At Odds* (New York, 1980), 357–60; Ronald Schaffer, 'The Montana Woman Suffrage Campaign, 1911–14', *Pacific Northwest Quarterly* 55 (January 1964), 12, and 'The Problem of Consciousness in the Woman Suffrage Movement: A California Perspective', *Pacific Historical Quarterly* 45 (November 1976), 490–2.

7 Mary Heaton Vorse, *Footnote to Folly* (New York, 1935), 168–9, and see her letters of the decade from 1910 in Vorse Collection, Walter Reuther Library of Labor History and Urban Affairs, Wayne State University, Detroit, Michigan.

8 C. P. Gilman, 'What is Feminism?', *Boston Sunday Herald*, 3 September 1916; Inez Milholland, 'The Liberation of a Sex', *McClure's* 40:4 (February 1913), 181; Judith Schwarz, *The Radical Feminists of Heterodoxy* (New Lebanon, NH, 1983); Elinor Lerner, 'Jewish Involvement in the NY City Woman Suffrage Movement', *American Jewish History* LXX (1981), 442–61; Eleanor Flexner, *Century of Struggle*, 240–93; Rosalyn Terborg-Penn, 'Afro-Americans in the Struggle for Woman Suffrage,' (unpublished PhD dissertation, Howard University, Washington DC, 1977), esp. 265, 275–6, and her 'Discontented Black Feminists' in Lois Scharf and Joan Jensen, eds, *Decades of Discontent* (Westport, CT, 1983), 261–6; MariJo Buhle, *Women and American Socialism* (Urbana, IL, 1981), 214–45; Sharon Hartman Strom, 'Leadership and Tactics in the American Woman Suffrage Movement: A New Perspective from Massachusetts', *Journal of American History* 62 (1975), 296–315; Ellen Dubois, 'Harriot Stanton Blatch and the Revival of American Suffragism', paper presented at the sixth Berkshire Conference on the History of Women, Smith College, Northampton, Mass., 2 June 1984.

9 Paula Baker, 'The Domestication of Politics: Women and American Political Society, 1780–1920', *American Historical Review* 89 (June 1984), 620–47; Ellen Dubois, 'The Radicalism of the Woman Suffrage Movement', *Feminist Studies* 3 (1975), 63–71. The literature on Progressivism is vast: Richard McCormick, 'The Discovery that Business Corrupts Politics', *American Historical Review* 86 (April 1981), makes an interesting beginning.

10 From *Senators vs. Working Women*, pamphlet published by Wage Earners Suffrage League of NY (1912), excerpted in Rosalyn Baxandall et al. (eds), *America's Working Women* (New York, 1976), 218.

11 Mary Beard to Alice Paul, letter of 1914 quoted in Barbara Turoff, *Mary Beard as Force in History* (Dayton, OH, 1979), 24.

12 Frances Kellor, 'Women in British and American Politics', *Current History* 17 (February 1923), 823; William Hard in 'What the American

Man Thinks', *Woman Citizen* (September 8, 1923), 17, quoted in William O'Neill, *Everyone Was Brave* (Chicago, 1968), 264.

13 For fuller discussion of the ERA controversy, see my article, 'Feminist Politics in the 1920s: The National Woman's Party', *Journal of American History* 71 (June 1984), 57–61.

14 Florence Kelley, 'The New Woman's Party,' *Survey* 47 (5 March 1921), 828.

15 Banks, *Faces of Feminism*, 103–17, 153–79.

16 See J. Stanley Lemons, *The Woman Citizen: Social Feminism in the 1920s* (Urbana, IL, 1973), 63–8; Lois Scharf, *To Work and To Wed* (Westport, CT, 1980); Joan Jensen, ' "All Pink Sisters": The War Department and the Feminist Movement in the 1920s', in Scharf and Jensen, *Decades*; Jacqueline Dowd Hall, *Revolt Against Chivalry: Jessie Daniel Ames and the Women's Campaign Against Chivalry* (New York, 1980).

17 See Dale Spender, *There Has Always Been a Women's Movement in This Century* (London, 1983); Ray Strachey, *The Cause* (London, 1928; repr. 1979), 5.

5 Feminism and Social Control: the Case of Child Abuse and Neglect

Linda Gordon

For the last hundred years, feminists have been important advocates of modern forms of social control. Yet contemporary feminist theoreticians and scholars have tended almost exclusively to condemn social control. This discrepancy is not merely between feminism's past and present; it also reveals a present-day lack of theoretical (or policy) integration between divergent goals. A study of the history of family violence provides a striking example of this discontinuity. The story of attempts to protect victims of domestic violence, almost all of them women and children, has disturbed my own anti-social-control orientation. It has not made me an enthusiast for expert administration of private life, but it has convinced me of the necessity for more sophisticated critiques, and specifically feminist critiques, of social control.

In this article I want to argue, not a defence of social control, but a critique of its critiques. My arguments derive from attempts to theorize actual historical events and I would like to make my case as it came to me, through the study of child abuse and neglect. When I began, six years ago, to study the history of family violence in the United States, I assumed I would be focusing largely on wife beating, since that was the target of the feminist activism which had drawn my attention to the problem (and particularly to the absence of any history about it). I was surprised, however, to find that violence against children represented a more complex challenge to the task of envisioning a feminist family policy and a feminist theory of social control.

Social Control

'Social control' is a concept usually attributed to the sociologist

E. A. Ross. He used the phrase (as the title of a collection of his essays) in 1901, referring to the widest range of influence and regulation imposed by society upon the individual.[1] Building on a Hobbesian view of human individuals as naturally in conflict, Ross saw 'social control' as inevitable. Moving beyond liberal individualism, however, Ross was arguing for social control in a more specific sense, that of active, deliberate, expert guidance of human life, not only as the source of past human progress but also as the best answer to an experience of the failure of older, familial and communitarian forms of control of individual impulse.[2]

Agencies attempting to control family violence are pre-eminent examples of the kind of expert social control institutions advocated by Ross and other 'progressive-era' reformers. These agencies, the most typical of which were the Societies for the Prevention of Cruelty to Children (hereafter SPCCs), were begun in the 1870s in a decade of acute international alarm about child abuse. They began as punitive and moralistic 'charitable' endeavours, characteristic of nineteenth-century elite moral purity reforms, blaming the problem on the depravity, immorality and drunkenness of individuals, these traits often traced to the innate inferiority of the immigrants who constituted the great bulk of the reformers' targets. By the early twentieth century the SPCCs took on a more ambitious task, hoping to reform family life and childraising according to a model of family health, not merely to cure family pathology. Describing the change slightly differently, nineteenth-century child protection agents saw themselves as para-legal, punishing specific offences, protecting children from specific dangers. In the early twentieth century they attempted ongoing supervision and direction of the family lives of those considered deviant.

These kinds of agencies were targets of condemnation by many activists and intellectuals of the New Left. In the United States the 'Second Wave' of feminism grew largely from this New Left, adopting its hostility to experts and its assumption that social control was in itself a reprehensible goal. Criticisms were directed especially at aspects of the welfare state, such as Aid to Dependent Children (a form of single-mother's pension in the United States), for providing the state with leverage to supervise women's private lives, and at medical and mental health professionals, whose controlling functions were often directed against rebellion or nonconformity, particularly among women. These criticisms usually distinguished an 'us' and a 'them', oppressed and oppressor, in a dichotomous relation. They suggested that the controlling was functional in relation to the material interests of a dominant group, and disfunctional or destructive in relation to the interests of the subordinate. Many such critics of social control acknowledged the material benefits produced by some such measures, such as unemployment insurance or telecommunications regulation. Their formula for evaluation of such measures was usually dichotomous, distinguishing between social amelioration and social control, the former representing concessions to demands from the bottom, the latter representing the imposition of an order beneficial to those on the top.[3]

Feminists have often repeated this line of criticism of social control, substituting gender for class or race categories in distinguishing the sides. Feminist anti-social-control critiques have contributed to, and been conditioned by, ignorance of the thick and complex history of feminist involvement in social control campaigns. In moral reform (anti-prostitution) and anti-alcohol movements, in progressive-era campaigns to reform the living and spending habits of the poor, in campaigns for industrial protective legislation and affirmative action, today in anti-pornography campaigns, feminists have often agitated for bureaucratic, professional and governmental control over individuals.[4]

In the United States feminists who were radicals (themselves very divided) attempted to blame the large liberal feminist movement (known as the 'bourgeois feminists') for this tradition. The marxist left encouraged an interpretation which condemned nineteenth-century feminism as bourgeois because of its middle-class base and its focus on legal reform, i.e. suffrage.[5] Left feminists claimed that it was these (past and present) liberal feminists who, in their attempts to seek advancement for privileged women within existing hierarchies, supported legalistic and professional controls as a means of solving social problems. To locate the problem simply with these liberal feminists was inaccurate and self-serving, as if they were the only individualists and statists, while we had creative communitarian solutions to loneliness, self-destructive behaviour, instrumental and self-aggrandizing behaviour, street violence, public squalor, neglect of the poor and elderly, exploitative commercialization. In fact, feminists of all political persuasions were vulnerable to the same contradiction: we had highly universalized concepts of the rights and freedoms which women could claim, and such broadly defined rights could not be adequately defended by relatively small communities. They required large-scale control. Furthermore, these rights were in fact influenced by 'scientific' knowledge, despite our critique of professionalism. In child welfare it is particularly obvious that 'rights' are conceptualized on the basis of historically changing possibilities. As medical care, education, good nutrition, decent clothing became available, they were accepted by child welfare workers, and implicitly by the citizenry, as among children's 'rights'.

It is inaccurate for radicals to claim immunity from the contradictions in the liberal feminist attempt to use the state to guarantee individual rights. The limitations of this separation of a left from a liberal feminist tradition became painfully clearer in the 1980s as a right-wing attack on the welfare state began to win momentum and political victories. Leftists had to defend the Aid to Dependent Children programme, target of so much feminist venom a decade ago. Socialist feminists became allies of the Planned Parenthood Federation in defence of 'choice' (as the liberals have labelled abortion rights in the United States), when a decade ago we were attacking its support for neo-imperialist population control policies, including sterilization. As tax-capping measures impoverished municipal and state treasuries, we had to defend the services rendered by the state and even de-emphasize the corruption, discrimination and humiliation involved in their actual distribution. The New Left critique of social control had been a product of prosperity and liberal government and has been temporarily discarded.

It would be better not to discard but to revise it. The critique of the domination exercised by social work and human services bureaucracies and professionals is not wrong, but its incompleteness allows for some serious distortion. I shall now summarize a case history, one of many which have influenced my thinking about social control.

In 1910 a Syrian family in Boston's South End, here called the Kashys, came to the attention of the Massachusetts Society for the Prevention of Cruelty to Children (hereafter MSPCC) because of abuse of a thirteen-year-old girl by her mother. Mr Kashy had just died, of appendicitis. Previously the family, like so many immigrants, had moved back and forth between Syria and the United States several times; two other children had been left in Syria with their paternal grandparents; in Boston, in addition to the central 'victim', whom I shall call Fatima, there were a six-year-old boy and a three-year-old girl; and Mrs Kashy was pregnant. The complainant was the father's sister, and indeed all the paternal relatives were hostile to Mrs Kashy. Their allegations were substantiated by the MSPCC investigation: Mrs Kashy hit Fatima with a stick or with chairs, bit her ear, kept her from school and overworked her, expecting her to do all the housework and to care for the younger children. When Fatima fell ill, her mother refused to let her go to the hospital. The hostility of the paternal relatives, however, focused not only on the mother's improper treatment of Fatima but on her custody rights in principle. It was their contention that the custody should have fallen to them after Mr Kashy's death, arguing that 'in Syria a woman's rights to the care of her [children] or the control of property is not recognized.' The paternal grandfather had rights to the children in their tradition, and he had delegated this control to his son, the children's paternal uncle. Apparently they had expected Mrs Kashy to bow to their rights, and her difficult economic and social situation would make it understandable that she might have. The complainant, the father's sister, was her landlady. Mrs Kashy lived with her three children in one attic room without water; she had to go to ground level and carry water up. The relatives offered her no help after her bereavement and she was desperate; she was trying to earn a living by continuing her husband's peddling, thus needing Fatima to keep the house and care for the children.

When Mrs Kashy resisted their custody claims, the paternal relatives called in as a mediator a Syrian community leader, publisher of *The New Syria*, a Boston Arabic-language newspaper. Ultimately the case went to court, however, and here the relatives lost, since their custody traditions conflicted with the new preference in the United States for women's custody. Fatima's preferences were of no help to the agency in sorting out this conflict; throughout the struggle she was ambivalent: sometimes she begged to be kept away from her mother, yet when away, she begged to be returned to her mother. Ultimately Mrs Kashy won custody but no material help in supporting her children by herself. As in so many child-abuse cases, it was the victim who was punished: Fatima was sent to an institutional home, and her relatives believed that she was treated abusively there.

If the story had stopped there one might be tempted to see Mrs Kashy as relatively blameless, driven perhaps to harsh occasional treatment and temper by her difficult lot. But thirteen years later, in 1923, the second daughter, now 16, was brought to the MSPCC by a 'school visitor' to complain of abuse by her mother and by her older, now married, sister Fatima. Since 1910 the second daughter had been sent back to Syria; perhaps Mrs Kashy had had to give up her efforts to support the children. Returning to the United States 18 months previously, the girl arrived to find that her mother intended to marry her involuntarily to a boarder. The daughter displayed blood on her shirt which she said came from a nosebleed brought on by her mother's beatings. Interviewed by an MSPCC agency, Mrs

Kashy was now openly hostile and defiant, saying that she would beat her daughter as she liked.

No single case is typical. Nevertheless, in its very complexity, the Kashy case exemplifies certain generalizations central to the argument here. One is that it is often difficult to identify a unique victim. Mrs Kashy was not only victimized by her isolation, widowhood, single-motherhood and patriarchal, hostile in-laws; she also exploited her daughter. It should not be surprising to see the oppressed Mrs Kashy as (also) angry and violent, but feminist rhetoric about family violence has often avoided this complexity. Indeed, Mrs Kashy's attitude to Fatima must be recognized as patriarchal: that children should serve parents and not vice versa.[6] This aspect of patriarchal tradition served Mrs Kashy. But in other respects the general interests of the oppressed group – here the Syrian immigrants – as expressed by its (male, petit bourgeois) leadership, were more inimical to Mrs Kashy's (and other women's) aspirations and 'rights' than those of the elite agency, the MSPCC. Furthermore, one can reasonably surmise that the daughters were also actors in this drama, resisting their mother's expectations as well as the male-dominated community's aspirations, in part as a result of the influence of New World ideas – an influence felt because it coincided with personal aspirations that were fully their own. None of the existing social control critiques can adequately conceptualize the complex struggles in the Kashy family, nor propose non-oppressive ways for Fatima's 'rights' to be protected.

Feminism and Child Abuse

Feminist theory in general and women's history in particular need a more complex view of social control that problems such as the Kashys require. The victimization paradigm that dominated the rebirth of feminist scholarship two decades ago, the pressure to describe and analyse the structures and methods of male domination, must be transcended. We can now look more closely at women's negotiations with, participation in, accommodation to and struggles against the manifestations of male domination. This move forward has been especially difficult in issues relating to social policy and to family violence particularly, because of the legacy of victim blaming. Defending women against violence is so urgent that we fear women's loss of status as political, deserving, 'victims' if we acknowledge women's own aggressions. These complexities are at their greatest in the situation of mothers, because they are simultaneously victims and victimizers, dependent and depended on, weak and powerful.

If feminist theory needs a new view of social control, thinking about child abuse virtually demands it. The child abuse cases reveal suffering which is incontrovertible, unnecessary, and remediable, and action in remedy seems self-explanatory. However severe the bias of the social workers attempting to 'save' the children and reform their parents – and I will have more to say about that bias below – one could not advocate a policy of inaction in regard to children chained to beds, left in filthy nappies for days, turned out in the cold. Furthermore, children in modern society, unlike women, lack even the potential for social and economic independence. Good social policy could address the problem of wife beating in part by empowering women to leave abusive situations, enabling them to live in comfort and dignity without men, and encouraging them to have high standards in their expectations of treatment by others. It is not clear how one can offer such empowerments to children. If they are to have 'rights' then some adults or groups must be accepted, by other adults, as speaking for them.

Women, who do the main parenting labour and have the greater emotional bonds with children, have fought for and largely won rights to child custody over the last 150 years. Yet the abusers and neglecters of children are often women. Indeed, child abuse becomes the more interesting and challenging to a feminist because in it we meet women's rage and abuses of power. Furthermore, child abuse is a gendered phenomenon, related to the oppression of women, whether men or women are the culprits, because it reflects the sexual division of the labour of reproduction. Rage against children is never abstract but is produced by specific, gendered expectations of how they should behave and what the caretaker expects of her/himself, exacerbated by feelings of failure or deprivation on the part of the adult when children engage in power struggles. Given that men spend on the whole so much less time with children than women, what is remarkable is not that women are violent towards children but that men are responsible for nearly half of the child abuse. But women are always implicated because even when men are the culprits, women are usually the primary caretakers who have been, by definition, in some ways unable to protect the children. When protective organizations remove children or undertake supervision of their caretakers, women often suffer greatly, for their maternal work is usually, trying as it may be, the most pleasurable part of their lives.

Yet in the last two decades of intense publicity about child abuse and the accumulation of massive clinical, survey, and research writing about the problem, the feminist contribution has been negligible. This is the more odd since in the First Wave of feminism, particularly in the period 1880–1930, the women's rights movement was tightly connected with child welfare reform campaigns. By contrast, the Second Wave of feminism, a movement heavily influenced by younger and childless women, has expended relatively little energy on children's issues. This omission has been particularly noticeable among the more radical women activists in the United States, despite a minor stream of campaigning for child care and, in the last few years, against sexual abuse of children. Feminist theorists have studied reproduction and the social organization of mothering in principle but not the actual experiences of child raising, and the movement as a whole has not made an impact on how child welfare issues are debated. When such issues are mentioned, there is often an assumption made that women's and children's interests always coincide, an assumption challenged not only by the facts of child abuse and neglect but also by the necessity sometimes of severing maternal custody in order to protect children.

Protecting Children

Child abuse was 'discovered' as a social problem in the 1870s. Surely many children had been ill-treated by parents before this, but new social conditions created an increased sensitivity to the treatment of children and, possibly, actually worsened the children's lot. Conditions of labour and family life under industrial capitalism may well have caused poverty and stress to bear more heavily on children. The alarm also reflected a growing class and cultural difference of perception regarding how children should be raised. The anti-cruelty-to-children movement grew out of an anti-corporal-punishment campaign, and both reflected a uniquely professional-class view that children could be disciplined by reason and with mildness. More generally it grew from widespread fears among more privileged strata about violence and 'depravity' among the urban poor, and in the United States these fears were exacerbated by the fact that these poor were largely immigrants and Roman Catholics, threatening the White Anglo-Saxon Protestant (WASP) domination of city culture and government. Above all, as I will argue in what follows, it grew from the disruption of earlier patterns of mothering (and secondarily fathering) by conditions of wage labour and urban life.

I studied the case records of several child-welfare agencies in Boston, including those of the MSPCC, one of the most influential of these agencies. The records strongly support the criticism that their work represented oppressive state and professional intervention into the working-class family. The MSPCC attempted to enforce culturally specific norms of proper parenting which were not only alien to the cultural legacy of the 'clients' but also flew in the face of many of the economic necessities of their lives. For example, MSPCC agents prosecuted cases in which cruelty to children was caused, in their view, by children's labour: girls doing housework and child care, often required to stay at home from school by their parents; boys and girls working in shops, peddling on the streets; boys working for organ grinders or lying about their ages to enlist in the navy. In the pre-World War I era, the enemy of the truant officers was usually parents, not children. To immigrants from peasant backgrounds it seemed irrational and blasphemous that adult women should work while able-bodied children should be idle. In another example of cultural disagreement, the MSPCC was opposed to common immigrant practices of leaving children unattended, and allowing them to play and wander in the streets. Both violated the Society's norm of domesticity for women and children; proper middle-class children in those days did not – at least not in the cities – play outside without being attended.

The style of mothering and fathering being imposed was new. Mothers were supposed to be tender, gentle, to protect their children above all from immoral influences, and the child savers considered yelling, rude language or sexually explicit talk to be forms of cruelty to children. Fathers were to provide models of emotional containment, to be relatively uninvolved with children; their failure to provide was often interpreted as a character flaw, no matter what the evidence of widespread, structural unemployment.

The MSPCC's model of parenting was, furthermore, culturally specific, and in practice as well as in rhetoric expressed disdain for the non-WASP nationalities. The exclusively WASP agents, for example, hated the garlic and olive-oil smells of Italian cooking, and considered this food unhealthy (overstimulating, aphrodisiac). They were unable to distinguish alcoholics and heavy drinkers from moderate wine and beer drinkers, and they believed that any woman who touched even a drop of spirits was a degenerate and an unfit parent. Many of these forms of depravity were specifically associated with Catholicism. Agents were convinced of the subnormal intelligence of most non-WASP and especially non-English-speaking clients, and the agents' comments and expectations in this early period could easily be transposed with similar views of blacks in the mid-twentieth century. These child welfare specialists were particularly confused by and disapproving of non-nuclear child-raising patterns: children raised by grandmothers, complex households composed of children from several different marriages (or, worse, out-of-wedlock relationships), children sent temporarily to other households.

The peasant backgrounds of so many of the 'hyphenated' Americans created a situation in which ethnic bias could not easily be separated from class bias. Class misunderstanding, moreover, took a form specific to urban capitalism: a failure to grasp the actual economic circumstances of this immigrant proletariat and sub-proletariat. Unemployment was not yet understood to be a structural characteristic of industrial capitalism. Nor were disease, over-crowding, crime and – above all – dependence understood as part of the system, but rather as personal failings.

This line of criticism only partially uncovers the significance of child protection, however. Another dimension is revealed by considering the feminist aspect of the movement. Much of the child-welfare reform energy of the last century came from women and was organized by the women's movement.[7] One manifestation of feminist influence was in diagnoses of the cause of child abuse. Most MSPCC spokesmen (and those who represented the agency in public were men) viewed men as aggressors and women and children, jointly, as blameless victims. Of course these 'brutal' and 'depraved' men were of a different class and ethnicity than the MSPCC agents, and of course the language of victimization applied to women and children was also one of condescension. Nevertheless, despite the definition of the 'crime' as cruelty to children, MSPCC agents were led to include wife beating in their agenda of reform.

Furthermore, the anti-child abuse campaign grew from a critique of violence and a campaign against corporal punishment rooted in feminist thought and in women's reform activity. Women's reform influence, the 'sentimentalizing' of the Calvinist tradition,[8] was largely responsible for the softening of childraising norms. The delegitimizing of corporal punishment, noticeable among the prosperous classes by mid-century, was associated with exclusive female responsibility for childraising, with women's victories in child custody cases, even with women's criticisms of traditionally paternal discipline.[9]

Not only was the anti-child-abuse lobby influenced and strengthened by feminism, but the very undertaking of protecting children was anti-patriarchal. A pause to look at the definition of patriarchy is necessary here. In the 1970s a new definition of that term came into use, first proposed by Kate Millett but quickly adopted by the United States feminist movement: patriarchy became a synonym for male supremacy, for 'sexism'. I use the term in its earlier, historical and more specific sense, referring to a family form in which fathers had control over all other family members – children, women, and servants – a control which flowed from the fathers' monopolization of economic resources. The patriarchal family presupposed a family mode of production, as among peasants, artisans or farmers, in which individuals did not work individually as wage labourers. That historical patriarchy defined a set of parent–child relations as much as it did relations between the sexes, for the children rarely had opportunities for economic independence except by inheriting the family property, trade or craft. In some ways mothers, too, benefited from patriarchal parent–child relations: their authority over daughters and young sons was an important value when women were denied access to other experiences of authority and independence, and women's old age was rewarded with respect, help and consideration from younger kinfolk.

The claim of an organization such as an SPCC to speak on behalf of children's rights, its claim to the licence to intervene in parental treatment of children, was an attack on patriarchal power. At the same time the new sensibility about children's rights and the concern about child abuse were symptoms of a weakening of patriarchal family expectations and realities that had already taken place. In this weakening, father-child relations had changed more than husband-wife relations. Children had, for example, gained the power to arrange their own betrothals and marriages, to embark on individual careers independent of their father's occupation (of course children's options remained determined by class and cultural privileges or the lack of them, inherited from fathers); by contrast a wage labour system was actually making women more dependent on husbands for sustenance and thus unable to risk direct defiance of a husband's wishes. The best women could hope for was a benign husbandly authority. Moral pressure might be placed on brutal men but, given the family system in which women remained economic dependents, there were few enforcement procedures available to check marital violence. Men could be and at times were prosecuted for assaults on wives, but a successful prosecution would leave a wife alone and unsupported and many wives naturally drew back from pressing criminal charges for this reason.

Early child-protection work did not, of course, envision a general liberation of children from arbitrary parental control or from the responsibility of filial obedience. On the contrary, the ideology of the SPCCs, and their inherent purpose, was so much to reinforce a failing parental/paternal authority as to limit it. Indeed the SPCCs tended to view excessive physical violence against children as a symptom of inadequate parental authority. Furthermore, then as now, the most common cases the Society encountered were those of neglect, not of assault. These neglect cases reflected particularly the withdrawal, albeit not always conscious or deliberate, of parental supervision and authority. Among the poor who formed the agency clientele, there was a great deal of desertion by fathers, and of inadequate provision even by fathers who were present; poverty was responsible for the great majority of neglect charges. Actual assaults on children, too, could reveal inadequate parental authority, stimulated as they often were by children's insubordination; disobedience and child abuse were mutually reinforcing. Many child neglect or child abuse cases ended with children being sent to reform schools on stubborn-child charges. Even when mothers were the bad parents, as they were in half the abuse and the majority of the neglect cases, their failure was part of the failure of a patriarchal family system, for women's mothering was an essential part of that system.

In sum, the SPCCs were part of a reconstruction of the family along lines that altered the old patriarchy, already economically unviable, and replaced it with a modern version of male supremacy. The SPCCs' rhetoric about children's rights did not extend to a parallel articulation of women's rights; their condemnation of wife beating did not include endorsement of the kind of marriage later called 'companionate', implying equality between husband and wife. Specifically, the new family and child-raising norms that underlay the SPCCs' work included:

1 That children's respect for parents needed to be inculcated ideologically, moralistically, and psychologically, since it no longer rested on an economic dependence lasting beyond childhood;

2 That the father, now as wage labourer rather than as slave, artisan, peasant or entrepreneur, had single-handed responsibility for economic support of his family;

3 That women and children should not contribute to the family economy, at least not monetarily;

4 That children instead should spend all their time in learning –

cognitive things from professional teachers, psychological and moral things from the full-time attention of a mother;
5 That women in turn should be entirely domestic and devote themselves to full-time mothering.

Feminism and Capitalism

This childraising programme points to a larger, perhaps ironic, historical relation: that the strengthening and 'modernization' of male domination was partly a result of the influence of first-wave feminism. That relation is often obscured by the use of ahistorical definitions of feminism. First Wave 'feminists' – not a word they yet used but one that is applied to them looking backward from the mid-twentieth century – rarely advocated full equality between men and women, and never the abolition of traditional gender or sexual division of labour. Allowing for differences of emphasis, the above five points constituted a feminist as well as a liberal reform programme in the 1870s. Indeed, in part organized feminism *was* a liberal reform programme, a programme for the adaptation of the family and the civil society to the new economic conditions, because, consciously or not, feminists felt that these new conditions provided greater possibilities for the freedom and empowerment of women.

Child protection work was an integral part of the feminist as well as the bourgeois programme for modernizing the family. Child saving had gender as well as class and ethnic content, but in none of these aspects did it simply or homogeneously represent the interests of a dominant group (or even of the composite group of WASP elite women, that hypothetical stratum on which it is fashionable to blame the limitations of feminist activity). The anti-patriarchalism of these agencies was an unstable product of many conflicting interests, including those of the client-victims. Understanding this illuminates the complex situation of feminism, as part of the development of a capitalist culture, even as it criticized the sexual privileges of the capitalist class and the degradation of women's traditional work by capitalist culture.

Usually the relation of feminism to capitalism is argued in dichotomous and reductionist fashion: feminism is the expression of the bourgeois woman's aspiration, an ultimate individualism that tears apart the remaining non-instrumental bonds in a wage-labour society; *or*, feminism is inherently anti-capitalist, deepening and extending the critique of domination to show its penetration even of personal life and the allegedly 'natural'. While there is a little truth in both versions, the truth is neither in between nor in a synthesis of the two, because at least one central aspect of feminism's significance for capitalism is missing entirely from this formulation: new conditions of motherhood. Industrial capitalism changed motherhood for women of all classes, even as motherhood remained the central identity for women of all classes. As the most universal aspect of the female experience, childbirth and childraising were, in the First Wave, the common referents by which feminist ideas were communicated. The working-class and even sub-working-class women of the child abuse case records were frequently 'feminists' in their conscious efforts to rid themselves of male domination. Their main motivation for doing so, the part of their identity that felt most crushed by personal and structural male supremacy, was their identity and work as mothers.

Child protection work simultaneously represented mothers' demands, but also made mothers vulnerable: by calling into question the quality of their mothering, already made more problematic by urban wage-labour living conditions, by threatening them with the loss of their children, with the breaking of their most permanent bonds. Of course, elite women figured more on the first side of this duality, for they had great impunity to treat their children as they liked. But poor women did not by any means figure only on the victim side, for they were often enthusiastic about defending children's 'rights' and correcting cruel or neglectful parents. Furthermore, they used an eclectic variety of arguments and devices simultaneously to defend their control of their children, and to defend their own or other children against perceived mistreatment. At times they mobilized liberal premises and cash-nexus relations to get greater mobility away from patriarchal households and to defend their custody rights; they were quick to manipulate bureaucrats and experts to attack the traditional patriarchal controls of other family members. Yet at other times they called upon traditional relations when community and kinfolk could help them retain control or defend children. Poor women often denounced the 'intervention' of outside social-control agencies like the SPCCs, but only when it suited them, and at other times they eagerly used and asked such agencies for help.

Let me offer another case history to illustrate this opportunistic and resourceful approach to social control agencies. An Italian immigrant family, let us call them the Amatos, were 'clients' of the MSPCC from 1910 to 1916. They had five young children from the current marriage and Mrs Amato had three from a previous marriage, two of them still in Italy and one daughter in Boston. Mrs

Amato kept that daughter at home to do housework and look after the younger children while she earned money doing home piece-rate sewing. This got the family into trouble with a truant officer, and they were also accused, in court, of lying to Associated Charities (a consortium of private relief agencies), saying that the father had deserted when he was in fact at home. Furthermore, once while left alone, probably in the charge of a sibling, one of the younger children fell out a window and had to be hospitalized, so that the mother was suspected of negligence.

Despite her awareness of these suspicions against her, Mrs Amato had gone to many different agencies, starting with those of the Italian immigrant community and then reaching out to elite social work agencies, seeking help, reporting that her husband was a drunkard, a gambler, a non-supporter and a wife beater. The MSPCC agents at first doubted her claims because Mr Amato impressed them as a 'good and sober man', and blamed the neglect of the children on his wife's incompetence in managing the wages he gave her. The Society ultimately became convinced of her story because of her repeated appearance with severe bruises and the corroboration by the husband's father. Mr Amato Senior was intimately involved in the family troubles, and took responsibility for attempting to control his son. Once he came to the house and gave the father 'a warning and a couple of slaps', after which the father improved for a while. Another time he extracted from his son a pledge not to beat his wife for two years!

Mrs Amato wanted none of this. She begged the MSPCC agent to help her get a divorce; later she claimed that she had not dared to take this step because his relatives threatened to beat her if she tried it. Then Mrs Amato's daughter (from her previous marriage) took action, coming independently to the MSPCC to bring an agent to the house to help her mother. As a result of this complaint, Mr Amato was convicted of assault once and sentenced to six months. During that time Mrs Amato survived by 'a little work and . . . Italian friends have helped her.' Her husband returned more violent than before: he went at her with an axe, beat the children so much on the head that their 'eyes wabbled' [sic] permanently; and supported his family so inadequately that the children went out begging. This case closed, like so many, without a resolution.

The Amatos' case will not support the usual anti-social-control interpretation of the relation between oppressed clients and social agencies. There was unity neither of the client family nor of the professional interveners. Furthermore, the interveners were often dragged into the case, and by individuals with conflicting points of view. Usually no one decisively 'won'. Collectively, of course, professional social work overwhelmed any representation of working-class or poor people's interests, but in specific cases the professionals hardly formulated definite goals, let alone achieved them. Indeed, the bewilderment of the social workers (something usually over-looked because most scholarship about social work is based on policy statements, not on actual case records) in many similar cases allowed the clients to go quite a distance towards achieving their goals. The social control experience was not a simple two-sided trade-off in which the client sacrificed autonomy and control in return for some material help. Rather the clients helped shape the nature of the social control itself.

Formulating these lessons about the inadequacy of simple anti-social-control critiques in some analytic order, I would make four general points. First, the condemnation of agency intervention into the family, and the condemnation of social control itself as something automatically evil, usually carry the assumption that there can be, and once was, such a thing as an autonomous family. On the contrary, no family relations have been immune from social regulation. Many sorts of formal and informal community pressure have served to maintain boundaries of acceptable behaviour. The notion of decreased family autonomy came, no doubt, from nineteenth-century developments: urbanization weakened com-munity sanctions, and created a norm of family autonomy which was both romanticized and also, to some extent, oppositional, expressing simultaneously the new sense of home as a private and caring space in contrast to that of the increasingly instrumental relations of the public areas, and a fear of women's autonomy. (The concept of family autonomy, in fact, as it is manipulated in contemporary political discourse, usually functions in opposition to women's rights to autonomous citizenship.) The Amatos' pattern of turning to relatives, friends and, when they could not help, Italian-American organizations (no doubt the closest analogue to a 'community' in the New World) was not adequate to the urban problems they now met. Yet even the violent and defensive Mr Amato did not question the right of his father, relatives, and friends to intervene forcibly, nor did Mrs Amato appear shocked that her husband's relatives tried, perhaps successfully, to hold her forcibly to her marriage. Family autonomy was not an expectation of the Amatos.

Second, the social-control explanation sees the flow of initiative going in only one direction: from top to bottom, from professionals to clients, from elite to subordinate. The power of this interpretation of social work comes from the large proportion of truth it holds, from the influence of social movements among the poor which have denounced attempts to mould and blame them, and perhaps from the rebellion of many social workers at being made into oppressors of clients. The case records show, however, that clients were not passive but, rather, active negotiators in a complex bargaining. Mrs Amato and Mrs Kashy were not atypical in their attempts to use 'social control' agencies in their own interest. Clients were frequently the initiators of agency intervention; even in family-violence cases, where the stakes were high – losing one's children – majority of complaints in this study came from parents or close relatives who believed that their own standards of childraising were being violated. In their sparring with social work agencies, clients did not usually or collectively win, because the professionals had more resources. But when social control is used as a simple explanation, it does violence to the actual experience of the clients which was neither a two-sided struggle nor a simple story of victimization.

To this argument it could be responded that it is difficult to define what would be a parent's 'own' standards of childraising. In heterogeneous urban situations child-raising patterns change rather quickly, and new patterns become normative. Certainly the child welfare agencies were part of a 'modernization' (in the United States called Americanization) effort, attempting to present new family norms as objectively right. However, in the poor neighbourhoods of these clients, poverty, crowding, and the structure of housing allowed very little privacy, and the largely immigrant clients retained autonomous family patterns, often for several generations.

Third, the active role of agency clients is often unrecognized because the family is conceived as a homogeneous unit, an integer. There is an intellectual reification here which expresses itself in sentence structure, particularly in academic language: 'The family is in decline', 'threats to the family', 'the family responds to industrialization'. Shorthand expressions attributing behaviour to an aggregate such as the family would be harmless except that they often express particular cultural norms about what 'the family' is and does, and mask intrafamily differences and conflicts of interest. Usually 'the family' becomes a representation of the interests of the family head, if it is a man, carrying an assumption that all family members share his interests. (A female-headed family is, in the common usage, a broken, deformed, or incomplete family and thus does not qualify for these assumptions regarding unity.) The outrage over the intervention into the family, often, was an outrage over a territorial violation, a challenge to male authority; or, expressed differently, an outrage at the exposure of intrafamily conflict and of the family head's lack of control. Furthermore, interventions actually were more substantive, more invasive, when their purpose was to change the status quo than if they had been designed to reinforce it. The effect of social workers' involvement was often to change existing family power relations, usually in the interest of the weaker family members.

Social work interventions were often invited by family members; but the inviters were usually the weaker members of a family power structure, women and children. These invitations were made despite the fact, well known to clients, that women and children usually had the most to lose (despite fathers' frequent outrage at their loss of face) from MSPCC intervention, since by far the most common outcome of agency action was not prosecution and jail sentences but the removal of children, an action dreaded least by fathers. In the immigrant working-class neighbourhoods of Boston the MSPCC became known as 'the Cruelty', suggesting eloquently the recognition and fear of its function. Yet its alien power did not stop poor people from initiating contact with it. After the MSPCC had been in operation ten years, 60 per cent of the complaints of known origin (excluding, for example, anonymous accusatory letters) came from family members, the overwhelming majority of these from women, children following second. These requests for help came not only from victims but also from mothers distressed that they were not able to raise their children according to their own standards of good parenting. Furthermore, women expertly manoeuvred to bring child-welfare agencies into family struggles on their sides. There was no Society for the Prevention of Cruelty to Women; in fact women like Mrs Amato were trying to turn the SPCC into just that. A frequent tactic of beaten, deserted or unsupported wives was to report their husbands as child abusers; even when investigations found no evidence of child abuse, social workers came into their homes offering, at best, help in getting other things women wanted – such as support payments, separation and maintenance agreements, relief – and, a⁺ least, moral support to the women and condemnation of the men.

Indeed, so widespread were these attempts to enmesh social workers in intrafamily feuds that they were responsible for a high proportion of the many unfounded complaints the MSPCC always met. Rejected men, then as now, often fought for the custody of children they did not really want, as a means of hurting their wives, and one way of doing this was to bring complaints of cruel treatment of children. Or they charged wives with child neglect when their main desire was to force the women to live with them again.

Embittered deserted wives might arrange to have their husbands caught with other women.

A fourth problem is that simple social-control explanations often imply that the clients' problems are not real but figments of social workers' biases. In child-neglect cases it is clear that one culture's neglect may be another culture's norm. For example, in many immigrant families it was expected that five-year-olds would care for babies and toddlers; to middle-class reformers five-year-olds left alone were considered neglected.

Social-control critiques are right to call attention to the power of experts not only to 'treat' social deviance but to define problems in the first place. But the power of labelling, specifically in the sources in this kind of study – the representation of poor people's behaviour by those whose self-definition is to be critical of that behaviour, coexists with real family oppressions. In one case an immigrant father, who sexually molested his thirteen-year-old daughter, told a social worker that that was the way it was done in the old country! He was not only lying, but also trying to manipulate a social worker, perhaps one he had recognized as guilt-ridden over her privileged role, using his own fictitious cultural relativism. His daughter's victimization by incest was not the result of oppression by professionals.

Feminism and Liberalism

The overall problem with virtually all existing critiques of social control is that they remain liberal and have neglected the feminist exposure of the limits of liberalism. Liberalism is commonly conceived as a political and economic theory without social content. In fact, liberal political and economic theory rests on assumptions about the sexual division of labour, and on notions of citizens as heads of family.[10] The currently dominant tradition of anti-social-control critique, that of the Frankfurt School, merely restates the same assumptions, identifying the sphere of the 'private' as producing a control that is somehow natural, productive of strong egos and inner direction, in contrast to the sphere of the public as invasive, productive of conformity and passivity. If we reject the social premises of liberalism (and marxism), that gender and the sexual division of labour are natural, then we can hardly maintain the premise that familial forms of social control are inherently benign and public forms malignant.

The critique of bureaucracies and professional experts has

identified many aspects of domination that are vital to recognize – not only the inevitable deformations of attempts to 'help' in a society of inequality, but also those that arise from the power to define what social order should be. But it is a critique of certain kinds of domination that often serves to mask other kinds, particularly those between men and women and between adults and children.

In fact, social control agencies such as the MSPCC, and more often, individual social workers, *were* able to help at times, specifically to help the weaker against the stronger, and not merely by rendering individuals passive. Again the discussion of results has been abstract, not marking exactly how they were able to help. Threats against or prosecutions of child abusers rarely changed adult behaviour, but had a greater impact on victims. Ironically, the MSPCC thereby contributed more to help battered women, defined as outside its jurisdiction, than abused children. Women had the emotional, physical and intellectual potential to leave abusive men, and often a tiny bit of material help, even a mere hint as to how to 'work' the relief agencies, could turn their aspirations for autonomy into reality. Moreover, women could sometimes get this help despite prejudice against them. Italian-American women might reap this benefit even from social workers who held derogatory views of Italians; single mothers might be able to get help in establishing independent households despite charity workers' suspicions of the immorality of their intentions. Just as in diplomacy the enemy of one's enemy may be *ipso facto* a friend, in these domestic emotional and physical spaces the enemy of one's oppressor may be an ally.

Moreover, the immigrant mothers, victims of racism, perhaps occasional beneficiaries of child-welfare work, were also part of the creation of modern child welfare standards and institutions. It is not adequate to diagram these individual interactions with social workers as a bargain in which one could get material help by giving up control. The control itself was invented and structured out of these interactions. So many of the MSPCC's early 'interventions' were in fact invitations by family members that the latter were in some ways teaching the agents what were appropriate and enforceable standards of child care. A more institutional example is the mothers' pension legislation developed in most of the United States between 1910 and 1920. As I have argued elsewhere, the feminist reformers who campaigned for that reform were influenced by the unending demands of single mothers, abounding in the records of child neglect, for support in raising their children without the benefit of men's wages.[11]

Not only this reform, but the entire progressive-era child health reform package, indeed the entire social programme of the women's rights movement, needs to be reconceived as not only a campaign for control spearheaded by elites, but also as a powerful if unsteady pressure for economic and domestic power in which poor and working-class women were active participants. Social control agencies were for them a tactic in their struggle to change the terms of their continuing, traditional, social control, which included but was not limited to the familial. The issues involved in an anti-family-violence campaign were fundamental to poor women: the right to immunity from physical attack at home, the power to protect their children from abuse, the right to keep their children – not merely the legal right to custody but the actual power to support their children, and the power to provide a standard of care for those children which met their own standards and aspirations. That family violence became a 'social problem' at all, that charities and professional agencies were drawn into attempts to control it, these facts were as much as product of the demands of those at the bottom as of those at the top.

Still, if these family and child-welfare agencies contributed to women's options, they had a constricting impact too. I do not wish to discard the cumulative insights offered by many critiques of social control. The discrimination and victim blaming which women encountered at the hands of professionals was destructive, the more so because they were proffered by those defined as 'helping'. Furthermore, it was not only scholars who saw professional intervention as weakening to individuals and families. Loss of control was an *experience*, articulated in many different ways by its victims, including those in these same case records. Often the main beneficiaries of welfare bureaucracies are those who hate them most. In wrestling with such bureaucracies one rarely gets what one really wants but rather another interpretation of one's needs. This is a contradiction that women, particularly, face and there is no easy resolution of it. There is no returning to an old or newly romanticized 'community control' when the remnants of community rest on a power structure hostile to women's aspirations. A feminist critique of social control must contain and wrestle with, not try to erase, this tension.

Notes

1 E. A. Ross, *Social Control* (New York, 1901).
2 Helen Everett, 'Social Control', *Encyclopaedia of the Social Sciences*, 1934; Herman Schwendinger and Julia R. Schwendinger, *Sociologists of the Chair: A Radical Analysis of the Formative Years of North American Sociology 1883–1922* (Basic Books, New York 1974), 203 ff.

3 John Ehrenreich, *The Altruistic Imagination: a History of Social Work and Social Policy in the United States* (Cornell University Press, Ithaca 1985).
4 Indeed, the dominant interpretation of this history, because not adequately discussed by feminists, has been antifeminist. For example, Christopher Lasch, *The Culture of Narcissism* (W. W. Norton, New York 1979) and *Haven in a Heartless World*; Ann Douglas, *The Feminization of American Culture* (Knopf, New York 1977); Jean Bethke Elshtain, *Public Man, Private Woman: Women in Social and Political Thought* (Princeton University Press, Princeton 1981).
5 A view effectively criticized by, e.g., Zillah Eisenstein, *The Radical Future of Liberal Feminism* (Longman, New York 1981); Ellen DuBois, 'Suffrage as a Radical Ideology', *Feminist Studies* Vol 3, 1–2, Fall 1975, and the same author's 'The Nineteenth-Century Woman Suffrage Movement and the Analysis of Women's Oppression,' in Zillah Eisenstein (ed.), *Capitalist Patriarchy and the Case for Socialist Feminism* (Monthly Review, New York 1978).
6 See below for the definition of patriarchy as I use it.
7 In Boston the MSPCC was called into being largely by Kate Gannett Wells, a moral reformer, along with other members of the New England Women's Club and the Moral Education Association. These women were united as much by class as by gender. Wells, for example, was an anti-suffragist; yet in her club work she co-operated with suffrage militants such as Lucy Stone and Harriet Robinson, for they considered themselves all members of a larger, loosely defined but nonetheless coherent community of prosperous, respectable women reformers. This unity of class and gender purpose *was* organized feminism at this time.
8 Ann Douglas, *The Feminization of American Culture*.
9 Robert Elno McGlone, 'Suffer the Children: The Emergence of Modern Middle-Class Family Life in America, 1820–1870,' PhD dissertation, UCLA, 1971.
10 Zillah Eisenstein, *The Radical Future of Liberal Feminism* (Longman, New York 1981); Joan B. Landes, 'Hegel's Conception of the Family,' in Jean Bethke Elshtain, (ed.), *The Family in Political Thought* (University of Massachusetts Press, Amherst 1982); Mary Lyndon Shanley, 'Marriage Contract and Social Contract in Seventeenth-Century English Political Thought', Ibid.
11 See my 'Single Mothers and Child Neglect', *American Quarterly*, Vol 37, 2, Summer 1985. All this material will be developed more fully in my book on the history of family violence and social control (New York, Pantheon, forthcoming).

6 Feminism and Welfare

Jane Lewis

Very few people today are unequivocally happy with the welfare state, whether they are on the political left or right, male or female. The New Thatcherite right is persuaded that welfare spending both curbs economic growth and erodes traditional systems of family support. The left finds itself caught between a defensive reaction to cuts (anticipated and real) in the level of service provision and state benefits, and the desire to make clear its own criticisms of a welfare state that is often not only paternalistic, but that has also failed to narrow the gulf between classes and create a more equal society.[1]

Feminists too have experienced tensions in formulating an analysis of the welfare state. Social policies have always referred to 'the family', to 'breadwinners', and to 'dependants', the concepts and assumptions being consistently patriarchal. The conviction that the state has never addressed women's needs in anything but an instrumentalist fashion – defining the needs of mothers, for example, in relation to a precise and prescriptive concept of motherhood as a social function[2] – allows some feminists to be largely dismissive of state welfare and to turn instead to the self-help alternative. Such an alternative has obvious limitations in terms both of the policy fields it can be applied to – health has probably been the most important – and of the number of people it can reach. A second feminist position is defensive, seeing the welfare state both as a crucial safety net, especially for the large numbers of poor elderly women and female single parents, and as an important source of female employment. The strong push from both the political right and left to expand the voluntary sector substantially and rapidly, with a view to saving money on the one hand, and offering a more diverse and less paternalistic range of choices on the other, is viewed by many as a strategy that would essentially increase the unpaid work of women in the community. A third feminist approach has been to recognize the inappropriateness of many of the principles underlying the structure of benefits and services and to call for radical reform to make sexual equality the priority, a position that inevitably comes into conflict with the more traditional priority of eradicating class inequalities. Despite its difficulties, it is this approach which has the greatest potential for changing the relationship of women to welfare.

In all their efforts to give priority to women's needs, and particularly in their attempt to rethink the framework of the welfare state, feminists face the problem that women's expressed interests in respect of social policies reflect the conflict they experience between their self-interest and their allegiance to family – to husband, children and kin. Historically, women have more often claimed benefits and services on behalf of their children than for themselves and have always been prepared to sacrifice their own welfare, whether in terms of leisure or food and clothing, to that of children and husbands. The fact that family relationships are a source of both dependency and emotional support and the home a locus of both love and labour that often borders on drudgery, means that women have sometimes perceived their interests to be the same as those of their men and sometimes as quite different. There are also profound differences between feminists on this score, most obviously between separatists who would have nothing to do with men and socialist feminists who believe that men must be part of the solution. More complicated are the divisions over motherhood. Those who believe in the importance of a female reproductive consciousness[3] are also concerned to protect and promote women's 'traditional' interests as mothers. Taken to extremes, this can sound remarkably like the New Right's emphasis on the importance of home, family and 'Victorian values'.

Thus, feminism has also experienced what is in fact an historical tension between an organization and practice that starts from women's claims as mothers and one that believes the main task to be the problem of defining and obtaining equality for women as individuals in the public sphere. Rarely in the history of feminism have these two positions been completely reconciled. The brief historical exploration of the relationship in Britain between feminist ideas, women's interests and social policy that follows makes these tensions more explicit. The task for feminists is to recognize that women relate to a much more complicated set of structures than men, and all of these structures play a part in determining their welfare; to be sensitive to women's conflicting loyalties; and to avoid making dogmatic claims on their behalf. Feminists interested in social policy must seek above all to *enlarge women's choices*, at the same time as forcing gender onto the social policy agenda. The second part of this paper makes some suggestions both as to what this means in current policy terms and regarding the importance of a feminist analysis in countering the New Right lobby, which is bent on turning the clock back as far as women's autonomy is concerned.

Feminists seeking to improve the welfare of women have always done so with a view to increasing equality between the sexes, but deciding exactly what constitutes equality for women has always been problematic. The majority of nineteenth-century feminists called for 'equal rights' in the belief that all women should ask for was the removal of barriers to equality, especially in law and in the workplace, and the same treatment as men. They expected to face a choice between, on the one hand, marriage and motherhood and, on the other, a career. The choice was often an agonizing one,[4] although some late-nineteenth-century women, such as the writer Cicely Hamilton, who deliberately chose celibacy and work, declared themselves happy with their lot.[5] These women urged that no special allowance be made for women workers who became mothers because that would be to ask for privileges that men did not have. Equality, in other words, was to be achieved on the terms set by men, although this does not seem to have struck women campaigners at the time as in any way problematic. Josephine Butler and fellow feminists registered their protest over protective legislation for women workers (which restricted their hours of work and the trades they might work in) in the following terms: 'this doctrine of Reproduction is not the essential aim of existence for either half of the human race'.[6] In other words, they rejected the idea that women should be protected as mothers at the expense of their right to work. The best 'welfare' for women in the eyes of these feminists was a 'fair field and no favour'. It was a line of thinking that persisted and offered an explicit challenge to the strengthening ideology of motherhood in the twentieth century. Cicely Hamilton was a founding member of the Open Door Council which was set up in 1926 with the aim of correcting 'the tendency of our legislators to be overkind to women who earn their livelihood; to treat them from youth to age as if they are permanently pregnant, and forbid them all manner of trades and callings in case they might "injure their health" '.[7]

In some measure there is a parallel between this kind of thinking and that of late-nineteenth- and early-twentieth-century male labour movement activists, who made the 'Right to Work', rather than state welfare benefits their first claim. There is certainly truth in the view that a well-paid job is the best form of welfare and there is no doubt but that the vast majority of women have always been consigned to the bottom of the labour heap. However, nineteenth-century women trade unionists were too conscious of the double burden imposed by paid work and domestic drudgery in the home to support the rigid views of middle-class feminists on protective legislation. Certainly oral evidence from the North West[8] suggests that women were pitied if they were forced to undertake paid employment in addition to the hard household labour that often involved heating the water for washing and cooking, pounding clothes in a dolly tub, mangling them with a hand wringer, cooking over a stove that had to be black leaded, and endless mending. In the early part of the century, women active in the labour movement, including female trade unionists, the wives of relatively well-paid workers in the Women's Cooperative Guild and middle-class women in the Fabian Women's Group, paid increasing attention to women's claims as mothers.

In her study of working-class marriage, Ellen Ross reached the conclusion that marital relationships in the early part of this century did not enjoin romantic love or verbal or sexual intimacy, but required financial obligations, services and activities that were gender specific.[9] Another influential interpretation of late-nineteenth-century family life has gone beyond this to suggest that the sexual division of labour between husband and wife was the best way of maximizing the welfare of the working-class family, that household work and childrearing comprised a full-time job for women during this period, and that men's fight for the status of breadwinner and the right to a family wage was the best strategy for raising the family's standard of living.[10] On the whole, it may be argued that in the early part of this century women accepted what present-day feminists have called the 'bourgeois family ideal' of a male breadwinner and female and child dependants. Social investigations of the period and such autobiographies of working-class women as we have emphasize the extent to which working women's worlds centred on their children and on holding the family together.[11] To this end they would take up casual employment as and when necessary, in the form of homework (making shirts or matchboxes, covering tennis balls, taking in lodgers), or by going out charring, but they defined their central responsibility in domestic terms. Working-class wives therefore supported their men in their fight for a family wage, even though this struggle was conducted at the expense of the woman worker. Evidence suggests that a majority of women were as firmly convinced as men of the justice of 'a woman's job and woman's rate'. When Ramsay MacDonald, who became the first Labour Prime Minister, investigated the printing trade early in the century he found that women in the trade rejected any suggestion that they might undertake tasks performed by men, as though something 'indelicate' had been proposed. He also reported the response of a female worker to the employer's request that she varnish books as: 'I know my place and I'm not going to take men's work from them'.[12] The belief in a 'natural' division of labour between the sexes, together with women's interest in keeping men's wages high, proved a powerful combination in supporting the family wage. Yet Labour women activists were also conscious that their needs as mothers were in practice rarely met.

In fact, men rarely earned a family wage. Booth estimated in 1889 that one-third of men did not do so.[13] The chief cause of poverty in the early twentieth century was low wages, and in addition, a large percentage of male wage earners had irregular employment as casual labourers. But families whose male breadwinner was temporarily debarred from earning through sickness or unemployment also suffered, especially before 1911 when a measure of health and unemployment insurance was introduced for the regularly employed. Nor was there any guarantee that wages would be shared equally amongst family members. The idea that working-class marriages worked in terms of a complementary division of tasks and mutual emotional and material support also often fell down in practice. Several writers have suggested the extent to which the implicit threat of violence may have bolstered a division of labour whereby the wife fulfilled her part, but the husband reserved a large part of his income for himself.[14] Female labour movement activists and suffragists were concerned that the wife should get her 'fair share'. In her pamphlet *Does a Man Support His Wife?* Emmeline Pethick Lawrence complained that a woman 'scrubs, cleans, stands over the wash-tub, makes and mends and cooks. More than all that she bears the long strain and the sharp ordeal of childbirth and becomes the sole minister to the manifold needs of her infant children', and yet her economic position was dependent on both the good fortune and the goodwill of her husband.[15] Rosalind Nash of the Women's Co-operative Guild also raised the issue of married women's essential economic dependency,[16] and several writers in both the suffrage journal, the *Common Cause*, and the Labour Party women's paper, *Labour Woman*, called for a scheme of wages for housework, whereby women would be given a legal right to a fixed proportion of their husband's wage.[17] Other feminists, including members of the Fabian Women's Group, felt uneasy at the thought of introducing market relations into family life and sought instead to achieve a

measure of 'endowment' for mothers from the state. The early call
for family allowances was thus envisaged as a payment to women for
their work in the home.

Feminists in the early part of the century thus began to grapple
with the key issues central to an analysis of women's welfare which
have come to dominate recent feminist thinking on the subject: the
implications of women's position in the family and the relationship
between paid and unpaid work. Both working women and feminists
active in the Labour movement accepted a system of sexual divisions
which conferred responsibility for childrearing and household
labour on women, and to this extent they showed little interest in
measures to improve women's leverage on the labour market, such
as day-care. Rather, they supported men in their struggles for a
family wage, but they were also prepared to make claims as mothers
for greater economic security, which necessarily involved asking for
a measure of economic independence. However, strategies for
achieving this, whether through legal entitlement to a proportion of
the husband's wage or through state endowment, brought the
tensions between women's self-interest and familial loyalties, and
between women's interests and those of men, into sharp focus.
Ramsay MacDonald, for instance, described the call for family
allowances as 'an insane burst of individualism' and declared that
'under socialism mothers' and children's right to maintenance would
be honoured by the family and not by the state'.[18]

Feminists and Labour movement activists did not pay as much
attention to the Liberal welfare reforms of 1906–11, usually regarded
by historians as laying the 'foundations' of the welfare state. The
most far-reaching of these reforms, National Insurance, which was
introduced in 1911, essentially excluded married women, who could
only join the scheme if they were insured workers in their own right.
The Fabian Women's Group pointed out that such a scheme of
contributory insurance was bound to exacerbate problems respecting
women's economic position, dividing those living as their husbands'
dependants from the small minority (ten per cent according to the
censuses of 1911 and 1921) who earned on their own account.[19] The
Women's Industrial Council (a group of mostly middle-class women
who devoted themselves to the investigation of working women's
problems) went further, to suggest that such a form of provision was
inappropriate for women and merely intensified 'the regrettable
tendency to consider the work of a wife and mother in her home of
no money value'.[20] Certainly these women were correct in their
perception that a social security scheme administered on a contributory basis through participation in the workforce would always

be of limited assistance to women, because of their marginal position in the labour market.

In fact, male and female workers had a great deal in common in terms of their attitudes towards early-twentieth-century welfare provision. As Pat Thane has pointed out, it was not a simple matter of working-class people welcoming or resisting state intervention, but rather that they asked in vain for non-intrusive, non-stigmatizing welfare.[21] Keir Hardie summed up their feelings during a House of Commons debate over school meals which was dominated by the fear that the measure would destroy the father's incentive to provide:

> He did not think the Hon. Gentlemen who had spoken so often that afternoon knew what it meant to them [Labour MPs] to sit there and listen to their wives being described as slatterns and themselves as spendthrifts. . . . It was absolutely untrue to say that they wanted their children to be quartered on the rates, but neither did they want children to be starved through the lack of ability on the part of parents through no fault of their own to provide them with food.[22]

Yet, while men and women thought alike at this fundamental level, they nevertheless experienced early state welfare provision differently, largely because of their different experience of family. Men and women drawing poor relief suffered stigma equally, but women were subjected to more intrusive welfare provision than men. For the early-twentieth-century state was anxious, for reasons of national and imperial security, to improve the welfare of mothers and children, and to that end a large number of officials started to knock on the doors of working-class homes in an effort to inculcate into mothers improved methods of infant care and domestic management. Many women resented the way in which people such as health visitors and school attendance officers threatened their domestic authority and privacy. It is this tradition of suspicion that Ferdinand Mount trades on in his recent book which calls for an end to all state intervention in the family:

> Our feelings are mixed even in the case of the most helpful of all public visitors. The District Health Visitor, who visits mothers with babies is often sweet and sensitive and genuinely useful. . . . But – and it remains an inescapable, embarrassing But – they cannot help being continuously aware that she is there as an inspector as well as an advisor. Her eye roams the room and the baby for evidence of dirt, neglect, even brutality. This kindly, middle-aged body has at her ultimate disposal a stalinist array of powers. . . .[23]

But Mount is wrong to deduce that working-class women have resisted all state intervention. Hannah Mitchell made it clear in her autobiography that she wished there had been infant welfare clinics in existence when her child was young.[24] As the Women's Cooperative Guild's appalling accounts of women's ignorance about health matters and their consequent suffering make clear, women wanted more information and help, but they did not want it imposed in ways over which they had no control.[25] Ignoring the fact that women needed more material resources, early twentieth-century welfare policies merely exhorted them to higher levels of child care and household management. Severe pressures resulted; for example, from 1906 mothers were told, at school medical inspections, what was wrong with their children and were given the responsibility, but not the financial resources, to get treatment (dependants were not covered by National Insurance). Mothers keeping older girls at home to look after the baby risked being summonsed before the School Management Boards by school attendance officers. As one active suffragist and settlement worker remarked, mothers were being 'ordered by law to perform the impossible and punished if they fail'.[26]

During the inter-war years the organized middle-class feminist movement took up the issue of women's position as mothers from the predominantly labour movement women who had discussed it prior to World War I. Under the presidency of Eleanor Rathbone, the National Union of Societies for Equal Citizenship (formerly the National Union of Women's Suffrage Societies) declared its determination to stop defining the equality of women on men's terms. Rathbone argued that nineteenth-century equal-rights feminists had ignored the fact that 'some aspects of our whole social fabric are man-made through generations to suit masculine interests and glorify masculine standards'.[27] Under her leadership, the National Union campaigned for protective legislation, family allowances and free access to birth control information. Nineteenth-century middle-class feminists had opposed birth control just as they had opposed protective legislation. Historians differ in their interpretations of why they did so, arguing on the one hand that they needed to maintain the link between sexuality and reproduction at a time when marriage was the prime source of middle-class women's livelihood, and on the other that their opposition was primarily ideological and moral.[28] In the first interpretation, women are seen to be acting in defence of their own interests within the family. In the second, they are portrayed as defenders of a more abstract idea of family, such as might be termed today 'traditional family values'. Certainly there is a

strong tradition of women taking the latter position; the Moral
Majority movement in the USA relies heavily on 'Right Wing
Women'[29] as well as men. But today's right-wing women do not
support the movement for greater equality between the sexes. Many
nineteenth-century opponents of birth control did so, and their
opposition must therefore be seen within the context of a society
which denied middle-class women options outside marriage.

The circumstances of working-class women, often struggling to do
jobs both inside and outside the home, were very different, and their
attitudes towards birth control were also different. Hannah Mitchell,
the working-class suffragist, had only one child, and recorded in her
autobiography that fortunately her husband 'had the courage of his
socialist convictions on this point'.[30] In the moving letters of
working-class wives collected by the Women's Cooperative Guild and
published in 1915, what comes across most vividly is their ignorance
of female physiology and sexuality, and desire for more information,
the difficulties they experienced in obtaining access to information,
and a lack of privacy in their homes that would have made the use of
female methods of birth control hard.[31] During the inter-war years,
when it was becoming more usual for middle-class women to seek
employment before marriage, middle-class feminists decided to
campaign for access to birth control information as a means of
furthering female autonomy. Family allowances would provide
women with greater economic autonomy and birth control would
give them greater sexual autonomy.

The new feminism of the inter-war years had little to say about
women's position in the workforce or the unfair way in which the
cuts in unemployment benefit during the Depression affected
married women; the Anomalies Act of 1931 assumed that a married
woman who left the labour force for whatever reason had effectively
retired. The assumption on the part of government and feminists
was still clearly that women would not combine marriage and
motherhood with full-time employment. Eleanor Rathbone believed
firmly that women were 'the natural custodians of childhood'.[32]
The concern of new feminists, like that of the women labour
movement activists before World War I, was to secure some real
improvement in the welfare of wives and mothers. In fact, the
government continued its efforts to educate mothers but did very
little to meet the real needs identified by feminists. Seriously ill
women became eligible to receive birth control information from
government clinics in 1930, but birth control did not receive official
sanction until 1967 and the campaign for family allowances rapidly
lost its feminist rationale. When allowances were finally introduced

in 1945 it was as a means of holding down wages and inflation.[33] Remaining representatives of the nineteenth-century tradition of equal-rights feminism broke with the National Union of Societies for Equal Citizenship in 1926 over the executive's insistence on redefining equality in ways that took account of women's reproductive capacities and family responsibilities. In essence, New Feminism had the potential to develop a radical analysis of women's position. Like Labour women before the War, new feminists were asking fundamental questions about the position of women in the family, but nevertheless failed to make strong enough analytical connections with the position of women in relation to other structures, especially in respect to the workplace and to educational institutions.

After World War II women's relationship to one of the key structures determining their welfare, the labour market, changed significantly. The percentage of married women aged 15–59 who were employed jumped from 10% in 1931, to 26% in 1951, to 49% in 1971 and 62% in 1980. In addition, an ever-increasing proportion of these women had young children. The demand for women's labour increased substantially after the War, particularly in the service and public sectors; indeed, women became a substantial proportion of those providing welfare in the new welfare state. It is not clear to what extent women were working for reasons of personal fulfilment, or to what extent they were doing as they had always done and were working primarily in order to make a contribution to the family economy. As Penny Summerfield and Patricia Allatt have pointed out,[34] family ideology was reconstructed at the end of World War II so that both employers and the state advocated part-time work for women as a means of enabling them to combine paid employment, marriage and motherhood without seriously undermining their home responsibilities. In the education literature distributed to the armed forces during the War, 'the family' was established as a value worth fighting for and the model of the family that was used integrated the bourgeois ideal of male breadwinner and dependent wife and children with the actual war-time experience of working men and women. Housewife and working wife were thus drawn together and the phrase 'working mother', which served to legitimize experience, was born.

The net increase in women's employment since 1961 is, in fact, entirely accounted for by part-time work. Thus, the majority of women remain supplementary wage earners and continue to see themselves as such, putting responsibilities to home and family first. However, their money is increasingly crucial to their families' welfare; in the mid-seventies four times as many families with children would have had incomes below the supplementary benefit level had not the wives, as well as the husbands, worked.[35] Despite women's status as secondary wage earners, women entering employment since 1960 have demonstrated an attachment to the labour force equal to that of men, and it appears that they will work for as many years as men, apart from breaks for childbearing.[36] And the recent government survey of women's employment in the 1980s indicates that an ever-growing number of young women expect to work throughout their adult lives, taking breaks only for maternity leave.[37]

Thus, the concept of a family wage, with its concomitant sexual division of labour, has become an increasingly contested ideal. However, the traditional assumption of a male breadwinner comprised one of the basic principles of the social security legislation passed immediately after the War. As a result, neither the contribution made by the wife to the family economy nor the entitlements due to her have been fully recognized by the social security system.[38] As paid employment has become a more significant part of women's lives, their interests in respect to legislative change have shifted, with more emphasis being placed on day-care provision, equal pay and the rights of part-time workers. Clearly, an increasing number of women want a share in paid employment, but this brings substantial conflict with the interests of men and problems in respect of the balance of change that can be achieved between the various structures that women relate to.

Greater equality for women in the workplace can only be achieved if substantial change is effected in respect of their domestic responsibilities. In other words, both unpaid and paid work must be shared. However, studies of the division of domestic labour show little evidence of any significant re-negotiation. Most working wives do the vast majority of cooking, cleaning and caring work in families, and their husbands do not spend significantly more time on domestic tasks than the husbands of non-working wives.[39] Nor has women's leverage on the labour market shown much improvement. The latest survey of horizontal occupational segregation shows that two-thirds of women are in jobs done only by women.[40] There is no evidence of an easing in either horizontal or vertical segregation since the passing of the Sex Discrimination Act in 1975, nor has there been any lasting improvement in women's pay since the full implementation of the Equal Pay Act, also in 1975. This lack of change has substantial secondary effects in terms of female poverty, both of elderly women, because women tend to do badly in terms of occupational pensions, and of single female headed households. Recent statistics from the USA show that since 1969 female headed families have experienced increasing poverty, while male headed families have experienced the reverse.[41] This trend is important in view of recent debates over the reform of family law, for example, where much has been made of the need to make divorce (which now ends one in four marriages) a 'clean break', meaning that divorcees should not get 'a meal ticket for life'. But this ignores the fact that marriage and motherhood effectively 'deskill' women and that it is women who continue to care for children and/or kin after divorce, as single parents.[42] When 'welfare' in our society is so dependent on the individual's relationship to the labour market, both in terms of the size of the wage and eligibility for benefits, women are seriously disadvantaged.

Recent feminist analysis of women's welfare, and the kinds of reforms necessary to improve it, has focused firmly on the way in which women's position in the family structures their position in the workforce. A twofold strategy has been put forward,[43] designed first to secure greater recognition of the contribution women make to the family economy, and second to improve women's position in the labour market. The first calls for disaggregation of the tax and social security systems, to cut through the web of assumptions regarding women's position in the family and their proper role in society, and to provide all women, irrespective of their marital and material circumstances, with greater individual autonomy and choice. Full disaggregation would, of course, mean that married women, or women cohabiting with men, who could not get a job could claim welfare benefits in their own right, and that men would no longer receive allowances for dependants under either the tax or social security systems. Households in which the man is rich would stand to benefit if the wife were willing to make herself available for work, thus bringing the goal of redistributing wealth into conflict with that of sexual equality. Such a strategy might also have the effect of forcing women with little or no job training, and who have previously occupied the socially acceptable role of housewife, onto a currently severely depressed labour market. The second part of the strategy calls for the adoption of positive action programmes, including affirmative hiring and education policies, and an increase in the social wage in the form of increased day-care provision and child benefit, in order to further undermine the idea of husbands as *the* breadwinners and to ease the burden of responsibility for domestic affairs that falls on women.

This analysis is both comprehensive and, in terms of a long-range strategy, hard to fault. Yet many women find it extremely threatening, as they fear, quite rightly, that some steps towards disaggregation may be taken (for example, in respect of alimony payments) without concomitant efforts being made to improve women's position in the labour force, especially at a time of deep economic depression when there is no government commitment to achieving sexual equality. After all, marriage remains a major source of livelihood for the majority of adult women. Women also continue to experience a tension between familialism and the desire for greater autonomy. For example, during the past few years, many Canadian feminists have campaigned vigorously for 'homemakers' pensions', explicitly calling for the recognition of the work women do in the home.[44] Similarly, many women would support the payment of women who care for elderly and infirm relatives or neighbours. A recent study shows that 'the majority of carers themselves believe that they are the right person to provide care and that care for elderly people is women's work'.[45] It is in many ways easier for government to give a measure of recognition to women's traditional work (the British government grants home responsibility credits in calculating pension entitlement) than it is to promote significant change in the sexual division of labour in order to improve women's position in the workforce and persuade men to do more of the caring work at home.

The problem of the feminist call for disaggregation is that it appears less a means of increasing the range of women's choices and more a prescription designed to force some women into what they consider uncongenial roles at great personal risk. The campaign to accord greater recognition to women's traditional work, on the other hand, runs the same risk as pre-War feminist campaigns to improve the lot of mothers, which is that traditional sexual divisions will be perpetuated. This does not mean that we should give up the struggle to develop policies that will both recognize women's complex allegiances and claims, and offer them more choice. And the feminist position must be flexible enough to accomplish this. It is crucially important in what is increasingly referred to as a post-industrial society to think about redefining and sharing work between the employed and unemployed and between men and women. For instance, incentives to care for the increasing numbers of frail elderly (in the form of social security or tax concessions for those taking part-time work in order to care) should be opened out, so men and women may choose the mix of caring work and paid employment that suits them best. The possibilities of genuine job sharing (that is, part-time work with full-time benefits) have yet to be explored, and while many policy analysts have floated the idea of a shorter working

week as a means of sharing paid work, few have talked about a
shorter working day that would also facilitate the sharing of unpaid
domestic work. Too often the questions that are posed about the
future of social policies are gender blind, concentrating for example
on the labour market and policies of job creation without considering
the problems women have in gaining access to the labour market and
the benefits it delivers. Similarly, in the last decade, both major
political parties have sought to make themselves parties of the
family, which has meant supporting policies to strengthen the
traditional bourgeois family ideal, irrespective of women's wishes.

In the present political climate, social policies are more likely to
deliberately ignore the issue of providing greater choice for women.
Indeed, recent years have seen an erosion of the provision of both
nursery education and maternity rights.[46] New Right writers
generally cherish 'traditional family values', which encompass the
traditional sexual division of labour. The bourgeois family ideal is
seen as fundamental to the family's crucial task of socializing
individuals with personalities and values conducive to entrepreneurial
capitalism and democracy.[47] Gender divisions have always been
perceived as 'natural' and therefore outside politics, and major
efforts to change them have thus always provoked an emotional and
often violent response, the struggle for the suffrage in the early part
of the century being the classic example. Feminist claims for female
autonomy inevitably clash with the present government's 'inter-
connected trinity of family, private market and voluntary sector'[48]
and with the interests of men. However, they are also threatening to
many women, because women's expressed interests cannot but
reflect the complex web of relationships they have with husbands,
children, kin, employers and the state. It is because women's claims
call for such radical rethinking that their legitimacy is so hard to
establish. The feminist vision of a more equal society requires a
process of re-definition and change in all areas of human activity.

Notes

1 Julian Le Grand, *The Strategy of Equality* (Allen and Unwin, London
  1982).
2 This idea is explored by Denise Riley, 'The Free Mothers: Pronatalism
  and Working Mothers in Industry at the End of the Last War in Britain',
  History Workshop Journal 11 (1981).
3 Mary O'Brien, *The Politics of Reproduction* (Routledge and Kegan Paul,
  London 1982).

4 For example, in the case of Beatrice Webb's decision to refuse marriage to Joseph Chamberlain: Barbara Caine, 'Beatrice Webb and the Woman Question', *History Workshop Journal* 14 (1982).

5 Cicely Hamilton gives her views of marriage in *Marriage as a Trade* (Chapman and Hall, London 1909).

6 J. Butler (ed.), *Legal Restrictions on the Industrial Work of Women from the Woman's Point of View* (Matthew and Sons, London 1874).

7 Quoted in Cicely Hamilton, *Life Errant* (J. M. Dent, London 1935), 288–9.

8 Elizabeth A. Roberts, *A Woman's Place: an Oral History of Working Class Women, 1890–1940* (Blackwell, Oxford 1984).

9 Ellen Ross, ' "Fierce Questions and Taunts": Married Life in Working Class London, 1870–1914', *Feminist Studies* 8 (1982), 578.

10 Jane Humphries, 'Class Struggle and the Persistence of the Working Class Family', *Cambridge Journal of Economics* 1 (September 1977).

11 See, for example, Magdalen Stuart Pember Reeves, *Round about a Pound a Week* (G. Bell and Sons, London 1913); and Joe Robinson, *The Life and Times of Francie Nichol of South Shields* (Allen and Unwin, London 1975).

12 J. Ramsay MacDonald, *Women in the Printing Trades* (P. S. King, London 1904), viii and 65–6.

13 Charles Booth, *London Life and Labour*, Vol I (Williams and Norgate, London 1889).

14 Nancy Tomes, ' "A Torrent of Abuse": crimes of violence between working class men and women in London', 1840–1875', *Journal of Social History* 11 (1978).

15 Emmeline Pethick Lawrence, *Does a Man Support His Wife?* (WSPU leaflet, London C 1911)

16 Rosalind Nash, *The Position of Married Women* (Women's Cooperative Guild, London, 1909).

17 An excellent discussion of the whole early debate over wages for housework and mothers' endowment is contained in Linda E. Walker, 'The Women's Movement in England in the Late Nineteenth and Early Twentieth Centuries', unpublished PhD thesis, University of Manchester, 1984.

18 Quoted by Hilary Land, 'The Family Wage', *Feminist Review* 6 (1980).

19 Fabian Women's Group, *How the National Insurance Bill Affects Women* (FWG, London 1911).

20 Women's Industrial Council, *Memo on the National Insurance Bill as it Affects Women* (TS, 1911, BLPES).

21 Pat Thane, 'The Working Class and State "Welfare" in Britain, 1880–1914', *Historical Journal* 27 (1984).

22 House of Commons Debates, 1906, vol. 166, col. 1385, also quoted in Thane, in *Historical Journal* 27.

23 Ferdinand Mount, *The Subversive Family: An Alternative History of Love and Marriage* (Allen and Unwin, London 1983), 1.

24 Hannah Mitchell, *The Hard Way Up* (Virago, London 1977).

25 Margaret Llewellyn Davies, *Maternity: Letters of Working Women* (Bell, London 1915).

26 Anna Martin, *Married Working Women* (NUWSS, London 1911), 8.

27 Eleanor Rathbone, *Milestones: Presidential Addresses at the Annual Council Meetings of the NUSEC* (NUSEC, London 1929).
28 The first position is taken by Linda Gordon, *Woman's Body, Woman's Right: a Social History of Birth Control in America* (Grossman, New York 1976), and Angus McLaren, *Birth Control in Nineteenth Century England* (Croom Helm, London 1978); the second by Carl N. Degler, *At Odds: Women and the Family in America from the Revolution to the Present* (Oxford University Press, New York 1980).
29 Andrea Dworkin, *Right Wing Women* (Women's Press, London 1983).
30 Mitchell, *The Hard Way Up*, 102.
31 Davies, *Maternity*.
32 Rathbone, *Milestones*.
33 John Macnicol, *The Movement for Family Allowances, 1918–45: a Study in Social Policy Development* (Heinemann, London 1980).
34 Penny Summerfield, *Women Workers in the Second World War* (Croom Helm, London 1984), and Patricia Allatt, 'The Family seen through the Beveridge Report, Forces Education and Popular Magazines: A Social Study of the Social Reproduction of Family Ideology in World War II', unpublished PhD dissertation, University of Keele, 1981.
35 CPRS, *People and their Families* (HMSO, London 1980).
36 Irene Bruegel, 'Women's Employment, Legislation and the Labour Market', in Jane Lewis (ed.), *Women's Welfare/Women's Rights* (Croom Helm, London 1983).
37 Jean Martin and Ceridwen Roberts, 'Women's Employment in the 1980s Evidence from the Women and Employment Survey', *Employment Gazette* (May 1984).
38 Hilary Land has argued this point forcefully in a number of places. See, for example, Hilary Land, 'Who Cares for the Family?' *Journal of Social Policy* 7 (1978).
39 Lisa Peattie and Martin Rein, *Women's Claims. A Study in Political Economy* (Oxford University Press, New York 1983), 71–2.
40 Martin and Roberts, 'Women's Employment'.
41 Martin Rein, 'Women, Reagan and the Welfare State', unpublished paper, 1984.
42 Hilary Land examines the recent family law debate further in 'Who Still Cares for the Family?' in Lewis (ed.), *Women's Welfare*.
43 *Rights of Women and Women's Legal and Financial Independence Campaign, 'Disaggregation Now', Feminist Review*, 2 (1979).
44 For a statement on this, see Louise Dulude (Chairman, Pensions Committee of the National Action Committee), letter to the *Globe and Mail*, 14 January 1984, 7.
45 H. Quershi and A. Walker, *The Caring Relationship* (Routledge and Kegan Paul, London forthcoming).
46 Miriam E. David, 'The New Right, Sex Education, and Social Policy: Towards a New Moral Economy in Britain and the USA', in Lewis (ed.), *Women's Welfare*.
47 For example, Brigitte Berger and Peter L. Berger, *The War over the Family: Capturing the Middle Ground* (Hutchinson, London 1983).
48 Malcolm Wicks, 'Enter Right: The Family Patrol Group', *New Society*, 24 February 1983, 297–8.

7 Feminism at Work

Heather Jon Maroney

The most important political phenomenon of the last two decades and one that will continue to mark the politics of the next has been the development of a new feminist consciousness and a movement for women's liberation.[1] In Canada and Quebec, as elsewhere in the advanced capitalist world, fifteen years of ideological and cultural struggle have resulted in the diffusion of the vital sense that women have rights and will not be bound by convention, prejudice or male privilege. Women's efforts towards collective self-definition have revalorized attributes and activities culturally coded as feminine. This transformation has begun to produce a positive atmosphere for girls growing to womanhood and women of all ages coming to feminism – a reorientation so profound that I (despite an instinctive feminism learned at my mother's knee as we changed our own flat tyres) could not have dreamed of it in the giggly, marriage-doomed fifties or even in the messianic cyclone of the sixties. This new-found self-confidence has been a source of inspiration for women in a wide range of social struggles and, increasingly, a radicalizing force for women as workers at the place of work. But, at the close of the seventies, although widely diffused, the new feminist consciousness remained uneven, politically embryonic, and in many cases reactive. More even than in most countries, in Canada and Quebec, feminist consciousness, like the organized women's movement, is fragmented along regional, sectoral and class lines.[2] Despite real advances these divisions have prevented feminists from developing a collective assessment of past actions or a coherent strategy on a bi-national scale.

The Two Waves of the Women's Movement

In one sense, the fundamental questions of strategy – the state, allies, the relation between sexual and class politics, and programme

– that confront the women's movement in the eighties have been on the agenda since the sixties.[3] They have, however, been given a particular urgency by the current political conjuncture. The deepening economic crisis and the rightward drift in state policies over the past ten years have provoked increasing trade union militancy. At the same time, in the confused ideological aftermath of the sixties, the restrictive cultural atmosphere engendered by the recession has allowed reactionary anti-labour currents – whose anti-feminist, homophobic, Christian fundamentalism is glossed as 'pro-family' – to mobilize social discontent in an attempt to overturn the cultural gains of the last fifteen years, especially those made by women.[4] In the face of this combination of resurgent class conflict and cultural backlash, no component of the broad left (from trade unions and social democracy through radical popular movements to the organized far left) has been able to develop an adequate strategy and programme. This lack of consensus complicates the development of strategy for the women's movement: we are compelled to elaborate our strategy with little sense of the direction our potential allies might take.

To this task, feminism brings diverse insights from two waves of radicalization: sixties women's liberation and contemporary working-class feminism. Against patriarchal ideology, women's liberationists claimed that women were *oppressed*. All relations between women and men – including institutionalized heterosexuality and the monogamous couple – were, whether women were conscious of it or not, structured and distorted by male power and privilege. What was particularly new in this analysis of male-female relations was the fact that it placed sexuality, marriage and the family at the centre, asserted that the long-term transformation of gender relations required sexual autonomy for women, and held that the rootedness of women's oppression in all social institutions required revolutionary transformation. From these insights several strategic principles were derived: the necessity of autonomy for the women's movement, the refusal to postpone women's struggles or to subordinate them to any state, party, class or male-dominated national movement interests, the defence of lesbian choice. These analytic and strategic acquisitions – much more than the classic demands for equal pay and equal work, reproductive freedom, and child care – are the legacy of sixties feminism for present practice.

In any contemporary evaluation, however, it must be recognized that the present women's movement differs markedly from that of the sixties. In Canada, two developments are particularly significant. A recent successful campaign to include equal rights for women in the Canadian Constitution has strengthened liberal feminism and its orientation to the state. But since the mid-seventies, a radicalization of working women – most immediately visible in several important public and private sector strikes – has profoundly altered the organizational and ideological balance of forces within the movement as a whole. This radicalization is significant not just in itself or in the opportunity that it provides for broadening the struggle, but because the widening of the class basis of feminism deepens our understanding of the way class and gender oppression condenses a global system of domination and opens up new ways to explore questions of strategy and theory that have long perturbed the women's movement and, indeed, blocked its development.

The rise of working-class feminism has not, however, been an unmixed blessing. The occupation of centre-stage by workplace struggles has helped to narrow the ideological focus by concentrating attention on economic issues at the expense of cultural and sexual liberation projects *even inside the women's movements itself* and so reinforced a general tendency in the left to economism.[5] Working-class feminism is also weighed down by the reformism which prevails in the three political spheres – trade unions, social democracy, and important sectors of the women's movement – which have so far conditioned its ideological development. But it is also important to remember that, despite the difficult conditions in which it emerged, working-class feminism grew out of militant struggle in the context of an already radicalized leadership of women who nurtured both its class and feminist consciousness. If its feistiness is maintained and if it is able to join forces with socialist and other feminist tendencies committed to overall social transformation, its radicalizing dynamic can profoundly alter class (as well as feminist) politics: broadening workplace struggles, overcoming antagonistic divisions between women and men in the working class, and introducing an anti-economist, anti-bureaucratic politics of liberation into existing working-class organizations.

Against this background, my aim here will be to trace the rise of working-class feminism, to show its contradictory significance in the women's movement, and to begin to explore its implications for socialist-feminist theory and practice.

The Growth of Working-Class Feminism

By the end of the seventies, working-class feminism in Canada had become a distinct current in the women's movement. In contrast to the university-based feminism of the sixties, it was rooted in the workplace and oriented, first of all, to the practical achievement of more concrete and, hence, more limited goals. It had its own outlook on what feminism should be: 'Of course jobs are a feminist issue: and equal pay and training. Getting women into non-traditional jobs is important right now, because of what will happen with tech change. Of course, in my union when they think they're getting down to the nitty-gritty real feminist issues, the men always ask "How's the day care in your town?" – the whole motherhood thing. They don't want to talk about sexual harassment or anything to do with sex. After all, it's not just cross-class, it's workers harassing workers. But unions give you power, and they educate you. It's the only way to unite the working class, through unions and working together.'[6]

Underlying the development of working-class feminism are dramatic increases in labour-force participation during the 1950s and 1960s for women over 25 with children. Women have risen from 17% of membership in trade unions in 1966 to 27% in 1976.[7] Although the most important single contribution to this increase in unionization was a top-down legislative conversion of provincial and federal staff associations into unions in a rapidly expanding public sector, women workers' readiness to unionize and their militancy in strikes testify to a consciousness that wage work is no longer an episode before marriage and childraising but a permanent feature of their lives, a recognition that is a crucial component of proletarian consciousness. In these recently formed Canadian public-sector unions of clerical and service workers, the combination of a relatively weak bureaucracy and a majority female membership has facilitated the entry and expression of feminist consciousness. As governments have sought to resolve their fiscal crisis through rationalization, semi-professionals like teachers and nurses have met increasingly proletarianized working conditions, pay restraints and job insecurity, have moved away from corporatist associations or professional aspirations and have affiliated to trade unions in great numbers. Despite their conservative and sometimes confessional origins, public-sector unions, particularly those in the Quebec Common Front, have proved to be both militant and relatively open to women's demands. In some cases, women teachers and nurses, traditionally ruled by an ethic of service and self-sacrifice, have raised explicitly feminist demands in contract negotiations.[8]

Two other developments have begun to bring more women into the trade union orbit and, this time, into the male-dominated heavy industrial unions. First, the entry of women into 'non-traditional' jobs in steel, mining, rail, manufacturing and forest products has been the focus of widespread propaganda by both government and labour, making a greater political impact than the restricted numbers of women would seem to warrant. For government 'affirmative action' promised a trendy, low-cost alternative to the enactment and enforcement of rigorous equal value legislation; selective promotion of a few both promotes individualism and serves the interests of formally qualified professional and managerial women.[9] Government publicity and human rights provisions notwithstanding, campaigns by coalitions of unions, socialist-feminists and job-seekers have been necessary to overcome actual employer barriers against female applicants.[10]

If, in this first instance, women have come into unions, in the second, the large industrial unions (especially United Steelworkers of America and United Auto Workers) have turned to women. With recession-induced instability and shrinking employment in the manufacturing sector, unions, forced to find new ways to secure a membership base, have supported organizing drives in small plants or moved to sign up clerical and service workers (at Blue Cross, Fotomat, in legal aid, and so on). Taken together, these developments imply the numerical feminization of the centres of male working-class power and of the labour movement as a whole. These inroads are, however, fragile as layoffs reduce or eliminate the numbers of women machinists, miners and smelter-workers.

As an organized expression, working-class feminism is partially structured by the existing labour movement and its ideology is most coherently expressed in groupings of feminists in the trade unions. Diverse in their political origins and experience, these nuclei can be divided into: politically self-conscious 'trade union feminists'; and women workers whose feminist (and trade union) consciousness has crystallized in the course of specific struggles. Within the first group a further distinction can be drawn between women working in established unions and those attempting to set up independent unions.

Trade Union Recalcitrance

In established unions, trade union feminists, often on staff, have set up or given new political life to official union committees on the status of women, worked for women's caucuses, and animated unofficial cross-union formations – like Organized Working Women (Ontario) – as a base to agitate against sexism. Highly developed caucuses leading to committees first appeared in Quebec, where they had led several campaigns: for equal pay legislation, for maternity and parental leave, against sexism in the schools, for women's liberation reports and resolutions which, in line with the 'ideological' character of the Centrale des Syndicats Nationaux and the Centrale des Enseignants du Québec, go far beyond workforce equality to call for abortion rights and the socialization of housework, and to criticize marriage as an oppressive institution.[11] Across Canada, their success has been marked by the establishment of equal rights committees in all the provincial labour federations, the establishment of the Canadian Labour Congress (CLC) women's conferences, and by rapid and dramatic changes in policy. Although the Quebec federations' concern with the global aspects of 'la condition féminine' is exceptional, many unions now have the essential elements of a programme for workplace equality through economic and social measures: equal value demands, across-the-board rather than percentage wage increases, affirmative action, day-care and parental 'reproductive' leave for childbirth, adoption or abortion.

Despite the advance represented by the institutionalization of these committees, the intersecting structures of sexism and bureaucratic power in the labour movement replicate and thus serve to reproduce prevailing gender structures. Even where the membership is predominantly female, women are consistently underrepresented in governing bodies and feminist forces are weak in relation to an entrenched male leadership. Although their paucity can be partially explained by the difficulties for women of adding a third set of union responsibilities to their double day of paid and domestic labour,[12] the independent effect of sexism must be taken into account. While the commentators in 'Women and Trade Unions'[13] recognize that many men in unions are supportive of, if sometimes confused by, women's attempts to redefine gender boundaries, they nevertheless point with remarkable consistency to sexism on the part of male workers, women's internalization of stereotyped behaviour, 'business unionism' and bureaucratic control as blocks to female participation.[14] Since the current leadership was politically and ideologically formed during the post-war defeat of feminism (and, incidentally, of the left), it owes its position at least in part to male privilege.[15] To put the question sharply, immediately equalizing women's representation in union power structures would require either that some male power brokers lose their positions of financial and sexual privilege or, an unlikely alternative, that the number of such positions be almost doubled to accommodate women. Thus the question of representativeness in general is raised by women's demands for equality. In the rank and file as well, a pro-woman economic programme has sometimes generated conflict between male and female workers.[16] Even if political education tends to homogenize the ideology of trade union *activists*, convention resolutions do not necessarily represent the view of the membership. As recently as 1971, many Quebec unionists still thought that men had a prior right to jobs and that women should, in any case, stay at home, union policy to the contrary.[17] Even allowing for economically irrational employer resistance, so-called 'women's issues' such as day-care, rights and benefits for part-time workers, and maternity leave seem sometimes to have been included in contract demands merely as bargaining points to be traded off.[18]

The resources of unions, never elastic, are particularly stretched by basic defensive tasks in the current recession, whether because of loss of membership from layoffs or intense strike activity. In this situation, continuing pressure from rank-and-file and more particularly women's caucuses is necessary to ensure that social concerns are taken up by the union.[19] In this regard, trade union feminism has passed through two stages of development. Having taken the first consciousness-raising and mobilizing step, it has gone on to formulate claims *from the point of view of women* as a special group: the right to work, equal pay, and so on. In agitating for the acceptance of these demands, women have sometimes breached gendered ghetto walls and created a class demand supported equally by, and understood to be in the interests of, women and men – again, equal pay is the classic case in point. Other innovative trade union policies, like a reduced working week without pay cuts or multi-patronal bargaining units, could also be sought in terms that educate female and male workers alike – in these cases, as a way to equalize paid labour and domestic labour in the household or to organize small workplaces of often female office and retail workers.

But at no point has feminism reformed the institutionalized forms of politics – bureaucratic by some accounts, patriarchal by others – which cyclically alienate women and impede their participation.[20] Formal norms of political procedure, for example, can be manipulated to define *what can be heard*, to block rank-and-file initiatives or to reinforce existing ideology. That bureaucratic responses are not limited to male power brokers but ingrained in union functions was shown at the 1980 CLC Women's Conference where a proposal from the floor for plenary discussions and time to evaluate the conference was blocked by the chair, a president of a national public sector union and a noted feminist; militancy was not stressed; and the discussion of how to acquire power was limited to lobbying.[21] Thus only a certain range of feminist complaint and militancy can be taken account of and women who have not yet learned the ropes (or those who go too far) are ruled out of court. Lest this process be thought of as simply one of self-censorship or internalized submissiveness on the part of women, it should be emphasized that 'ruling out' not only takes place from the chair of conventions but is often backed up in private by threats or promises about future union careers or outcomes in private life. On balance, trade unions provide organizational continuity, material resources, and an established constituency in contrast with the more ephemeral, poorer, yet creative, self-directed and consciously holistic structures of the autonomous women's movement. Nevertheless, formal democratic norms have provided a means for trade union feminists to take advantage of the political and ideological space created by general feminist agitation, whether that be as a result of real sensitivity to women's needs or merely to their explosiveness.

Trade union feminists are caught in a contradictory situation. Their position inside the labour movement is vulnerable and their room to manoeuvre depends upon the extent of feminist radicalization and trade union militancy of women in the rank and file – which, in turn, exists in a complex relation with general feminist and class mobilization. In isolation, trade union feminists, especially union staff, are not only subject to the usual pressures of bureaucratic and reformist integration of normalized union practice, but must also bear the brunt of sexism inside the unions. On the other side, feminist peers outside the labour movement often expect that a maximal programme for women's liberation can and should be propagated without modification in the trade union arena and that any failure to do so amounts to a sell-out of women's interests. The task has been complicated by the existence of real resistance among rank-and-file women (let alone men) to sexual and cultural issues 'expressed in feminist jargon' – particularly to abortion and lesbian rights. The resources that have been available to staff women have been far from adequate to carry out general consciousness-raising programmes on these questions (or even on basic trade unionism) among the workers whose interests they are supposed to represent. And, although their position allows them to speak with the political weight of the trade unions in the broader women's movement, what they say is restricted by the ideological horizon of the constitutency that they represent. Overall, they must mediate between the feminist movement, including its working-class component, and working-class sexism and sexual oppression.

The Check to Feminist Syndicalism

A second grouping of trade union organizers located mainly in British Columbia has adopted a feminist-syndicalist approach by attempting to construct exemplary independent unions in female-dominated industries – for example, the Service, Office and Retail Workers Union of Canada (SORWUC) among restaurant, office and bank workers, and the Association of University and College Employees (AUCE), both formed in 1972. The initial success of their organizing drives demonstrated how lessons derived from sixties women's organizing – small group consciousness-raising, a stress on democratic, anti-hierarchical principles, and feminist policies of day-care, equal pay and promotion – could be applied to the class ends of union solidarity; in the process, they disproved the contention of malestream trade unions that service and clerical workers were too difficult to organize.[22] Relying on support from women's groups, the social-democratic New Democratic Party, and CLC and Congress of Canadian Unions (CCU) locals and members of long-term leafleting campaigns and essential financial support during strikes, feminist-syndicalist organizers urged women workers to unionize (along with men) not just for economic defence but to combat their special exploitation in the labour market as women.

Since 1978, however, the limitations of feminist syndicalism have become clear. First, employer resistance in the banking sector successfully used both threats and co-optation to limit the union drive.[23] In the face of what turns out to have been a tactical error in deciding to organize on a branch-by-branch basis, coupled with a financial inability to gain first contracts in certified locals and to carry cases through the Canadian Labour Relations Board, most of the bank locals were decertified, the United Bank Workers dissolved, and several hundred women left without union protection. Secondly, SORWUC, unable to mobilize adequate support from outside the CLC and unwilling to 'compromise' the democratic constitution as the price of entry for CLC power, eventually split on the question of integration into the central, with those opposed to the move bitter about what they saw as raiding by rival (and johnny-come-lately) CLC affiliates. Faced with similar financial and political weaknesses, AUCE has voted to lobby the CLC for admission as an independent union in order to protect the democratic and feminist aspects of its constitution. In evaluating their tactics in British Columbia, we have to weigh organizing skills, willingness to organize small work units, and a capacity to create union organizers out of women workers against a purist reaction against 'big' unionism. Some of SORWUC's financial weaknesses may be offset by its adhesion to the CCU, which is largely based in British Columbia, but it still remains in opposition to the CLC and, thus, isolated from the largest female-dominated public sector unions.

Along with its organizational character, feminist syndicalism encapsulates an ideology and strategy of workplace organizing to create changes necessary for women's social liberation. As a perspective generated by the material conditions of class and sexual oppression, it is to some degree shared by other feminists in trade unions even if they reject the project of building independent women's unions. The conflict between sexism and feminist radicalization within workers' organizations means that women need and want a political base outside the control of the labour movement's male hierarchy to fight for their needs: in short, feminism. On the other hand, divisions also continue to be created between organized women workers and others in the autonomous women's movement by the institutional framework of the labour movement, by the special needs of working-class women for whom the time pressures are extreme, and by class differences. Often impatient with the consensus styles of work and the diffuseness of global 'demands' that have tended to characterize the programme and tactics of sixties-based feminism, trade union feminists sometimes reject movement attempts to formulate global analyses and strategy: in short, syndicalism. A strategy of building independent women-controlled unions has long had currency among feminists.[24] Despite the 'failure' of its first attempt, SORWUC has already had an ideological impact on women's groups and labour groups and has plans for another bank drive.

Radicalization Through Struggle

In addition to these two consciously organized variants, working-class feminism has also arisen in the course of strikes. Two strikes in Ontario – at Fleck in 1978 and at the International Nickel Company in 1978–9 – spectacularly illustrated how feminism among working-class women strengthens economic struggles and how their mobilization can have an important political impact on the women's movement.

At Fleck, an automobile parts plant, a newly certified UAW local composed overwhelmingly of women struck for a first contract and over wages, union security and working conditions. As the strike dragged on for months it took on an increasingly class-political tone as a battle about the right to unionize. The UAW, the parent union, rallied to its support with plant-gate collections and busloads of mostly male workers for mass picketing. At the same time, it became a test case for feminism, and socialist feminists in particular saw it in these terms. The general potential for radicalization in the interplay of class and feminist forces was manifested in this strike. By its very nature, a strike situation is an intensive consciousness-raising process. With work rhythms disrupted, the opportunity and the necessity to think collectively and strategically break through the fatigue, political passivity and mystification of normal production. Militant strike action by women is also an objective challenge to their economic exploitation, their individuation into the illusory privacy of the family, and the ideological construction of women as passive dependants protected by men which is at the core of women's place in the contemporary capitalist sexual division of labour. At Fleck, the strikers explicitly articulated this challenge. They attributed management and police harassment to a complacent assumption that they would be easily intimidated because they were women; instead, maintaining that men would not have been able to hold out so long, they saw their own capacity to resist arising from their *solidarity as women*. By mobilizing union women's committees and groups from the autonomous women's movement for picket-line and financial support, trade union feminists brought a feminist perspective to the strike and, more importantly, legitimated 'the women's movement' in the eyes of the strikers (and other unionists), at the same time as non-union feminists were given a deeper understanding of class conflict. Finally, the Fleck strike shows the importance in such radicalization of the interplay between 'spontaneous' struggle and conscious intervention 'from the outside'. As well as the crucial role played by trade union and other feminists in this regard, some journalists also brought a feminist concern to their investigation and reporting of the strike, eliciting the strikers' responses to their situation as women and playing back through the media an ideologically more sophisticated version of the strikers' own feminism.

Historically, the Fleck strike helped to popularize a militant feminist ideology. The intensity of the struggle, and the determination and sharpness with which sex and class lines were drawn, gave it the kind of drama that makes news. The strikers' individual and collective courage, conviction and humour caught the imagination of people well beyond the organized labour and women's movements. They became popular working-class heroines with a message that captured the essence of working-class feminist ideology: women have the right to work; wages are a woman's concern; unionization is a basic weapon; women can find strength from one another in struggle. For feminist strategy, the lesson that they confirmed was that, given the right political conditions, self-organization in struggle will radicalize, mobilize and broaden feminist consciousness and action.

If the Fleck strike showed the radicalization of women at the point of production, then the strike in Sudbury against INCO demonstrated a different possibility; the role of class-conscious feminism in promoting solidarity between the union and the community. During a previous strike in 1958, a mass meeting of 'wives' had been manipulated to make it appear that they were in favour of immediate and unfavourable settlement. In 1979, however, partly at the initiative of members of a local women's centre, a women's committee, 'Wives supporting the strike', was formed to counter the reputation and repetition of '58. Mobilizing the power of women in the community and including aspects of normally private 'domestic' work (children's clothing, Christmas parties, layettes, community suppers) in an overall programme of strike defence partially and conjuncturally overcame the structural split in the working-class community between wage-work and housework which is expressed as conflict between women and men. But the resolution was not complete. With the mobilization of women, however, new conflicts were generated. From the power base of the wives' committee, some women pressed, against union opposition, for a greater voice in the direction of the whole strike. An important political issue was thus posed: what should the relation of wives' committees be to strike steering committees when both women and men are dependent upon wages and men's working conditions indirectly affect women's household work? Family and marriage relations were affected by the partial sublation of gender conflict. A preliminary study[25] indicates that, despite the added tensions of economic hardship, family relations were considered to be more satisfactory when men spent more time in the household. Some of the readjustments were precarious, with men pressuring their wives back into the kitchen after the strike. After some initial compliance, however, many women have sought part-time work and become reactivated in local women's committees.[26]

Problems of Socialist-Feminism

A strong socialist component has made an important contribution to
the development of a class-conscious current in this Second Wave of
the women's movement. Marxist women's liberationists saw the
campaign for reproduction rights which culminated in the 1970
Abortion Caravan as an opportunity for class as well as feminist
organizing. When leafleting at factories and offices met with
indifference or hostility and, more importantly, failed to catalyse
parallel working-class women's organizations, they explored other
avenues. In line with the workerism which seemed to offer a solution
to militants of the revolutionary youth and student movements,
some sought unionized jobs and, later, jobs with unions where they
pushed women's issues. Others, on the west coast, initiated
SORWUC. In part this entry into the labour movement was made
possible by the particular character of the Canadian scene. By
comparison with the USA, there are fewer feminist activists in some
of the state sector unions, but the trade unions are more open and
the labour movement's affiliation to a social-democratic party
provides a leftish ideological cover; thus, movement between sectors
is possible. Socialist-feminists in unions, however fraught their
situation, have been able to link feminists of different generations
and class backgrounds.

As individuals, socialist-feminists have consistently worked for
and provided leadership in union, child care, abortion, lesbian rights
and equal pay campaigns, but socialist-feminist organizations in
Canada have had, with one exception, a more precarious fate.
Operating from a mainly ideological basis of unity, these organizations have lacked the focus of single-issue campaigns and the
institutional cohesion of the self-help services that also evolved from
the initial phases of the women's liberation movement. Externally,
they have generally met with hostility from the mixed Leninist
left, suspicion from the labour movement, and opposition from
radical and liberal feminists. Given the immense theoretical and
practical difficulties of working through their commitment to
struggle on two fronts – against patriarchy and against capitalism –
and the heterogeneity of the membership, socialist-feminist groups
have time and again run into difficulty. Unable to agree upon a
'correct' and effective programme of action, they have dwindled into
theoreticism, split or been reduced to passivity. Throughout the
seventies, many of the women activists, organizers and theorists who
might have helped pull these groups together were tied up in far-left

groups. Those in some far-left organizations were hostile to and boycotted such efforts; the initiatives of others were widely suspect because of their affiliation to mistrusted 'male-dominated' Leninist groups. After the defeats of the seventies, the radicalization of working-class women provided a pole for the reconstitution of the women's movement.

At present, working-class and socialist feminists together form a strategically located, mutually dependent, but functionally differentiated nucleus for a class-conscious current in the autonomous women's movement. Although trade union feminists are the critical links for this nucleus, they have not been an independent leadership for the women's movement as a whole. Socialist-feminists have effectively supported working women's struggles, single-issue and national campaigns (most notably the promotion of International Women's Day as a unitary day of protest and celebration),[27] have contributed to the development of theory, strategy and ideology, and have consistently sought to play a leadership role for both class-conscious and other feminist forces. But they have little permanent organization, no coordination at the level of the Canadian state, and no publication. There are also tensions in the current's whole development and its homogeneity should not be overestimated. Only in British Columbia and Saskatchewan have there been province-wide organizations that included both unionized and non-unionized women.[28] In other centres in Ontario, city-wide socialist-feminist organizations exist.[29] Even on IWD, the day of symbolic unity, political differences have developed over the relative weight to give demands for abortion rights and maternity leave or how to present demands for lesbian rights.[30] As well as contradictory evaluations of the political impact of these issues by organizers, these disagreements reflect real unevenness of political development of the constituencies involved. For, if trade union feminists are caught between the differing expectations of the bureaucracy and the rank and file, socialist-feminists, lesbian and straight, are similarly placed in a conflictual relation with labour and other feminist and socialist currents.

The influence of working-class feminism on the women's movement has not all been in the direction of economism. Working-class and déclassé lesbians, for example, have fought to have the labour movement defend the freedom of sexual orientation and to oppose the New Right. Links made on the picket line have been maintained and serve to homogenize the politics of the current. Part of the reason that union women initially came to Toronto IWD celebrations was simple reciprocal solidarity. Through such activities, trade unionists have come to a greater awareness of non-economic aspects of feminism and have, in turn, become leaders able and willing to defend these issues to other women. At a recent IWD, two women from Fleck were talking about the Lesbian Organization of Toronto whose presence was signalled by banners, picket signs and buttons. While one was uneasy about the presence of 'all those lesbians', her friend responded, 'Well, that's the women's movement, and you'll just have to get used to it.'

Sexual Harassment and Cultural Radicalization

The popularization of feminist analyses of sexuality, rape and violence has set the stage for the class transformation of earlier concerns with sexual objectification. Sexual harassment on the job has come to be considered a major women's issue in the labour movement. Unlike other women's issues, however (such as day-care, maternity leave, equal pay), sexual harassment focuses directly upon sexuality and upon the antagonism which pits women, individually and collectively, *against men as agents of their oppression*. Since women are harassed not just across class lines by men in supervisory positions but also by fellow-workers, this issue is potentially explosive inside the working class.

Although, strictly speaking, sexual harassment is a feminist issue of sexual politics, it has a class dimension as well. 'Quid pro quo' harassment by a supervisor tells women that they hold their jobs only at their bosses' pleasure, reinforcing both class and gender subordination.[31] Although supervisors are also implicated, the more prevalent form, 'harassment as a condition of work', is in large part carried out by co-workers through unremitting comment on a woman's appearance, sexual activities and desires – real or fantasied – often in a joking manner which men aver as 'harmless' and even flattering to women.[32] Such statements assert that a woman's sexuality is not hers alone but an aspect of her public personality which belongs by right to any man who wishes to appropriate it through comment.

The direct result of sexual harassment is to keep women in line (in culturally specified places and ways) or to keep them out of where they are not supposed to be. In the labour force, sexual harassment strengthens both vertical hierarchy and horizontal divisions to maintain women in their traditionally inferior position. It is the intimate way in which working-class men police their privileged position in the labour force and let women know they are transgressors on male territory, particularly when they enter non-traditional jobs. Culturally sexist attitudes and behaviour also prevent women's full participation in unions: feminist activists in particular are attacked as 'lesbians' and their clothing is scrutinized. Even if all men do not harass or support harassment by silence, its pervasiveness cautions women against trusting men. Structurally, sexual harassment pits all men against all women at the same time as it makes working-class women the target of cross-class sexism. The net result is to reinforce male solidarity across class lines, to blur class divisions through working-class sexism, to fragment the solidarity of a working class that has two sexes, and to reinforce class domination.

How this issue is resolved depends in large part on political choices made by working-class feminists. Union officials are likely to try to contain some of its more radical elements on the understandable grounds that unions are, after all, organizations for economic defence and not for liberation struggles. Opening up the full dimensions of this question may indeed initially be 'divisive', if not on the convention floor then on the shop floor. But the full exploration of this issue holds the potential to strengthen unions. Even in the short run, active educational campaigns under the control of rank-and-file women would increase their participation and provide them with some of the political experience and clout necessary to occupy other leadership positions.[33] An understanding of the full implications of this issue *at all levels* of the unions would be an important step in carrying out in the medium term the ideological and organizational reforms that are needed to correpond to the increase in female membership.[34]

More than just equalizing the division of mundane tasks, the generalization of feminist consciousness in the working class requires breaking through the psychological barriers of prevailing gender types and adopting liberated norms. All aspects of femininity and masculinity, including sexuality, must be reformed if women, men, and the relations between them are to change. To underestimate the importance of this struggle is to underestimate the depth and complexity of the interpenetration of sexual oppression and class domination and to ignore the strength and persistence of the unconscious psychological forces that sustain them both. To neglect feminism is to run the risk of replicating the experience of post-revolutionary societies where, despite formal legal equality for women, the material bases for their double burden of paid and domestic labour, their secondary public status, and the emotional bases of machismo and sex-negativity make women dependent upon marriages and families that continue to oppress them. To fear feminism is also to neglect the countervailing forces of class solidarity – whether from shared experience of economic struggle or the ties of kinship and community – that bind women and men alike into class. Finally, beyond even its implications for class solidarity, feminist struggle against the deep sexual fears at the root of sexism is necessary for social reconstruction. 'Speaking bitterness' provides, on a mass scale, an essentially psychotherapeutic moment where the violence that festers in the repression of sexuality and the cultural denigration of the feminine can be released. Without such a moment, the eroticization of daily life that women's sexual autonomy implies cannot be realized and the possibility of freely expressed libidinal lives for children scarcely imagined.[35]

Canadian Feminism: A Turning Point

As a result of the radicalization of women workers that I have described here, the women's movement in Canada and Quebec has reached a turning-point. The possibility has opened up for a decisive expansion of 'Second-Wave' feminism's social base, and at the same time the opportunity has been uniquely created for a fusion between the two modes of social opposition, 'cultural' on the one hand, class-based on the other, which normally traverse the contradictory universe of advanced capitalism in mutual isolation. The turn, however, to a class-conscious feminism has not been made by the movement as a whole; nor, correlatively, has working-class feminism articulated the full range of programmatic concerns that sixties feminism itself placed on the historical agenda.

The price of not completing the turn is the continued dominance of liberal feminism and the exclusion of socialist-feminism from mainstream political debate. Actually, the most anodyne forms of state-sponsored feminism, or radical feminist ideology wedded to reformist tactics, have succeeded in presenting themselves as feminism *tout court*. Socialist feminists were uninterested or in disarray at the time of the discussion on the Constitution in 1982, while better-organized liberal feminists successfully lobbied for the inclusion of an equal rights plank in the Bill of Rights. This achievement should not be discounted; it succeeded where the more protracted effort of the US pro-ERA (Equal Rights Amendment) lobby failed. However, despite its popular resonance, it made only a limited appeal for equality within the juridico-political framework of the capitalist economy and state. An opportunity was missed to campaign for constitutional guarantees for reproductive freedom, the rights to equal work, pay, unionization, self-determination for national minorities, freedom of sexual orientation and basic economic security for children as important prerequisites for women's equality, particularly for oppressed minorities, and to point out the role of the state in reproducing gender-stratified class hierarchies. Even more recently, liberal and radical feminists and politicians at all levels of government have joined together with Christian fundamentalists in an anti-pornography campaign which, because it offers state censorship as a solution, has a practical appeal for many people partially radicalized by feminist critiques of sexual exploitation and harassment. These developments have helped to legitimate the Canadian state as amenable to women's issues and to align the politics of sexuality on the right.[36]

In order to challenge this recuperation of feminism, it is not enough to denounce it; it is necessary to develop an alternative pole of attraction by furthering the unification of the two moments of left-feminist radicalization of the sixties and seventies. The project of building a distinct socialist-feminism, which the political integration of these groups both requires and facilitates, itself arose in a particular political and economic con- (or dis-) juncture; where, if you like, the last rose of sixties radicalism met Godzilla, the world-wide recession. Today the economic situation in Canada is changing as technological change and deindustrialization put work as such in question. Paradoxically, this shift may contain possibilities for extending the cultural critiques of gender and family within the workers' movement as a whole, thereby expanding the political base for class-conscious feminism. By way of completing this brief strategic *tour d'horizon*, let us take up these points in turn.

Feminist Ideologies: Integration or Impasse

The key strategic objective is to develop an expanded feminism which incorporates the strengths of each of the generations of feminists while overcoming the one-sidedness specific to each. On the one hand this means recuperating the insights of sixties theory, particularly with respect to sexual and cultural issues; conversely, it means giving it a wider social base. In many ways the development of working-class feminism has already confirmed and extended the socialist-feminist effort to pose questions and find answers alike in feminist and Marxist terms; that is, by demonstrating that capital and 'patriarchal' privilege do structure gender asymmetries in the labour force *and* the household and that both economic and sexual structures are manifested in women's oppression. But the political underdevelopment of working-class feminism, combined with the need to root it in the trade unions on the one hand and to carry out economic struggles on the other, created continuing pressures to relegate sexual and cultural issues to secondary importance. Thus, while there seems to be general agreement in current strategic discussions that the insights of sixties feminism should be retained, there seems to be much less clarity about how to do so. Still, the legacy of sixties feminism, in the changed circumstances brought about by the mobilization of working-class women, means correlatively that feminist theory must undergo a process of class transformation, particularly with respect to the family, which nevertheless preserves the irreducible importance of sexual and cultural freedom.[37]

A starting-point for the necessary work of correction is to realize that the women's movement of the sixties was ideologically limited by its restricted social base – specifically the absence of significant numbers of working-class and unionized women. If its analysis of culture and sexuality was strong, its understanding of the state and class politics was not. Formulated as a call to 'smash the family', feminist analysis could not explain why working-class *women* as well as men have fought to defend the possibility of family life. Thus, sixties theory, produced by a particular contradictory dynamic of class and sex struggle, was often age- or class-biased and too abstract to serve as a basis for policy formation. All the same, it *did* contain crucial insights not easily available to working-class activists.

Workplace-based struggles do not generate an insistence on the positively liberating aspects of eroticism or on the need to challenge the family as an institution. On the contrary, as contemporary capitalist developments undermine family stability, and as the fall-out from the 'disco-*Goodbar*' commodification of sexuality and from rising rates of social violence produces a climate of fear and uncertainty, one reaction is to defend it. But defensive responses to maintain the illusory privacy of individual family life against impersonal economic rationality are not the only reason for protectiveness about families. As Humphries and Luxton have pointed out, kinship networks have also traditionally provided a support base for working-class struggles.[38] Their steady disintegration in late capitalism thus has a mixed import for class-based politics.

Although there has been a tension between feminist and class politics throughout the history of the women's movement, its form of expression has varied radically according to the circumstances. Much of the sixties emphasis on sexuality and the family as a site of conflict between women and men reflected not just the characteristics of feminists as individuals or the specific character of the cultural conjuncture, but the student/youth social composition of the new left where female-male relations revolved intensely in a movement-defined space that was simultaneously political, erotic and emotional. In contrast, feminists who are in the labour force are placed in another powerful relation with men as fellow-workers, union and class members. This surely makes their gender situation even more complex – both richer and more confusing. Ehrenreich has put the dilemma well: 'We are all pulled in at least two directions. On the one hand, as feminists, we are drawn to the community of women and to its political idealization as a sisterhood of free women. It is this sisterhood, this collectivity of women, that we believe to be the agent of revolutionary change. On the other hand, we are pulled by . . . "fleshy, familial ties" to a community of men and women – fathers, lovers, brothers, sons, neighbours, co-workers – out of which comes our sense of class solidarity.'[39]

By now, however, an accumulation of common experience has created the conditions to overcome differences between the two generations of feminists that arose out of their different work and sexual histories. While 'middle-class' feminists have entered the workforce for a variety of biographical and financial reasons, feminist critique has been diffused through the mass media, co-optative educational reforms, trade union projects and so on to other working women. In addition, the issue of sexual harassment has been a vehicle for women workers to confront the ways in which their (economic *and* sexual) oppression is reproduced through maintaining and exploiting female sexual vulnerability. Thus, the fusion of initially different emphases on personal and work life has proceeded, without, however, producing an explicit theoretical or political elaboration. Understanding Ehrenreich's double bind is, I would argue, crucial to left feminism's further progresses.

Feminism and Trade Unions in the New Conjuncture

Today the economic conjuncture in Canada is changing in ways that may help to advance these theoretical and strategic issues by moving the questions of work and family to centre-stage in the labour movement. Like most of the advanced capitalist world, the Canadian economy is undergoing a process of structural transformation that seems likely permanently to reduce labour requirements, creating rising unemployment and producing enormous social dislocation and suffering. Whether as a result of technological change or deindustrialization resulting from a shift in the global division of labour, high levels of unemployment have already hit workers of all ages, sectors, skill and educational levels. In particular, an 'alarmingly high rate of unemployment among female clerical workers' – as high as 26% in 1985 and 46% in 1990 – has been projected for the main area where women found work in the expansionist 1960s.[40] If these labour reductions are introduced simply in the interests of capital, the consequences for women workers and their movements could be disastrous: sharpening gender inequalities in work, wages and social power, eroding the membership base of unions and undermining the capacity to resist.

Coming to grips with this problem presents an important opportunity for feminists and unionists because it poses the questions of work, gender and family in one integrated moment. First, simply in order to carry out defensive struggles it is necessary for the labour movement to combat primitive sexism generated by competition over the remaining jobs, a consequence of unregulated but systematic disemployment. Although women experience disproportionately high rates of unemployment that are often disguised by underemployment in part-time, seasonal or underqualified work or by being swallowed up in family membership,[41] their continuing visibility as workers provokes attacks that they are 'responsible' for the loss of male jobs. To deal with job loss in general, Canadian trade unions have already initiated a call for the reduction of the working week in order to redistribute employment more equitably and in order simply to work less. To be effective, such a campaign must take on the question of women's and men's relationships to work and 'family'. In the short run, demands for the redistribution of work must also find ways to integrate affirmative action and equal pay policies that have only recently become part of the labour movement's *active* policy. To be effective in the long run, however, what is required is a reconsideration of the nature of work in late capitalist society. Gorz has suggested that in conditions of job scarcity the possession of a job becomes a social privilege that serves to fragment sections of the working class – to confer privilege on the traditional organized proletariat which is politically fragmented from the unemployed and the new mass workers.[42] Indeed, possession of a job/salary or 'breadwinner power' has long been a material basis of male privilege within the family.

Whatever the success of efforts to redistribute work, the social effects of economic transformation may also affect relationships within families and marriages. For men, a loss of work puts not only economic survival but also personal identity at issue. Deprived of 'breadwinner power', men will be willy-nilly 'freed' from a hitherto forced reliance on a masculine ethic of work, stripped of a material base of male power, and faced with the prospect of rebuilding individual character structure and relationships with women on something other than these patriarchal bases.[43] Simple resistance is, of course, possible, but so are other outcomes. As part of a complex process, some men will, through an interest in their wives' wages, move to support equal pay while others who find themselves conjuncturally dependent or unemployed over the long term may, like the Sudbury miners, become more responsible for domestic and child care activities, with positive results for family relations. Given the real need and widespread acceptance of women's right to work, women are likely to resist measures reminiscent of the 1930s which scapegoat them or solve the crisis on their backs. At the same time, since they are well aware of the costs *and* benefits of the double day and the wage, they are also likely to use any opportunities to press for greater equality both in the workplace through unions and in the guerrilla struggles that go on with regard to domestic and emotional life – that is, those who choose to maintain permanent and particularly child-raising relationships with men.

While neither the social transformation of masculinity[44] nor the sharing of domestic labour resolves the question of the family, together they promote greater equality. Similarly, while even a highly sophisticated and militant campaign to redistribute work and to gain some benefit from technological change will not cause class structure to melt magically away, it does introduce important debates into the labour movement. And if heightened consciousness of the perniciousness of sexual oppression does not mean liberation, or only makes present situations sometimes seem too much to bear, without this awareness no progress is possible. With these questions on the agenda, whether as a result of feminist agitation or economic transformation, the mixed and labour left must respond to issues in the reconstruction of culture that have been a feminist concern for some time now; indeed, the task of forging an opposition bloc on feminist and socialist bases becomes more pressing.

Notes

1 The effects of this transformation appear everywhere in women's writing: in fiction by Nicole Brossard, in Mary Daly's philosophical poetics, and in Dorothy Dinnerstein's provocative psychology. For a

discussion see Catherine Stimpson, 'Neither dominant nor submissive', *Dissent* (1980).

Much of the material for this piece was gathered from interviews with trade union feminists. Since some of them wish to remain anonymous, I have not attributed any statements. I would like to thank Gay Bell, Deidre Gallagher, Meg Luxton, Gail Scott, Wally Seccombe and Andrew Wernick who read and commented on an earlier draft; the women who offered their views on the women's movement; and all those who offered much-needed support as I went through the identity crisis of facing its past and future. An earlier version of this paper was presented at the 'Socialism in the 1980s' conference, Vancouver, January 1981.

2 The federated pan-Canadian state is, first of all, riven by the effects of unresolved national questions with regard to Quebec, Acadian, Inuit, Dene and the many Indian nations. Secondly, the ten provincial governments, as well as those of the territories, control labour, education, family law, most human rights provisions, and some aspects of cultural policy, while other specific aspects of educational and research funding, human rights, divorce law and taxation are federal responsibilities. Finally the population is gathered into dispered regional economic and political centres across the continent. These political and economic conditions obviously affect the women's movement in all sorts of practical and political ways. For example, the two most consistent campaigns in Quebec and British Columbia for repeal of the *same* federal law on abortion were carried out in isolation from each another. National meetings – on, for example, day-care – almost always require federal funding, which brings with it attempts at political control. Finally immigrants – particularly women – are often isolated by language and intimidation.

3 The terms of the debate were largely defined by Sheila Rowbotham, Lynne Segal and Hilary Wainwright in *Beyond the Fragments* (London, Merlin Press 1979). Also, see Varda Burstyn, 'Toward a socialist party, marxist-feminist', *Canadian Dimensions*, June 1981.

4 The fact that these forces are also anti-labour is the conjunctural basis for an alliance of unionists, feminists, and lesbain and gay liberationists.

5 Barbara Haber, 'Is the personal still political?', *Feminist Studies* 5:3 (1980) and Beatrix Campbell, 'A feminist sexual politics: now you see it, now you don't, *Feminist Review* 5 (1980).

6 Interview December 1982. For a similar statement from US women, which points to equal pay as a feminist issue, stresses the difficulties of media-distorted 'feminist jargon' and points to unions as 'the main tool that women have, that workers have', see District 65, 'Union women of feminism', *Heresies* 9, 1980, 85.

7 Julie White, *Women and Unions* (Ottawa, Canadian Advisory Council on the Status of Women 1980); 27% of the female workforce is unionized in comparison with 43% of the male labour force and over 60% of the female membership are in public sector unions. In the decade following 1966, female membership increased 160% in comparison with 40% for men.

8 Public health nurses, Toronto, and hospital workers, Winnipeg, demanded equal pay for work of equal value, as have hospital and

clerical workers, nurses and teachers in Quebec's Common Front. For historical material, see Judi Coburn, ' "I see and am silent": a short history of nursing in Ontario' and Elizabeth Graham, 'School marms and early teaching in Ontario', both in J. Acton (ed.), *Women at work: Ontario 1850–1930*, (Toronto 1974).

9 Dorothy Gillmeister, 'The equal opportunity fantasy: a hard look at voluntary affirmative action', *Status of Women* 6:2 (1980).

10 For example, with Steelworkers, at Stelco in Hamilton. The list includes a joint campaign by machinists and local women in St Thomas, a Women into Rail campaign, and the integration of the sawmills in B.C. These situations deserve to be studied in depth.

11 The major reports to conventions of the *centrales* include CSN 'La lutte des femmes: combat de tous les travailleurs' (1976) and 'La lutte des femmes: pour le droit au travail social' (1978); CEQ 'Condition féminine' 1974; and Fédération des Travailleurs du Québec, 'Femmes et syndiqués,' 1973.

12 Mona-Josée Gagnon, 'Les femmes dans le mouvement syndical québécois', *Sociologie et Société* 6:2 (1974).

13 Special issue, *Resources for Feminist Research* (RFR) 10:2 (1981).

14 Debbie Field, 'Women's Committees in Unions', RFR 10:2 (1981) 8–9.

15 Women's struggles against exclusion from the auto industry in the US met with at least an ambivalent response from their union. (Nancy Gabin, ' "They have placed a penalty on womanhood": the protest actions of women auto workers in Detroit area UAW locals, 1945–47', *Feminist Studies* 8:2 (1982).) It is likely that similar exclusions occurred in Canada.

16 Unionization, of course, benefits women and men economically; cf. Morley Gunderson, 'Male-female wage differentials and the impact of equal pay legislation', *Review of Economics and Statistics* 57 (1975); White (1980), 57. Nevertheless, higher-paid skilled workers have refused to bargain for across-the-board increases which effectively erode their own income, particularly with respect to peers, in an inflationary period.

17 René Geoffrey and Paule Ste-Marie, 'Le travailleur syndiqué face au travail rémunéré de la femme', *Études pour la commission royale d'enquête sur la situation de la femme au Canada*, no. 9, Ottawa.

18 Recently, however, benefits for women have been strike issues in the context of a pro-natalist policy. The Quebec public sector Common Front obtained the best maternity/parental leave provisions in the country – 20 weeks full pay (instead of 15 weeks at 60% with an obligatory loss of two weeks' salary provided by federal insurance benefits) with up to two years' job security – the Canadian Union of Postal Workers struck unsuccessfully for maternity benefits among other issues; in 1980 CAIMAW (affiliated to the mainly BC based Congress of Canadian Unions – membership about 40,000 – which has a good record on women's issues) held out for seven months in a strike for equal pay for work of equal value for seven female data processors; equal pay became an issue in a strike by Vancouver Municipal Workers later in 1981.

19 Janet Routledge, 'Women and social unionism', RFR 10:2 (1981).

20 Grace Hartman, 'Women and the unions', in G. Matheson, (ed.), *Women in the Canadian Mosaic* (Toronto 1976); Peter Warrian, 'Patriarchy and the trade unions', paper presented at the Committee on Socialist Studies, Ottawa June 1981; Lynn Frogett, 'Feminism and the Italian Trade

Unions', *Feminist Review* 8 (1981).

21 Micki McCune, 'Fighting for our rights: the CLC women's conference', RFR, 10:2.

22 Jackie Ainsworth et al. document earlier attempts by UBC clerical workers to organize with CLC public sector (Canadian Union of Public Employees) and private sector (Office and Professional Employees International Union/Office and Technical Employees Union) in 'Getting organized: in the feminist unions', in M. Fitzgerald et al., *Still Ain't Satisfied: Canadian Feminism Today* (Toronto, Women's Educational Press 1982).

23 The Bank Book Collective, *An Account to Settle* (Vancouver, Press Gang 1979).

24 Meredith Tax, *The Rising of the Women* (New York, Monthly Review Press 1980); Patricia Marchak, 'The Canadian labour farce: jobs for women', in M. Stephenson, ed., *Women in Canada* (Toronto, New Press 1973).

25 Henry Radecki, *One Year Later: The 1978–79 Strike at INCO: The Effects on Families* (Sudbury, Ont., SIS Laurentian University 1979).

26 Meg Luxton, 'The home: a contested terrain', in M. Fitzgerald et al., *Still Ain't Satisfied*.

27 In Montreal, International Women's Day celebrations were held by the unions as a 'fête populaire' with little political content in 1973 and 1974; in 1975, women from the inter-central *commission féminine* along with those from abortion and health work, day care and the far left held a teach-in which led to several co-operative demonstrations. In 1978, drawing on the Montreal example, women in the Revolutionary Marxist Group – now defunct – promoted IWD celebrations/demonstrations to link up with union women across English Canada. Some centres, notably Vancouver, had already begun to mark IWD.

28 B.C. Federation of Women, Saskatchewan Working Women.

29 Despite the pressures described above, the International Women's Day Committee (Toronto) has a five-year history of militant action and self-education to its credit. There are also groups in Hamilton and Sudbury.

30 These were roughly on union/non-union lines. In Montreal in 1976, the union women demonstrated for maternity leave; the *groupes autonomes* for abortion rights. Lesbian rights were an issue in Toronto in 1978 and 1979.

31 The typology of Harassment is taken from Catherine A. MacKinnon, *Sexual Harassment of Working Women: A Case of Sex Discrimination*, New Haven 1979.

32 Women's Rights Committee, 'Sexual harassment in the workplace', discussion paper, B.C. Federation of Labour, March 1980. For a useful report on union practice, see Marlene Kadar, 'Sexual harassment as a form of social control', in M. Fitzgerald et al., *Still Ain't Satisfied*.

33 Women are vulnerable here because they are isolated and often because, untrained by unions, they may break shop-floor standards. Sexual insult playing on homophobia can of course be used against men, but, whether it's a woman or a man who is called 'a stupid cunt', the insult is misogynist.

34 Some unions have held sexual harassment workshops, offered assertiveness training, adopted resolutions and so on. But Kadar concludes: 'Apart from the high profile and very positive influence of the National Union of Provincial Government Employees . . . the unions, despite

good intentions, have not held their own in this area' 176. Women are often discouraged from reporting incidents, particularly against fellow-workers.

35 Kate Millet, *The Basement* (New York, Simon & Schuster 1979), illustrates a negative outcome of this relation in her discussion of the torture and murder of a young girl accused of being sexually promiscuous.

36 It is important to stress the contradictoriness of these developments. On the one hand, the kind of equality 'in and under the law' promised by the Bill of Rights is, as Juliet Mitchell points out, a limited form of equality that cannot challenge class inequalities under capitalism ('Women and equality' in J. Mitchell and A. Oakley, eds., *The Rights and Wrongs of Women*, (Penguin, Harmondsworth 1976)). It has also given Judy Erola, now the minister responsible for women in the Liberal government, 'wide non-partisan support' according to one commentator, Penny Kome, in *Canadian Forum*. But victories are more energizing than defeats and liberal feminists in particular now have a legal basis and an organizing precedent to carry out the legal reforms that have been in their bag for some time now. Its impact on developing feminist consciousness on a wider scale remains to be seen and the whole question deserves to be studied.

37 There are signs of this work beginning in Britain with Michele Barrett and Mary McIntosh, *The Anti-Social Family* (London, Verso 1982); Lynn Segal, ed., *What is to be Done About the Family* (Penguin, Harmondsworth 1983). In Canada, Meg Luxton's excellent study, *More than a Labour of Love: Three Generations of Women's Work in the Home* (Toronto, Women's Educational Press 1980), and her follow-up work discuss strategies for housewives.

38 Jane Humphries, 'The working-class family, women's liberation, and the class struggle: the case of nineteenth-century British history', *Review of Radical Political Economics* 9:3, 1977. See also Luxton, *More than a Labour of Love*.

39 Barbara Ehrenreich, 'A funny thing happened on the way to socialist-feminism', *Heresies* 9, 1980, 5.

40 Official unemployment rates were already about 12% in May 1980. On micro-technology see Heather Menzies, *Women and the Chip* (Montreal 1981).

41 Pat Armstrong and Hugh Armstrong, 'Job creation and unemployment for Canadian women', paper presented at the NATO Symposium, 'Women and the world of work', Portugal 1980.

42 It is appropriate to discuss André Gorz's *Farewell to the Working Class* (Boston 1982), because it was one of the key texts discussed by top union leadership at the CLC winter school in 1983.

43 As the European peasantry was freed from the land by the development of capital.

44 This transformation has already been underway since the 1950s as a result of changes in the nature of work, the commodification of male sexuality on a well-defined feminine model, and women's and experts' demands; witness the spate of books like Mark Feigan Fasteu's, *The Male Machine* (New York, Delta 1975).

8 Feminism, Motherhood and Medicine – Who Cares?

Ann Oakley

> People believe a little too easily that the function of the sun is to help
> the cabbages along.
>
> *Flaubert*

Both the institution and the experience of motherhood have been
important topics for all feminist movements. Different social
perceptions of motherhood's biology give rise to different definitions
of women's social role as mothers, and provide a range of agendas
which can then, in turn, be reacted against. What is striking is that,
at each historical moment, the dominant definition of motherhood
asserts an exclusive morality – there is only one 'right' way to be a
mother, whether it is to have many children or only one, whether it
is to stay at home or provide for one's children through paid labour
outside the home. Here, though, class is, as always, the great divide.
Dominant definitions are those of the 'ruling' classes. Within the
world of working-class women, very different views and practices
may prevail.

This chapter has two objectives. First of all, it explores some of
the historical intersections between feminism and motherhood.
Secondly, it contends that the revolutionary potential of motherhood
for feminist politics cannot be understood without considering the
political significance and power of the mother-child relation as
experienced by women. Since, in the twentieth century, motherhood
has also become a medicalized domain, it is important to see how
medicine has accommodated itself to, and built itself around, a
knowledge of this reproductive 'fact'. Medicine has technicalized the
love of mother and child, at the same time as it has set up a structure
of services for mother and child which emphasize surveillance, not
caring. This has had profound consequences for the health of

women, and also for the knowledge-base of medical science itself. But in addition, it can be said that medicalized motherhood presents a new challenge to feminism; for absorbed into the medico-scientific domain, historically unprecedented chances of reproductive 'success' enter into women's knowledge about motherhood at the same time as they are required to give up their personhood in the process of becoming mothers.[1] Of course the arrival of artificial conceptional techniques serves to underline this need of modern medicine to deem irrelevant the mother's individuality, while preserving the appeal to be acting somehow in the fundamental interests of women, to be benefitting their welfare as a group.

Feminism and Motherhood – Some Historical Positions

Historically speaking, feminist commentary on motherhood has mostly had the character of a response; it has not specialized in initiating new themes. Since motherhood has changed historically, the projects within motherhood that have been entered into the vocabulary of feminine protest have also changed over time. Thus, during some periods 'safe' delivery in institutions has occupied women's collective attention; during others it has been the right to have a baby at home; sometimes legalization of abortion has been a key issue. Elsewhere the pronatalist rights of women in specially disadvantaged groups have needed to be protected, while at times feminists have shone the spotlight on the dire state of women's legal position as mothers within marriage, also concluding that the 'protection' of motherhood demands the economic independence of *all* women. But in each case what has tended to happen is that feminists have used a particular (and class-differentiated) vision of the status quo in order to define a different projected future for motherhood.

When we ask, what do feminists say about motherhood? we are therefore asking historical questions not only about what motherhood is and what feminism is like: we are also asking about the relationship between the two. To do this is no easy task. On the other hand, it is not difficult and is therefore tempting, to talk on a superficial level about motherhood – one sign of this facility is the enormous popular, academic and political attention given to motherhood in the twentieth century, especially in the post-war era.[2]

'To be a good mother' said Mary Wollstonecraft quite unequivocally in *A Vindication of the Rights of Woman* (1792) 'a woman must have sense, and that independence of mind which few women possess who are taught to depend entirely on their husbands. Meek wives are . . . foolish mothers'.[3] That women should be mothers, and good mothers, was not in doubt for Wollstonecraft, who was writing at a time when upper-class women did little actual child rearing. It was against the view of femininity as decorative idleness that she rebelled, insisting that it was wrong for women to relegate the care of their children to nurses, servants and boarding schools, that 'many children are absolutely murdered by the ignorance of women'[4] and that those women who did not breastfeed their children were scarcely worthy of the title 'mother' at all. (On this point Wollstonecraft made an interestingly modern observation about the health and contraceptive implications of lactation: 'did women suckle their children they would preserve their own health and there would be such a interval between the birth of each child, that we should seldom see a houseful of babes.'[5]) According to Millicent Fawcett, who wrote an introduction to the 1891 edition of the *Vindication*, Wollstonecraft's exaltation of the 'truly feminine' and her own character as 'the essentially womanly woman, with . . . motherly and wifely instincts strong within her' were responsible for keeping the English women's rights movement 'free from the excesses and follies that in some other countries have marred its course'.[6] Yet it is enlightening to realise that, a century before, Wollstonecraft's 'womanly' position on motherhood would have shocked many – even leaving aside the irregularities of her own personal life.

Eighteenth- and early-nineteenth-century feminism focused more on the political, economic and psychological effects of women's enforced dependence on men than it did on either the burdens or the health-promoting effects of motherhood. Most of the women active in feminist politics were childless or relied on servants for childcare. In America, Elizabeth Cady Stanton, with seven children, complained repetitively about the difficulty of finding good household servants, but it was the move to the dull factory town of Seneca Falls for her husband's new job that immortalizes the town in feminist history. The 'Declaration of Sentiments and Resolutions' adopted by the 1848 Seneca Falls Convention says nothing about the injustices suffered by women as mothers, except that the rule of male supremacy gives guardianship of the children to fathers in divorce cases, and that is 'contrary to the happiness of women'.[7] Stanton herself defended the 'extravagance' of having seven children, saying she would not be without any of them, while her colleague Susan B. Anthony, herself childless, complained that too much intelligent feminist energy was going into 'baby-making'; after all, one or two children rather than ten sufficed to show that women were able to combine motherhood with personhood.

On the other side of the Atlantic, Millicent Fawcett bore out Susan B. Anthony's point by having only one child. However, in the era when domestic servants were not hard to come by (and no one had yet articulated the irony of one woman's fight for liberation being another woman's domestic oppression), it was not children but men who got in the way of women's participation in the public world. Both Fawcett and her activist contemporary Emmeline Pankhurst were able to take up feminist campaigning when widowhood validated their choice of another function in life. Less socially privileged women may have campaigned with one hand tied behind them, to use Hannah Mitchell's phrase; but women's hands were tied first and foremost by an unequal sexual division of labour, rather than as a result of childbirth.

For many women at the time, there was no need to protest against large families as such. Provided one could close one's eyes to the high rate of maternal mortality – one mother died for every 250 or so births – then large families were benefits, not hazards, for those privileged enough publicly to articulate a point of view. For working-class women, the practical and all-consuming daily labours of childbearing and childrearing would have caused the silent protest of endless fatigue, but scarcely left time or energy for debating the relative weights of the different causes of women's oppression. But it did not follow, either, that feminism necessitated an articulation of the desirability of birth control and its facilitating technologies. Stanton and her co-soeurs did not see why feminism should be responsible for a falling birth-rate; and indeed, it seems that it was not.[8] Family size began to decline before nineteenth-century feminism got off the ground, and the early birth-control movement produced propaganda which appealed to both sexes. The panic about population decline was something feminists did not wish to be associated with – nor were they.

Wollstonecraft had said, and Fawcett had repeated, that 'Women cannot really be good . . . mothers if charming accomplishments and domestic tasks are to be considered their highest virtues'.[9] Somewhat later Charlotte Perkins Gilman contributed the observation that housework itself had little to recommend it from the child's point of view. Rather ironically (given the subsequent twentieth-century 'pathologization' of motherhood) one of the reasons for Gilman's observation was the desire to call mothers bad as well as good: 'Our eyes grow moist with emotion as we speak of our mothers', she wrote in *The Home* (1903) '. . . Our voices thrill and tremble with pathos and reverberation as we speak of "the mothers of great men". . . . [But] *Who*, in the name of all common sense, raises our huge and growing crop of idiots, imbeciles, cripples, defectives and degenerates. . . . Are the mothers to be credited with all that is good and the fathers with all that is bad?'[10] Instead of demolishing the idea of the maternal instinct, Gilman sketched it as an incompetent designer of effective childrearing methods. One reason for this, she felt, was the encapsulation of women and motherhood within the home, a place of arrested social development.

It was the very acceptance of motherhood as the duty of women that led to an alternative version of its socialization – outside the unhappily sheltered confines of the family home, and within a more collective and less kin-oriented version of the social order. 'She does not wish to be free of her babies' asserted Ada Nield Chew in an article called 'The Problem of the Married Working Woman' (1914) '. . . but she could collectively make provision for the care of her own and other babies much better than she can do by remaining an untrained domestic worker. . . . No woman is individually good enough, however fiercely maternal her passion, to have the unaided care, day and night, of a baby'.[11] The nurseries envisaged by Chew would provide 'a new and glorious field of work to women, in which their special sort of human genius would have scope for development'. Out of one prison into another, motherhood was to define women's public, as well as their private, lives. Perhaps all this means is that idealized charters for social change are liable to be contextually limited. It is a matter of one step at a time – what one generation perceives as liberation may be taken apart as a further agenda for oppression by the next.

Nineteenth- and early-twentieth-century feminism thus stated a variety of positions about motherhood. On the whole, the struggle to render women citizens overshadowed the need to understand motherhood in relation to women's overall situation, psychology or future and as differentiated by class, ethnicity and economics. Motherhood remained essentially unproblematic. In part this was because it wasn't necessary to defend women's right *not* to have children. Population statistics, the surplus of women over men, the fact that women's single status was a socially acceptable option – these meant that women didn't need to demand the right to remain childfree. The perceived problems of women's situation were, rather, those to do with public institutions, the law, government, the professions, education, citizenship. These areas of inequality had to be addressed first, before control of biological fertility and the power of mother-child relationships could become significant political questions.

After the close of the First World War, many governments embarked on an era of acceding to the demands of women's rights movements, or recognizing that women – along with everyone else – were entitled to move into the twentieth century. The legalization of sex equality that took place during this period was one factor that eventually turned feminists' attention to motherhood. But equally important was the rising star of medicine. Medicine, under the title of the maternal and child health movement, was beginning to colonize a new area of women's lives, at a time at which the theoretical and practical significance of this area to women's position as a whole had scarcely been grasped by anyone.

Motherhood and Medicine

In Britain and other countries in the early 1900s, the modern capitalist state began to take a serious interest in the health and welfare of its people. Some countries had, of course, developed a concern before this time, but provision of medical services tended to come under the heading of public relief of destitution; the state's duty to provide medical care was limited to its duty to relieve poverty.[12]

The early 1900s saw an increasing preoccupation with the quality of national populations, which bred an interest not only in preventing premature and untimely death, but in furthering health.[13] Infant mortality was defined as preventable, and thus came to be seen as something that responsible policy-makers should prevent. Children became objects of medical discourse just as, and partly because, they had already been incorporated into a system of state educational surveillance. Moreover, there was concern not only with the prevention of death, but with the furtherance of all dimensions of health. The period that saw the emergence of the professions of paediatrics (The British Paediatric Association, founded 1928) and obstetrics and gynaecology (The British College of Obstetricians and Gynaecologists, founded 1929) also saw the birth of psychological medicine. It was no longer enough to consider the behaviour of bodies on the one hand, and to set aside a residual category of the insane who could be classed along with the poor and the otherwise morally deranged on the other.[14]

In early twentieth-century medical discourse mental instability, which began to be recognized as a condition different from madness at the end of the nineteenth century, took a leap forward into its modern guise by appearing as 'nerves' and 'neurasthenia'. Medicine thus became concerned with the mind.[15] There was nothing sophisticated about the early 'psychological' insights of medicine, and there is even a certain historical continuity in medical perceptions of mental states – for example, the biological attribution of 'neurasthenia' to masturbation in the nineteenth century is neatly matched by the attribution of postpartum depression to hormonal condition in the twentieth.

When postpartum depression first appeared in medical language it, too, did so as a symptom of primary genital derangement.[16] Towards the end of the nineteenth century, the growth of the child-centred family had begun to implicate women's feelings about their children in at least the symptomatology, if not the epidemiology, of postpartum depression. By this time infanticide had been placed in a category of its own as 'temporary madness', and from 1864 in Britain, the practice was followed of avoiding the death penalty when a woman was accused of killing her own child within a year of its birth.[17] As it developed over the years the implication of this view was that childbirth necessarily induced mental disturbance. By the 1970s the advice literature for new mothers was studded with the message that it is normal to be depressed, and if you aren't, perhaps there is really something wrong with you. Even the Department of Health tells mothers to expect depression after childbirth – this expectation being one plank in the platform of making childbirth safer.[18]

These developments in medical thinking have been detectable in medical writings but have been also concretely realized in practice. For example, concern with the child as a measure of the nation's prosperity led to an entirely new system of child health care in the years leading up to the First World War. 'Given a healthy and careful mother' said the Chief Medical Officer of the Board of Education in 1914, 'we are on the high road to securing a healthy infant; from healthy infancy we may expect healthy childhood; upon healthy childhood may be laid the foundations of a nation's health'. Against this doctrine was set the reality of the current practice of motherhood – as medically perceived: 'Many women have had no instruction at all in infant care before their children were born, and they have been dependent for advice on family traditions and on hints given by neighbours and relatives. It is certain that infant mortality and suffering would be materially reduced if all women could have some training in the management of infants'.[19] There was thus no escaping the conclusion that the prime necessity was inducing mothers to bring their children for medical supervision.[20]

A supplementary system of home visiting was designed to help overcome this problem, but the reluctance of working-class mothers to enter their children into the medical surveillance system did not simply disappear in response to the moral exhortations uttered by the upper-class ladies who came to persuade them. This is a good concrete example of class differences in women's perceptions and experiences of motherhood which coexist with, and persist through, periods of great social change overall in the *institution* of motherhood.

The early twentieth-century protection of child health could not rely on such modern instruments as developmental assessment and immunization. Much of it was environmental in nature, which meant that the task of professional service-providers was to survey the child's domestic safety, nutrition and general hygiene. But such an ideology and practice depended upon a prior stigmatization of mothers as ignorant.

As one official British report quite uncompromisingly put it, 'In every stratum of society self-indulgent, extravagant, idle and ignorant women are to be found, and they represent a serious amount of national weakness'. However, 'ignorance is less serious if the mothers are teachable.'[21] The allegation of maternal ignorance was unsubstantiated by evidence collected by women's organizations,[22] and was, importantly, qualified by recognizing the difficulty of being a successful mother in appalling social conditions. (The same report that referred to 'idle and ignorant women' also went into much detail about the condition of back streets in built-up areas, observing that liquid horse manure and human excrement turned them into 'quagmires of filth, giving for a disgusting odour').[23] But despite these qualifications, to call mothers ignorant was, and is, a powerful statement of patriarchy's need to control women and motherhood. To say that women do not know anything about motherhood is to cast aside their individual identity and authenticity. Since the ideology of maternal ignorance is combined with a continued sanction of the biological and social rightness of female parenting, women are tied to a place they cannot know by themselves. This is probably the most critical aspect of motherhood's fate in the twentieth century – that women's own knowledge of it has become, in the professionalised image, inauthentic. Stripped of its internal authenticity, motherhood becomes an exercise in professional consultation, an axis of self-doubt, and a black hole into which 'liberated' women disappear only to be besieged by visions of all they gave up (or never had) in order to fulfil this one great intimate destiny.

In the first decades of the twentieth century the formula for professionalized motherhood was instructional campaigns combined with medical surveillance. At first the medical surveillance covered childbirth and child health only, then a more sophisticated epidemiology of health and illness took the medical spotlight back to the prenatal period. At last the mother's own corporeal existence (even if not what Frances Power Cobbe deemed her 'immortal soul'[24]) became visible. At the same time a new priority took its place alongside the preservation of infant health – the prevention of maternal death. As a British Ministry of Health Report on Maternal Mortality put the problem in 1924, looking back to 1900, the general death rate had been cut by a third, and the infant mortality rate halved, yet the rate at which mothers died from childbearing was much the same as it had been since national statistics began to be collected. Childbearing was the third most important cause of death in the age group 15–45.

Avoidable maternal deaths were thus a matter of everyday occurrence. The author of this report, Dr Janet Campbell, put the primary reason for this appalling state of affairs as inadequate professional attendance at delivery and during pregnancy. Campbell also said that:

> Insanitary surroundings have probably much less direct influence upon puerperal mortality than might be supposed . . . employment of married women has probably little direct influence upon the maternal death rate . . . the double strain of housework and outside employment, however, may impose too heavy a burden upon the mother. . . .[25]

Her general message, that doctors, midwives and the inertia of the public health authorities were to blame – was not popular; and her location of the problem of maternal death within the context of women's situation as a whole was a facet of governmental reporting on the maternity services that was rapidly to fall out of fashion. Nevertheless, the point was that the failure of the maternal death rate of decrease provided a *raison d'être* for a period of rapid professional growth on the part of the specialist obstetricians, who practised until they were word-perfect the argument that no one else was qualified to survey motherhood, and that in order to do so they had further to institutionalize motherhood by enclosing it within the hospital.

The period from the 1920s to the 1960s is a particularly interesting one from the point of view of the dialectic between feminism and medicine on the topic of motherhood. Organizations such as the

Women's Co-operative Guild passed on to organizations such as the Association for Improvements in the Maternity Services (founded in 1960), a definite agenda pressing for more medicalization in the interests of women's safety and psychological comfort. Demanding a trained midwife and medical antenatal examination in the 1920s was equivalent to demanding a hospital bed for childbirth in the 1960s, in the sense that both were perceived at the time as genuine requirements of women, and both opened the door more widely on medicine's advance into motherhood's domain. In the 1920s and 1930s the argument was couched in terms of procuring greater safety for women and babies. Although this point was still there in the 1960s, a new rhetoric had been added: that of 'choice'. Liberal-feminist ideology feeds on a statement about the rights of women in medically managed reproduction which was not there earlier, perhaps because it didn't need to be.

Why Medicalization?

Explanations of why this medicalization of motherhood has occurred in the way it has can be offered on a number of different levels. One approach, which is predominantly the one adopted within medicine[26] is to say that it happened because this was the only rational route to solid improvements in maternal and child health. That this type of explanation will not serve is indicated by even a cursory look at the literature evaluating the effectiveness and efficiency of medicine.[27] A. L. Cochrane's well-known table showing the decrease in mortality with (a) increasing hospital confinement rates, and (b) reduced length of post-partum hospital stay is a good illustration of the famous philosophical flexibility of statistics.[28] Whereas one index of maternal care may be positively related to improved health outcomes, another may be negatively related. It is not a very long step from here to the contention that social engineering contributes as much as, or more than, intensified medical care to the promotion of better health.[29]

Another view about the reasons for the medicalization of motherhood cites the professional and masculinist imperialism of the medical profession. While we may dispute the strength of this motive, and the details of its translation into practice, there is clearly some truth in it; for, once a given professional group exists, it is in the interests of that group to promote its own occupational welfare and identity. 'Legitimate control over work'[30] to use sociologist Eliot Friedson's phrase, is required for a separate occupational identity.

The expert must have public agreement of his/her status as expert, although, underlying this, it is equally clear that expertise may be 'a mask for privilege and power'.[31] Histories of the 'rise' of obstetrics and gynaecology as a distinct medical specialism show that the competition between the early male obstetricians and the community of female midwifery was part of a more profound sexual conflict in society at large; the prohibition against women in medicine was part of a misogynous distaste for women in public life, and intimately connected with that ideology of women which permitted mutilating and dangerous genital surgery in the name of 'science'. When J. Marion Sims, America's 'Architect of the Vagina', bought black female slaves and housed them in a hut in his own backyard in order surgically to experiment upon them, the end he had in view was not mass improvement in the reproductive destinies of women, but the building up of sufficient personal prestige to gain acceptance as physician to wealthy upper-class women.[32]

To say that such episodes in the history of reproductive care for women are bizarre aberrations having nothing to do with main-stream medical developments is to ignore one important insight of the sociology of knowledge: that studying the untypical is very often the best way to learn about the typical.[33] The very fact that gynaecological surgery as practised by Sims in late nineteenth-century America was so practised is an index of underlying medical ideologies towards women, and so is the remark of one gynaecologist in the 1970s to the effect that he rarely succeeds in operating on women without getting at least a semi-erection.[34] Yet, what on a personal basis may be experienced as domination and power may not always be thus represented in paradigms of knowledge and expertise publicly expressed by the profession. While nineteenth-century doctors spoke quite unashamedly about women's biological inferiority and weakness, those in the latter part of the twentieth century have exchanged a vocabulary of outright domination for a softer litany that speaks instead of 'monitoring', of the need to watch carefully for possible pathologies, and of women's own interests in subjecting themselves and their fetuses to this systematic clinical gaze. For example, according to one medical manual for pregnant women, 'The maternity services, as represented by the doctor and midwife, have cheerfully and gladly accepted the responsibility of looking after the pregnant woman . . . complete antenatal care is the ideal type of preventive medicine for which doctors have been searching for many generations. Complications can be recognised sufficiently early to be corrected . . . even for those who are destined to have a perfectly normal pregnancy, labour and delivery, helpful guidance, reassurance and information will help to make their pregnancy a pleasure. . . .'[35] For the patriarchal language of power and control has been substituted a language of careful vigilance, which appeals in its seductiveness precisely to the maternal within women, but which does not necessarily index either greater care or greater effectiveness on the part of the medical service thus advertised.

Yet a third explanation of the medicalization of motherhood takes as important factors external to medicine and to the unfolding of gender roles. The twentieth century in the industrialized world is increasingly characterized by the growth of monopolistic power among the professions. Medicine is but one example:

> Professionals assert secret knowledge about human nature, knowledge which only they have the right to dispense. They claim a monopoly over the definition of deviance and the remedies needed. For example, lawyers hold that they alone have the competence and the *legal* right to provide assistance in divorce. Gravediggers become members of a profession by calling themselves morticians, by obtaining college credentials or by increasing the standing of their trade by electing one of themselves president of the Lion's Club.[36]

Within the field of childbirth it is possible these days to see competing professionalisms at work in quite anarchic ways. For example, the rise of 'unqualified' midwifery may lead to charges of 'incompetence' that obstetricians would never make about their peers; and lawyers are proving invaluable beneficiaries of the obstetrical claim that mothers do not understand their fetuses' best interests.[37]

Like all such puzzles, the truth of the matter probably lies in a combination of elements from all three explanations. Because one is about science, one is about gender relations, and one about the public division of labour, our difficulty in integrating them is partly a consequence of that theoretical chasm Margaret Stacey identified as the 'two Adams'.[38] Adam and Eve in the Garden of Eden add up to one account of the division of labour (between the sexes) while Adam Smith generates another, whose points of intersection with the first are unclear, to put it mildly.

The Power of Falling in Love

That motherhood has called forth this repertoire of response from the state and the medical profession points to its social importance, and also indexes something of the political realities of feminism. Yet the extent to which feminists in the postwar era have publicly commented on prevailing social and medical definitions of motherhood has been very limited. As many people have pointed out, the women's movement articulated an implicitly, if not explicitly, negative evaluation of motherhood for many years before it was able to articulate the positive side. Much of the early energy of organized feminism went into those aspects of medical practice – abortion and contraception – which benefited non-motherhood rather than those affecting the experience of motherhood itself. By the time pregnancy and childbirth and their medicalization became a major feminist project, other social movements had begun to take a careful look at what medicine was doing to mothers. The consumer movement in maternity care, well under way in Europe and North America by the mid 1960s, was joined by the alternative/self-help health movement. Sometimes, therefore, it has been hard to tell just which items in the current commentary on medicalized motherhood have a uniquely feminist stamp about them and which do not. But there does remain a sharp underlying ideological divide within each particular position on childbirth (pro-home delivery, anti-home delivery, pro-analgesia, anti-analgesia, and so forth). This divide is, at least to some extent, between those who hold pronatalist, pro-domestic views of women, and those who take the line that the medicalization of childbirth needs to be challenged or improved, not on the basis of women being particular kinds of people, but rather on the basis of women being people with basic human rights to dignity, privacy, freedom from assault, and the help and support of those whom they love and trust rather than those whom they do not know 'from Adam'.

If we say that the medicalization of motherhood would not have happened in the way and to the extent that it has without motherhood being a source of power for women, then we must probe beneath the superficial layer of biological explanations to find out why this is so. If biology does not explain the social patterning of sex differences, then can it really be called upon to explain something as complex and important as the institution of medicalized motherhood? Biological arguments, never popular with feminists or any other radical political movement, can hardly be dismissed in one sphere while being counted on for support in another.

Once we move away from the apparently 'hard' ground of biology, other kinds of explanations do, indeed, suggest themselves. Unlike the other structures of women's oppression, motherhood involves a dyadic relationship. The twentieth century has yielded many philosophies of mothering, which characterize it and women in different ways. There have also been different schools of thought on the nature of relationships between men and women. Theories of social relations do not, however, tend to see mothering and heterosexuality within the same conceptual framework.

In his book *Falling in Love* the Italian sociologist Francesco Alberoni describes a remarkable insight into the social phenomenon of 'love' which deserves to be considered in relation to motherhood. Alberoni says that falling in love is a collective movement of exactly the same type as the Protestant Reformation, the French Revolution, or feminism itself. It brings together in a social relationship individuals who were formerly not united. And it brings them together in such a way that the collective force generated is marked by 'solidarity, joy in life and renewal'. The extraordinary intimacy experienced by people who have fallen in love is akin to that felt by participation in great political movements: one's sensory world expands, becomes more intense, the boundaries between people become diffused, ordinary human selfishness is replaced by an unusual altruism, and everyday routines and language become inappropriate to the description and working out of a relationship that cancels time by becoming 'an eternalisation of the present'. But, more than anything else, falling in love is a 'nascent state', 'the revelation of an affirmative state of being', and 'an experience of authenticity, of transparency, of truth'.[39]

While this describes a phenomenon occurring to most adults in their relationships with one another at least several times in a lifetime, it is also how many mothers talk about their relationships with their newborn infants.[40] Even the expectation of falling in love, of the excitement of getting to know and 'possessing' a new person, the attunement to someone else's needs, the mutual physical pleasure in one another – even these are present in women's accounts of 'motives' for wanting a baby and of their feelings during pregnancy. The desire to have further children is in part a desire to recreate this unparalleled intimacy, although the idea that in motherhood women, otherwise a socially disadvantaged group, possess something of their own, is also important. This positive side of motherhood is as hidden as its negative side. Bad experiences are called deviance, and good ones are held out to be synonymous with the romantic view of mother-and-child in a field of daisies, with blond hair (and white nappies) softly blowing in the wind. Feminist writers on motherhood such as Adrienne Rich have therefore had a good deal to say about the devalued 'good' side of motherhood,[41] although the psychological parallels between adult heterosexual falling in love and mother-child falling in love are not generally themselves articulated.

Almost as a direct recognition of, and response to, the veiled power of this relation, a new goal of medicine in relation to motherhood has emerged over the last 15 years.[42] From the preoccupation with preventing mortality and physical morbidity, the practitioners of perinatal medicine have moved to a statement of their need to facilitate a phenomenon called 'bonding'. In the 1970s, based on the animal evidence, experimental studies were carried out with human mothers which were interpreted as showing that mothers and neonates separated after delivery did not do as well in psychological terms as those who were not separated.[43] These studies were then used to justify changes in obstetric and midwifery practice so that many more mothers did have a chance to hold their babies after birth before they were removed to the hospital nursery, and to breastfeed them, an exercise which had been accepted for a long time as making successful long-term breastfeeding considerably easier.

'Bonding' is now part of the language of hospital obstetrics. It is, of course, deeply interesting that the discovery of bonding came only after childbirth had been medicalized and removed to the hospital. The unmonitored bonding of mothers and babies in home deliveries had never evoked comment from the medical profession – nor, significantly, did the invention of the need for mother-baby bonding in hospital give rise to the reply that mothers and babies might be better off at home. (There is an analogy here with other recent psychosocial discoveries of medicine, for instance the helpfulness of social care during labour,[44] which needs to be actively promoted in hospital while it probably proceeds quietly on its way at home.)

There are multiple methodological flaws in the maternal-infant bonding studies,[45] but these are ultimately unimportant. What is important is, firstly, that 'bonding' theory made falling in love simply another phase in the pregnancy-birth process. For the doctor's job was no longer merely to deliver a labouring mother, it now included 'Helping Mothers to Love Their Babies', as a leader in the *British Medical Journal* put it.[46] In other words, the domain of motherhood deemed relevant to medicine was extended, and there was now something else that mothers could not do by themselves, but only with medical help. Secondly, bonding theory provided an acceptable excuse for hospitals and clinicians to reform their routines in line with the demands of the consumer movement, which had become much more vociferous by the mid 1970s. Simply to accede to consumer demands would have challenged the profession's claim to practise scientifically; but bonding theory enabled change without loss of face. But, thirdly, this new addition to medicine's perspective on motherhood gave a scientific veneer to the professional recognition that the falling in love mothers and babies do is a phenomenon simply bursting with revolutionary power. There was, after all, something powerful about motherhood that needed to be acknowledged, and could not merely be contained within the structure of hospitalized childbirth and the persuasive litanies of antenatal surveillance. The medical invention of bonding theory was thus one mode of recognizing that women are important, and that if their importance is not neatly defined and circumscribed by the medical and other professions, then the danger is that women will simply define their own importance in their own way.

Who Cares for Mothers?

Although reproductive medicine has been increasingly pushed by the 'consumer' movement, by feminism, and by the concerns of other professional groups, into recognizing psychosocial dimensions of motherhood, much of the contemporary critique of this medicine adds up to the complaint that doctors do not care. Thus we find in surveys of women's attitudes to prenatal surveillance the recurrent theme of a service provided by a series of strangers that is lacking in sensitivity to mothers' needs, marked by more of a respect for clinic routines than for the individuality of the patient, and so over-concerned with the possibility of biological pathology as to be oblivious of major psychological or social morbidity.[47] Caring attitudes from staff for mothers in labour are similarly less common than mothers would like them to be.[48] Infertility treatment, now infiltrated by the 'magic bullets' of in-vitro fertilization and embryo transfer, shares with prenatal care, in the form of new technologies such as chorion villus sampling, a preoccupation with physical cure rather than psychological care (and these technologies, for this reason, combined with their other profound social implications, have led to a great deal of comment from feminist quarters). Pregnancy loss – either early in pregnancy or late – is especially likely to provoke in medical staff a response that is seen by women as uncaring – though many women recognize that (at least with respect to early miscarriage) the very commonness of the event is what leads to the dismissive attitude. Like the common cold, a miscarriage is normally a self-curing illness. Yet the fact that many women experience pregnancy loss makes it, from their point of view, precisely more, and not less, important.[49]

We can identify here a conflict between two sets of perceptions about what is important in the process of becoming a mother; but, of course, it is also true to say that those who become mothers and those who help them to do so are united in a concern that the result of the process should be a live, healthy baby. However, the sense in which there is a contradiction between the different sets of perceptions points to something more important than itself, which is the existence of two major cultural dilemmas of our time: one relates to women, and one concerns the dominant paradigm of 'scientific' knowledge that pervades all our social, educational, medical and political institutions.

Caring as a concept isn't easy to define, but clearly relates to that range of human experiences having to do with feeling concern for, and taking charge of, the well-being of others. Caring is both who you are and what you do – it is both love and labour. In the former sense, to love is part of women's psychology, and in the latter to perform caring work is part of women's situation within a gendered division of labour.[50] One of the consequences of the medicalization of motherhood is that women's capacity to care about themselves and their children has been subject to a process of erosion and devaluation. Yet those professions which have assumed this responsibility, have reworked the notion of caring beyond all recognition, so technical services in the pursuit of physical, quantifiable ends are overwhelmingly what 'caring' for motherhood has come to mean. At the same time, women are subjected to a paradox highlighted in feminist social policy analysis, namely the idea that when money runs out it suits the state and the 'caring' professions to make women in the community responsible for shouldering the welfare of the elderly, the mentally and physically sick, and the disabled. Defined as incapable of caring properly from one point of view, women are filled with a surfeit of caring from another.

The second cultural dilemma is addressed by Fritjof Capra in his book *The Turning Point*. Capra identifies three social transitions currently in progress across the world: first, the gradual decline of patriarchy; second, a change in the world's energy resources as coal, oil and natural gas are used up and the era of solar energy is in sight; and third, a 'paradigm shift' – 'a profound change in the thoughts, perceptions and values that form a particular vision of reality'.[51] Capra believes that together these transitions will radically alter the world's social, economic and political systems. However, their timing is not necessarily in phase, and different groups of people are important in each. Capra argues that women, as represented by the feminist movement, are a major catalytic force in this transformation.

Within western culture a particular way of knowing the world prevails:

> Our culture takes pride in being scientific; our time is referred to as the Scientific Age. It is dominated by rational thought and scientific knowledge is often considered the only acceptable kind of knowledge. That there can be intuitive knowledge or awareness, is generally not recognised. This attitude, known as scientism, is widespread, pervading our educational system and all other social and political institutions.[52]

The scientific paradigm was born in the sixteenth and seventeenth centuries, when Newtonian physics and Cartesian rationality replaced the softer and more organic logic of a world view based on religion and an Aristotelian respect for nature. A desire to predict and control events gradually replaced a less intrusive quest for meaning and significance. This displacement of one paradigm by the other has been associated with a drive towards complex technologies, rather than ecological solutions to human needs. The mother who receives electronic fetal heart rate monitoring and epidural analgesia in labour is a manifestation of the same set of values as those responsible for developed countries spending three times as much on armaments as on health care. Men go to the moon while 35 per cent of the world's population lacks safe drinking water.

Within medicine itself the shift from a subjective to an objective mode of knowledge is demonstrated in a process spanning four centuries. In the beginning doctors gathered 'facts' about patients' conditions from patients themselves. Now they use many intermediary devices to do so: the thermometer, the stethoscope, the ultrasound scanner, the microscope, the electrocardiograph. What is transformed in this process of change is not only the nature of the facts collected but the social relations of health care, and at times this is a most conscious project, as in the contentions of the French inventor of the stethoscope, Laennec, to the effect that patients cannot be trusted to tell the truth and doctors must be provided with the technical means to know better than the patient. Social distance even becomes marked by spatial distance, so that the stethoscope is equipped with a long flexible tube and not a short rigid one – the doctor must not come too close to the patient.[53]

Applying Capra's paradigm shift to the particular case of motherhood, medicine and feminism, we can say that the institution of motherhood is trapped in the tension between two paradigms. The scientism of medicine has pulled motherhood one way in the twentieth century, while feminism has more recently begun to push it in another direction. The fact that earlier in the century feminists tried to co-opt medicine in the attempt to make motherhood safer is not incompatible with this view; the requirement then was for basic health services to be accessible to mothers and babies so that deaths due to such elementary causes as infection, haemorrhage and induced abortion might be avoided.[54]

A variety of evidence could be cited to support this interpretation of motherhood's current position, and the conclusion to this chapter will briefly cite two such examples: (1) the status of 'social' interventions in motherhood; and (2) the ethics of informed consent in research.

Between Two Paradigms

Just as medical services for mothers remain largely unevaluated in terms of effectiveness and efficiency, so social interventions have only recently come to be considered worthy of scientific investigation. Can 'hard' outcomes such as perinatal mortality, rates of caesarean section and the incidence of low birth-weight and preterm delivery be improved by social as opposed to clinical forms of care? 'Care' is no easier to define in this context than in any other, but non-clinical social interventions include such activities as health education, childbirth preparation exercises, 'marital' counselling, dietary advice and the provision of continuity of care within the context of standard medical services. A recent analysis[55] of 29 such studies showed statistically significant effects of social as opposed to clinical forms of care on the incidence of instrumental/operative delivery and prolonged labour. The incidence of low birthweight delivery also appeared to be influenced to some extent. In addition, and not surprisingly, the satisfaction that women feel with both their childbirth and motherhood experiences, was significantly improved following social care in pregnancy.[56] This 'knowledge' fits easily within the social-scientific literature on the importance of social relations in shaping people's lives,[57] though less easily within an epidemiological framework which emphasizes the need to identify causal factors behind poor health. It is almost totally incompatible with the clinical paradigm which relies heavily on a mind-body divide ruling such an explanation *a priori* out of court.

In a different way the politics of motherhood caught between two paradigms is illustrated by the troubling issue of informed consent. Medicine has always meant research, but the importance of research comes to the fore especially when the evidential basis of medical practice is challenged, as it is today. Currently about one in ten of all patients in Britain is the subject of what are known technically as randomized controlled clinical trials (RCTs).[58] Many patients are so without their knowledge, because medical researchers in Britain and some other countries contend that by and large it is no more necessary to ask for patients' consent to participate in research than it is to consult them about the ordinary treatment they will have. RCTs have become popular in perinatal medicine but have met criticism from the consumer movement, both on the issue of informed consent and on the general ethics of experimentation on mothers and foetuses. One recent problematic case was the multi-centre Medical Research Council trial on vitamin supplementation in women at risk of having babies with neural tube defects: many women felt the case for vitamins already proven, so that experimentation (with vitamin and no-vitamin groups) was not justified.[59] Yet consumer organizations in the maternity care field demand more evaluation of medical practice at the same time that they possess their own unevaluated certainty about motherhood. They want both to have their cake and eat it: to practice one paradigm and promote the other – to 'know' what they 'know' and also demand that knowledge in that other scientist sense, be sought.

The pursuit of medical knowledge in the form of RCTs may be the last fling of the scientist paradigm, the death struggles of a doomed and inappropriate world-view. But taking a good, hard look at the medicalization of motherhood may rescue us from that bleak fate and provide the impetus for a new paradigm to be established and accepted by all the actors in the drama of motherhood. At the moment it is, in fact, hard to make sense on the subject of motherhood because whatever one says relates to the two prevailing different paradigms. For example, the very notion that I've introduced in this chapter that part of the importance of motherhood is that mothers and babies fall in love with one another, can be taken as something that is self-evidently true on the experiential level – it's something women say about motherhood, yet on the other hand the same idea of love is wrapped in cultural trappings. Is love a luxury possible only when one is freed from material oppression? Is the appeal to love thus only what one class says happens in the world, and thus to be disbelieved for its imperialist overtones? Even more fundamental an objection is the role of love in heterosexual relationships; again, real at the level of lived experience, but used and abused as a a way of making women do what men want: 'she did it all for love'. To speak of love between mothers and children may thus be to locate women in yet another enclosure from which they may escape only by denying their identity as women.

The fact that it is not possible to make an informed choice between these two different interpretations is only one small sign of the mess we're in. Whatever else feminism is, it's therefore not about providing short-term solutions to social problems. Many of the questions feminism raises about motherhood will take a long time to be answered.

Notes

I should like to thank a number of people for help with generating and organizing the random thoughts in this chapter. Particular thanks go to Emily Oakley for one of the original inspirations, to Jennie Popay for trying to bring me down to earth, to Sandra Stone for making it all look more impressive than it really is, and to Marty Wagner for lending me his copy of *Falling in Love*, and for many conversations about this topic over many years.

1 This statement takes a particular side in two important contemporary debates – the debate about whether medicalization of motherhood *has* brought about real gains for women, and that about whether women 'need' to experience autonomy or control in the process of controlling motherhood. With respect to the first point, I am sure that the gains in terms of improved survival and health for women have been substantial (even if not as great as they are sometimes made out to be). On the second point, I believe that the desirability of childbirth being so 'managed' as to enable women to feel some control over the process is quite compatible with the existence of social class differences in 'models' of childbirth. (See M. K. Nelson, 'Working-class Women, Middle-Class Women and Models of Childbirth', *Social Problems* Vol 30, 3 (1983), 284–97).

2 Some examples are V. Barker and M. M. Skaggs, *The Mother Person* (Severn House, London 1977); J. Bernard, *The Future of Motherhood* (Penguin Books, New York 1975); D. Breen, *Talking with Mothers* (Jill Norman, London 1981); A. Dally, *Inventing Motherhood* (Burnett Books, London 1982); S. Downrick and S. Grundberg (eds), *Why Children?* (The Women's Press, London 1980); S. Yudkin and A. Holme, *Working Mothers and Their Children* (Sphere Books, London 1963).

3 M. Wollstonecraft, *A Vindication of the Rights of Woman* (Everyman, London 1929), 106.

4 Ibid., 209.

5 Ibid., 211.

6 M. G. Fawcett, 'Introduction' to M. Wollstonecraft, *A Vindication of the Rights of Woman* (T. Fisher Unwin, London 1891), 23.

7 'Declaration of Sentiments' and 'Resolutions' adopted by the Seneca Falls Convention in 1848 in W. O'Neill, *The Woman Movement: Feminism in the United States and England* (Allen and Unwin, London 1969), 109.

8 J. A. Banks and O. Banks, *Feminism and Family Planning in Victorian England* (Routledge and Kegan Paul, London 1964).

9 H. Fawcett and M. G. Fawcett, *Essays and Lectures on Social and Political Subjects* (Macmillan, London 1872), 200.

10 G. P. Gillman, *The Home* (1903) cited in O'Neill, *The Woman Movement*, 129.

11 Ada Nield Chew, *The Life and Writings of a Working Woman*, ed. D. Nield Chew (Virago, London 1982), 231.

12 S. Webb and B. Webb, *The State and the Doctor* (Longmans Green and Co, London 1910).

13 See A. Oakley, *The Captured Womb: a history of the medical care of pregnant women* (Blackwells, Oxford 1984).

14 A. T. Scull, *Museums of Madness* (Penguin, Harmondsworth 1982).

15 D. Armstrong, *Political Anatomy of the Body* (Cambridge University Press, Cambridge 1983).

16 S. Day, 'Towards a Social History of Postnatal Depression', unpublished paper, Child Care and Development Group, Cambridge, 1981.

17 C. Damme, 'Infanticide: the worth of an infant under law', *Medical History* Vol 22 (1978), 1–24.

18 Department of Health and Social Security, *Reducing the Risk – Safe Pregnancy and Childbirth* (HMSO, London 1977).

19 Board of Education, *Annual Report for 1914 of the Chief Medical Officer of the Board of Education* (HMSO, London 1915), 25.

20 Local Government Board, *Forty-Fourth Annual Report. Supplement 1914–15 Maternal Mortality*, (HMSO, London 1916).

21 Local Government Board, *Thirty-Ninth Annual Report. Supplement on Infant and Child Mortality* (HMSO, London 1910), 73.

22 For example, *Maternity: letters from working women*, ed. M. L. Davies, (G. Bell and Sons, London 1915; reprinted Virago, London 1978).

23 *Thirty-Ninth Annual Report*, 87.

24 F. Power Cobbe, '*The Final Cause of Women*', cited in P. Hollis, *Women in Public: The Women's Movement 1850–1900* (Allen & Unwin, London 1979), 23.

25 J. Campbell, *Maternal Mortality* Reports on Public Health and Medical Subjects. No. 25. (Ministry of Health; HMSO, London 1924).

26 For example, T. Cianfrani, *A Short History of Obstetrics and Gynaecology*, (C. C. Thomas, Springfield, Illinois 1960).

27 See, for example, M. Enkins and I. Chalmers (eds.), *Effectiveness and Satisfaction in Antenatal Care*, (Spastics International Medical Publications, London 1982). A valuable commentary on this issue is K. Figlio, 'The Historiography of Scientific Medicine: an invitation to the human sciences', *Comparative Studies in Society and History* Vol 19, 3 (1977), 262–86.

28 A. L. Cochrane, *Effectiveness and Efficiency* (The Nuffield Provincial Hospitals Trust, London 1971).

29 See T. McKeown, *The Role of Medicine* (Blackwells, Oxford 1979).

30 E. Freidson, *Profession of Medicine* (Dodd, Mead & Company, New York 1972), 82.

31 *Ibid.*, 337.

32 J. Barker-Benfield, *The Horrors of the Half-Known Life* (Harper & Row, New York 1976).
33 An example would be the study of families experiencing acute illness: F. Davis, *Passage Through Crisis: polio victims and their families* (Bobbs Merrill, New York 1963).
34 D. Scully, *Men Who Control Women's Health* (Houghton Mifflin, Boston 1980).
35 G. Bourne, *Pregnancy* (Pan Books, London 1975), 121–2.
36 I. Illich, 'Disabling Professions', in I. Illich, I. K. Zola, J. McKnight, J. Caplan and H. Shaiken, *Disabling Professions* (Marion Boyars, London 1977), 19.
37 R. G. De Vries, *Regulating Birth* (Temple University Press, Philadelphia 1985).
38 M. Stacey, 'The Division of Labour Revisited, or overcoming the two Adams' in P. Abrams, R. Keen, J. Finch, P. Rock (eds.), *Practice and Progress: British Sociology 1950–1980* (Allen and Unwin, London 1982).
39 F. Alberoni, *Falling in Love* (Random House, New York 1983), 4.
40 See, for example, A. Oakley, 'Normal Motherhood: an exercise in self-control?' in B. Hutter and G. Williams, *Controlling Women* (Croom Helm, London 1981).
41 A. Rich, *Of Woman Born* (Virago, London 1977).
42 C. Ounsted, J. Roberts, M. Gordon and B. Milligan, 'Fourth Goal of Perinatal Medicine', *Bristol Medical Journal*, 20 March 1982, 179–82.
43 See W. R. Arney, *Power and the Profession of Obstetrics* (University of Chicago Press, Chicago 1982), Chapter 5, for a review; also R. G. De Vries, ' "Humanising" childbirth: the discovery and implementation of bonding theory', *International Journal of Health Services*, 1984, 89–104.
44 R. Sosa, J. Kennell, M. Klaus, S. Robertson, J. Urruta, 'The Effect of a Supportive Companion on Perinatal Problems, Length of Labour and Mother-Infant Interaction', *New English J. Med.* Vol 303, 11 (1980).
45 See Arney, *Power and Profession of Obstetrics*, for a discussion.
46 Leading article 'Helping Mothers to Love Their Babies', *British Medical Journal*, Vol 2 (1977), 595.
47 For one such survey, see J. Garcia, 'Women's Views of Antenatal Care' in Enkins and Chalmers (eds.) *Effectiveness and Satisfaction*.
48 S. Kitzinger's *Good Birth Guide* (Fontana, London 1979) provides a manual of those aspects of care positively evaluated by some consumers.
49 See A. Oakley, A. McPherson and H. Roberts, *Miscarriage* (Fontana, London 1984); S. Borg, J. Lasker, *When Pregnancy Fails* (Routledge and Kegan Paul, London 1972).
50 H. Graham, 'Caring: a labour of love' in *A Labour of Love* (eds.). J. Finch and D. Groves (Routledge and Kegan Paul, London 1983).
51 F. Capra, *The Turning Point* (Bantam Books, New York 1983), 30.
52 Ibid., 39.
53 S. J. Reiser, *Medicine and the Reign of Technology* (Cambridge University Press, Cambridge 1978).
54 Some of the early reports of the Confidential Enquiries into Maternal Deaths make salutary reading. See A. Macfarlane and M. Mugford, *Birth Counts* (HMSO, London 1984), 199–209.

55 A. Oakley, D. Elbourne and I. Chalmers, 'The Effects of Social Interventions in Pregnancy', Paper given at INSERM conference on Prevention of Pre-Term Birth: new goals and practices in perinatal care, Evian, France, 19–22 May 1985.
56 I recognize the paradox of citing the concept of 'statistical significance' in a discussion of the pros and cons of the 'scientist' paradigm!
57 See B. H. Gottliebs (ed.), *Social Networks and Social Support* (Sage Publications, Beverly Hills 1981); L. F. Berkman, 'Assessing the Physical Health Effects of Social Networks and Social Support', *Ann. Review of Pub. Health* Vol 5 (1984), 413–32.
58 On the issue of informed consent in general, see C. Faulder, *Whose Body is it?* (Virago, London 1985).
59 See the Newsletters of the Associations for Improvements in the Maternity Services, 1983–4.

9 Feminist Perspectives on Legal Ideology

Deborah L. Rhode

Almost since its inception, feminist ideology has been in tension with the liberal traditions from which it grew. Early feminist theorists grounded their case for female emancipation on liberal notions of equal rights. Within this framework, individuals were entitled to pursue their own vision of self-fulfilment, unconstrained by gender. Yet, as feminists, these theorists also presupposed some recognition of women's collective interests and identity; they assumed the common bonds that liberalism seeks in large measure to transcend. Moreover, some strands of feminism have always had more radical roots. Both in theory and in practice, the movement's demands have included not simply equal entitlements within existing social structures but a different set of structures. As contemporary theorists have increasingly recognized, if feminism is to achieve its objectives of full equality between the sexes, it must transcend the focus on individual rights that remains at the core of liberal ideology.

The tension between feminist theory and liberal thought has been apparent in a variety of historical and cultural contexts, but nowhere has it been more graphically demonstrated than in the last century of Anglo-American legal ideology. To the question 'What is Feminism?' this jurisprudential tradition provokes a representative answer: because liberal legalism neither raises nor resolves certain fundamental questions concerning woman's status. To be sure, as the experience in the United States over the last decade makes evident, a focus on individual entitlements can be of enormous significance in challenging the most overt forms of sexual discrimination. But to rely on that paradigm as a framework for true sexual equality is to misread the legacy of liberal legal ideology. Equal rights are, at this historical moment, too restricted in legal content and too divisive in political connotations to serve as an adequate feminist agenda.

In part, the difficulties arise from the indeterminacy of equality as a societal vision. Liberal jurisprudence draws heavily on Aristotelian premises; equality results from treating similarly situated individuals similarly, and drawing distinctions based on real differences. The problem comes in specifying what counts as a difference. On that point, neither legal thought nor liberal feminist theory has offered a coherent answer.

Early women's rights advocates often based their claims on natural rights, while remaining wedded to natural roles. John Stuart Mill, who provided the analytic framework for many feminists as well as legal theorists, advocated equal entitlements for women in the public sphere, but left unchallenged their unequal obligations in the private sphere. Although denouncing 'ascribed statuses', Mill accepted conventional allocations of domestic responsibilities as 'the most suitable division of labour.'[1] Women who chose to marry would 'naturally' renounce 'all other objects and occupations' inconsistent with household responsibilities. For those lacking exceptional talents and adequate servants, domesticity was a full-time vocation. Yet as long as marriage was a matter of 'individual choice', not necessity, Mill's liberal principles were satisfied.[2] Equality, thus conceived, offered women the option of public or private pursuits. It did not demand re-examination of the terms of that choice, the social structures which constrained it, or the assumption that only women should be required to choose.

Similarly, the first American feminists frequently asserted woman's equal 'inalienable rights' while accepting her unequal domestic role. Like Mill, these theorists emphasized individual autonomy: woman ought not to be condemned to a 'separate sphere'. Yet once she had chosen marriage and a family, certain consequences seemed naturally to follow. Many of the most ardent advocates of egalitarian legal principles saw 'no excuse for neglecting any home duty for the most desirable foreign pursuits.'[3]

Moreover, as the campaign for legal rights progressed, its androgynous principles became less pronounced. Rather, women were cast as separate but equal; their purportedly distinctive attributes became a rationale for participation in public life. With their 'high code of morals', women would purify politics.[4] To many of these early feminists, it followed that woman's access to equal legal rights would of itself transform society. Enfranchisement, they often assumed, would secure parity in wages and work; it would open to women the 'colleges, the professions and all the opportunities and advantages of life.'[5]

However expedient in the short term, such claims left a less fortunate legacy. The fixation with formal civil rights to some extent deflected attention from the broader economic and social forces that shaped women's lives. For much of the nineteenth and early twentieth centuries, the liberal equal rights agenda remained one step removed from the problems and priorities of those most in need of assistance. Particularly in America, where activists lacked strong working-class ties, the feminist focus on certain limited legal entitlements often seemed somewhat beside the point. For the average middle- or lower-class women, issues of family law, poverty, welfare, health care, working conditions, birth control, domestic roles, and spousal brutality assumed far greater significance than any constitutional recognition of equal status. So too, feminists' cele- bration of women's distinctive attributes helped perpetuate the stereotypes on which antifeminism rested. As the evolution of nineteenth- and early twentieth-century legal ideology makes clear, women's purportedly natural roles remained a ready basis for denying their natural rights.

Drawing on the same notions of 'real differences' that feminists alternatively celebrated and condemned, Anglo-American jurispru- dence declined to enforce a 'fictitious equality'.[6] The clearest exposition of woman's distinctive destiny came as male professionals contemplated her intrusion into their own separate sphere. What is striking about virtually all of the legal decisions concerning female entry into male universities and vocations is the utter lack of self- consciousness with which an exclusively male judiciary decided questions of male exclusivity. To Justice Bradley of the United States Supreme Court in 1873, woman's 'proper timidity and docility unfit[ted] her for many of the occupations of civil life', including practice at the bar. Her 'paramount destiny' was mother- hood; this was 'the law of the Creator'.[7] Although the precise method of divine communication was never elaborated, it was apparently accessible to other nineteenth-century jurists both in America and abroad. English courts lumped women together with the insane, the insolvent, and occasionally the inanimate, as unsuited for the 'intense labour' of professional vocations.[8] Nor was this separate spheres ideology confined to nineteenth-century cases involving professional advancement. Until the late 1950s, the House of Lords resisted feminine incursions, and as recently as 1961, the United States Supreme Court invoked women's place at the 'center of home and family life' to justify their categorical exemption from jury service.[9]

Moreover, although legal ideology celebrated woman's domestic realm, it declined to grant her sovereignty within it. When denying woman's access to professional opportunities and political entitle-ments, courts and legislators talked reverently of her custody over the home. But when that custody was in fact at issue, the rhetoric suddenly shifted. It was the husband's prerogative to determine the couple's domicile and standard of living. The sanctity of domestic life appeared to demand a circumscribed role for both women and the law. Even today, courts generally decline to enforce marital support obligations until a marriage actually terminates. As long as the couple lives together, their home remains a 'domain into which the king's writ does not seek to run', whatever the hardship of a dependent wife.[10]

Comparable delicacy has characterized judicial and prosecutoral attitudes towards chastisement, the common law euphemism for wife beating. In cases of 'mere impulsive violence' and no permanent injuries, parties have often been left to 'forget and forgive'. For, however great 'the evils of ill temper', they have been thought 'not comparable with the evils that would result from raising the curtain and exposing to public curiosity and criticism the nursery and the bed chamber'.[11]

Until that curtain is raised and the personal becomes the political, the likelihood of achieving significant social transformation remains remote. For women to obtain equality in fact, they cannot simply rely on equality in formal rights – the core of the liberal legal agenda. Nonetheless, Mill's legacy lingers on in many of the leading feminist organizations. America's National Organization For Women (one, if not the largest, of the world's feminist coalitions), defines its primary objective as equal opportunity and freedom of choice.[12] Yet true equality and personal autonomy will remain illusory as long as individuals' socialization, education, and material circumstances vary widely. As a vast array of social science research makes clear, women's capabilities and aspirations are heavily influenced by gender stereotypes and conventional role expectations, as well as by various wealth-related factors.[13]

Moreover, parity in formal rights cannot begin to secure parity in actual opportunity as long as rights remain restricted to those that predominantly upper-middle-class male legislators and judges have been prepared to regard as fundamental. In the United States, for example, the list of constitutional entitlements has been interpreted to include the right to bear arms or sell 'artistically redeeming' pornographic magazines, but not, if one is indigent, the right to obtain an abortion, child care, health services, or equal educational opportunities.[14] Women are, at least in theory, protected from discrimination on account of sex in employment but not from discrimination on account of sexual preference or non-marital sexual activity.[15] And, in fact, in the two decades since passage of statutes requiring equal salaries and vocational opportunities, female workers' economic position relative to men's has not fundamentally improved. Women are entitled to equal pay for equal work but not to comparable pay for comparable worth; that male parking attendants receive higher salaries than female child care attendants is a matter beyond the scope of conventional equal opportunity analysis.

Nor is the United States an atypical example. Many developed countries have equal pay legislation, but none has anything close to equal pay.[16] Most grant women the same abstract entitlements to pursue political and professional careers, yet nowhere are the sexes evenly represented in positions of power, prestige, and economic reward.

Individual rights-oriented strategies have succeeded largely in guaranteeing equal opportunities for advancement in male-defined structures under male-defined criteria. The principal beneficiaries have been females who are willing and able to conform to the male biography, those who accept the competitive, hierarchical structure of the workplace, together with the price that such conformity exacts in the home. For example, according to a representative sampling of recent articles, the route of 'success' for an American woman attorney is to remain ready to work evenings and weekends and never to request special favours because of family commitments.[17] Those who succeed are those who acclimate to work environments structured by and for men. Through that process of acculturation, individuals tend inevitably to lose the incentive or perspective necessary to challenge the underlying structures and the purportedly neutral standards by which merit is assessed. Thus the culture perpetuates itself, legitimized by the presence of a small percentage of women.

The challenge now is to move beyond liberal legalism, to demand not simply equality in form but equality in fact. Drawing on their more radical roots, feminists must employ law to seek not simply access to, but alteration of, existing social institutions. They must demand an expanded conception of legal rights while recognizing the limitations of legal strategies. A more constructive approach will require focusing attention less on gender difference, and more on the disadvantages that have followed from it.

An obvious example involves the way courts have coped with the relationship between women's productive and reproductive roles. During the mid 1970s and early 1980s both English and American judges determined that discrimination on the basis of pregnancy did not constitute unlawful sex discrimination because men and women were not similarly situated. Since there was 'no masculine equivalent of pregnancy', there was 'no risk from which men were protected and women were not'. In the United States, the Supreme Court added the somewhat novel view that discrimination on the basis of pregnancy did not even involve 'gender as such'. According to a majority of Justices, employers were entitled to treat childbirth-related disabilities as involving 'additional risks' and 'unique characteristics' and to distinguish between 'pregnant women and non-pregnant persons' in granting benefits.[18] At no point did the court explain what made pregnancy more 'unique' than the male reproductive conditions entitled to coverage. Moreover, to characterize pregnancy as a 'unique' risk both assumed what should have been at issue and made that assumption from a male reference point. Men's physiology set the standard against which women's claims appeared only 'additional'.

The notion that distinctions based on pregnancy are not distinctions based on 'gender as such' obscures the most basic physical, cultural, and historical meanings of reproduction and the disadvantages that have flowed from it. In western industrialized countries like the United States, approximately 85 per cent of female employees can expect to become pregnant at some point in their working lives, and maternity politics have been highly inadequate.[19] Nor have traditional equal protection paradigms worked to secure better alternatives. In the United States, the immediate response to the Supreme Court's pregnancy decisions was a pregnancy discrimination statute, which required that women 'affected by childbirth and related conditions be treated the same as other persons not so affected but similar in their ability or inability to work.' Although that legislation has promoted some positive reforms, its similarly situated framework has once again deflected attention from more basic issues. In effect, the statute prevents employers from singling out pregnant workers for special disadvantages. It does not affirmatively require or encourage provision of disability benefits or support structures that would enable women to accommodate work and family obligations. The scope of British protective statutes has been similarly inadequate.[20]

A comparable point can be made about other legislative and doctrinal developments. Many of the problems of greatest concern to women – poverty, violence, child care, reproductive freedom, comparable worth – do not find the sexes 'similarly situated'. To make significant progress toward equality between them will require more expansive legal strategies and societal commitments. As the pregnancy illustration suggests, the problems of reconciling productive and reproductive roles are not satisfactorily addressed through conventional anti-discrimination doctrine. The point is not simply to prohibit dissimilar treatment under current employment structures but to promote alternative structures – ones that are more hospitable not only to pregnant women but to working parents. On a practical level, what that entails is a cluster of legal regulations, tax incentives, and government subsidies directed towards a cluster of issues: guaranteed leaves, job security, flexible working schedules, part-time employment, and adequate child care. On a more theoretical level, that agenda implies a broader commitment to traditional female values of collaboration, co-operation, and caretaking. Given the role constraints that have limited male as well as female experience, both sexes have a stake in such a reconstructive enterprise. The ultimate issue is not simply equality of treatment between men and women but the quality of life for both of them.

How best to pursue that agenda will vary considerably across cultures, but focusing on matters such as a constitutional guarantee of equality is of limited value. The American campaign for an equal rights amendment suggests the limitations of that strategy; the experience is, in historian L. B. Namier's phrase, 'a good illustration of how things do not happen'. Conceived in the early 1920s as a measure to unite women, the Equal Rights Amendment served often to divide them. During the first part of the century, leading women's rights advocates bitterly divided over the merits of mandating equality in circumstances of social inequality. In the view of some feminists, such a constitutional provision would invalidate beneficial protective labour legislation regulating women's wages, hours, and working conditions. Other feminists emphasized the likelihood that women would be 'protected' out of desirable vocations. Too often, the amendment became a vehicle for ultimately unproductive legal and political debates over the extent to which female workers were naturally different from males and in need of special solicitude. Women ended up fighting each other over the value of protection rather than uniting to challenge the social and economic conditions that made protection so valuable.

Again in the 1970s, the Equal Rights Amendment proved highly divisive, although the dispute centred less on concrete consequences than on cultural values. Anti-feminists of the New Right cast the provision as an assault not on gender discrimination but on gender differences. Equality signalled the onslaught of a 'unisex' society, a vision that aroused anxiety in various quarters. To many women,

158   *Feminist Perspectives on Legal Ideology*

particularly those who had defined their lives in accordance with traditional feminine values or who lacked meaningful vocational choices, the rhetoric of rights appeared elitist, irrelevant, or profoundly unsettling. Liberal feminism's focus on professional advancement and its perceived devaluation of domestic pursuits seemed to enshrine a vision of liberation as confining as the stereotype it sought to supplant. Ironically enough, it was the opponents rather than the supporters of equal rights who were able to dignify the traditional feminine role that society as a whole had undervalued.

Thus transformed, the equal rights debate inevitably became trivialized. Proponents became enmeshed in pointless disputes over gender differences rather than gender domination. At a time when millions of women were victims of poverty and violence, millions of dollars were invested in arguing over whether an equal rights amendment would prohibit separate bathrooms. In an effort to allay the impression that homemakers generally opposed equal rights, liberal feminists launched culinary campaigns designed to match their foes muffin for muffin. Legislators were barraged with brunches and brioches from all constituencies, while the press often characterized the campaign as an internecine battle between rival Hausfraus.[21]

After a ten-year struggle, the amendment was narrowly defeated, but it is by no means clear at this juncture how much that loss should be lamented. Formal legal guarantees are often more a catalyst than a source of change. Given the process and principal agents of constitutional adjudication, an abstract legal mandate is of itself unlikely to work major social transformation. Yet if, in the battle for equal rights, women gain valuable lessons in *realpolitik* and the limitations of their own influence, such campaigns may ultimately be vindicated. Without a fundamental reordering of societal institutions and values, women cannot begin to achieve true parity in vocational opportunities, economic security, and social status. To achieve that reconstruction, feminists must attain political leverage and push beyond the agenda of liberal legalism. They must focus more attention on issues of class as well as caste, on structural changes in the family and the workplace, and on strategies for fundamental reallocations in wealth and political power. The objective, as Juliet Mitchell has suggested, must be a transformation of production, reproduction, socialization, and sexuality.[22] If law is to be significant in that endeavour, it must build on broader feminist values that transcend the liberal individualist legacy.

Notes

1 John Stuart Mill and Harriet Taylor Mill, *Early Essays on Marriage and Divorce*, in *Essays on Sex Equality*, (ed.) Alice Rossi (University of Chicago Press, Chicago 1970), 67, 76; John Stuart Mill, *The Subjection of Women*, in *On Liberty, Representative Government, and the Subjection of Women*, (ed.) M. Fawcett (London 1912), 483.
2 Mill, *The Subjection of Women* 484, 514–15. See Susan Okin, *Women in Western Political Thought* (Princeton University Press, Princeton 1979).
3 Caroline Dall, *College, Market, and Court* 128–9. See also Antoinette Brown Blackwell, *Relation of Women's Work in the Household to Work Outside* 1873, quoted in Aileen Kraditor, (ed.), *Up From the Pedestal: Selected Writings in the History of American Feminism* (Quadrangle Books, Chicago 1968) (domestic work remained 'nearest and dearest' to 'average womanhood'). Also Angelina Grimké, Letter to Anna Weston, 15 July 1838 (Boston Public Library) (necessary for feminists to show they were not 'ruined as domestic creatures'.)
4 See Susan B. Anthony and Ida Husted Harper (eds.), *History of Woman Suffrage*, Vol IV (Hallenback Press, New York 1902), 39. Similarly, Jane Addams cast women as municipal, housekeepers. Jane Addams, 'Why Women Should Vote,' in Frances M. Bjorkman and Annie G. Porritt (eds.), *Women Suffrage: History, Arguments, and Results* (National Woman Suffrage Company Inc., New York 1915), 131–3.
5 'The Ballot, Bread, Virtue, Power,' *Revolution*, Vol II (January 1868), 1.
6 *Quong Wong v. Kirkendall*, 223 U.S. 59 (1912).
7 *Bradwell v. State*, 83 U.S. 130, 141–2 (187). See also *Lockwood v. United States*, 9 Ct. Cl. 346, 355 (1875), and *In the Matter of Goodell*, 29 Wisc. Rep. 232, 244 (1875).
8 See cases discussed in Albie Sachs and John Hoff Wilson, *Sexism and the Law* (Robertson & Co., London 1978), 6–44.
9 Ibid., 33; *Hoyt v. Florida*, 368 U.S. 57 (1961).
10 *Balfour v. Balfour*, L.R., 2 K. B. 571 (C. A. 1919). See *Miller v. Miller*, 78 Iowa 177 (1889); *McGuire v. McGuire*, 157 Neb. 226, 59 N.W. 2d 336 (1953).
11 *State v. Rhodes*, 61 N.C. 445, 448 (1858).
12 See Betty Friedan, *It Changed My Life* (Dell, New York 1977), 124; Maren Lockwood Carden, *The New Feminist Movement* (Russell Sage Foundation, New York 1974), 104.
13 See, e.g., Michelle Zimbalist Rosaldo and Lousie Lamphere (ed.), *Woman, Culture, and Society* (Stanford University Press, Stanford 1974); Alice M. Jaggar, *Feminist Politics and Human Nature* (Rowman and Allanheld, New Jersey 1983), 194–7.
14 Compare United States Constitution, Amendment 2 (right to bear arms) with *Miller v. California*, 413 U.S. 15, 22 (1973) (states may proscribe pornographic material only if it, *inter alia*, lacks serious, literary, artistic, political, or scientific value) with *Harris v. McCrae*, 448 U.S. 297 (1980) (no right to subsidized abortion); *San Antonio Independent School District v. Rodriguez*, 411 U.S. 1 (1973) (no right to equal educational expenditures).

15 See cases discussed in Judith Baer, *Equality Under the Constitution: Reclaiming the Fourteenth Amendment* (Cornell Press, New York, 1984), 225–52 and Mary Dunlap, 'Toward Recognition of a "Right to be Sexual," ' *Women's Rights Law Reporter* Vol 7 (1982), 245–9.
16 See J. Mitchell, *Women: The Longest Revolution* (Pantheon, New York 1966), 57; Sachs and Wilson, *Sexism and the Law*.
17 See e.g., Nell B. Strachan, 'A Map for Women on the Road to Success', *American Bar Association Journal* Vol. 70 (1984), 95; Steven Brill, 'The Women Problem', *The American Lawyer* (February 1983), 8.
18 *Turley* v. *Allders Dept Stores Ltd*, IRLR 427 [1978]; *Geduldig v*. Aillo, 417 S.S. 484, 496–7 n. 20 (1974); *General Electric Co.* v. *Gilbert*, 429 U.S. 125, 135–6 (1976); See also *Reaney* v. *Kanda Jean Produce Ltd.* [1980], ICR 66; David Pannick, 'Sex Discrimination and Pregnancy: Anatomy Is Not Destiny', *Oxford Journal of Legal Studies* Vol 3 (1983), 1.
19 See Sheila B. Kammerman, Alfred J. Kahn and Paul Kinston, *Maternity Policies and Working Women* (Columbia University Press, New York 1983); Wendy Welsen Williams, 'Equality's Riddle: Pregnancy and the Equal Treatment Special Treatment Debate', *New York University Journal of Law and Social Change* 13 (1984–5).
20 See 42 U.S.C. §2000e; Katherine O'Donovan, *Sexual Division in Law* (Weidenfeld and Nicolson, London 1983), 166–73.
21 See Deborah L. Rhode, 'Equal Rights in Retrospect', *Journal of Law and Inequality: A Journal of Theory and Practice* Vol 1 (1983) 1–72.
22 Juliet Mitchell, *Women's Estate* (Penguin Books, New York 1971).

10 Women's Work: Women's Knowledge

Hilary Rose

Feminism has been preoccupied with the distinctive activity of women – with our labour in the world. In bringing this labour out of nature and into history, feminism has uncovered both distinctive social relations around gender and a distinctive relationship to nature. My task in this paper is to show, through a discussion of women's work, the domestic labour debate, and the arguments around patriarchy, how a feminist epistemology – 'feminist stand-point'[1] as others have termed it – is grounded in the labour of women. In this claim the developing epistemology of feminist materialism finds both echoes and support in the materialism of Marx. His critical method enabled him to go behind the appearance of things, to what he spoke of as their essence. Above all he was able to go behind the appearance of freedom in the labour market in which buyers and sellers freely bought and sold, to reveal the systemic relations of domination and subordination which are located within the capitalist mode of production itself. For feminism the task has been to go behind – above all in personal life – the appearance of love and the naturalness of a woman's place and a woman's work, to reveal the equally systemic relationships of the sex-gender world.

The key to this particular feminist method is a theory of labour. What has this to do with knowledge? The point is that for materialist theory, human knowledge and human consciousness are not abstract or divorced from experience or 'given' by some process separate from the unitary material reality of the world. Human knowledge, whether of the arts or the sciences, comes from practice, from working on and changing the world. As people work on nature and transform it, they gain knowledge of how nature – including their own nature – is organized and may be explained. Knowledge initially derives from the basic needs of human survival, the need for food, for shelter and so forth. What distinguishes humans from other animals is their self-consciousness of this knowledge; human activity transforms nature continuously and in doing so performs that characteristically human activity of production. Science in this sense is organized knowledge of the world derived from practice upon it. As Mao Tse Tung put it:

> If you want knowledge you must take part in changing reality. If you want to know the taste of a pear you must change the pear, taking it into your mouth and chewing it. If you want to know the structure and properties of an atom, you must make physical and chemical experiements to change the state of an atom. If you want to know the theory and methods of revolution, you must take part in revolution.[2]

Because science derives from labour, it is clearly shaped and formed by the purposes and direction of that labour. Labour in a capitalist society is alienated; capitalist and worker confront each other with different knowledges derived from their different class positions – which define them differently vis-à-vis each other and nature. Ruling-class ideas are ideologies designed to preserve the *status quo*; science, as transformative knowledge, comes out of the revolutionary practices of the working class. Real knowledge is history from below. It is not merely a question of achieving a balanced view of the world, but of transformative knowledge imbued with an understanding of the dynamic of history – the history of humanity and the history of nature.

To understand the specificities of masculinist knowledge and the exclusion of women from it, and to understand the transformation of knowledge made possible by a feminist epistemology, it is therefore necessary to return to the particular nature of women's labour in the world and the division of labour between the genders. Both masculinist and feminist knowledge and epistemology derive from the sex-gender division of labour. Masculinist knowledge takes the form of a peculiar emphasis on the domains of cognitive and objective rationality, on reductive explanation, and on dichotomous partitioning of the social and natural worlds. It is this masculinist knowledge which has produced today's deadly culture of science and technology and which seeks to relegate women and women's knowledge to the realm of nature. By contrast, a feminist epistemology derives from women's lived experience, centred on the domains of inter-connectedness and affectual rationality. It emphasizes holism and harmonious relationships with nature, which is why feminism has links with that other major social movement of our time, ecology. Feminist knowledge transcends masculinist knowledge, just as materialism, as proletarian knowledge, transcends ruling class ideology. To understand feminist knowledge, a 'feminist science', we have to begin with women's work.

Labour's Pursuit of Time

Getting hold of the labour process of women's work – remembering that it exists as 'not men's' – gives us a way of looking at words like 'intuition', 'sensitivity', 'inter-relatedness' and all those other womanly words about which many of us have held complex and contradictory feelings. In order to do this, I have to speak of women's labour in a rather theoretical way; in actuality it is complicated by race, class, nationality, age, to say nothing of all those contingencies of personal biography.

Above all, if we consider the labour of women, we must begin by acknowledging that, although we are just over half humanity, we do much more than half the labour of the world. There is a depressing consistency in the international time-budget studies which have over the last decade or so mapped out the gross inequality between the hours worked by women and by men. While the double shift of paid and unpaid labour seems, at an everyday level, sufficient explanation as to why women were denied access to the time-demanding arena of public life, it does not explain how the ideological conjuring trick has been performed successfully for so long. The sheer effort of taking women's work, above all housework, out of nature and into culture[3] was paralleled by the effortless and near total erasure of women within the masculinist construction of culture. Thus, where the inter-war edition of the *International Encyclopaedia of the Social Sciences* devoted a substantial number of pages to women, the 1968 edition managed without a single reference.

Even now, two decades after Betty Friedan and the other pioneers of the Second Wave, we are faced with the contradiction that, while the history of the organized labour movement acknowledges the reduction of hours of work as one of its key objectives, and now increasingly sees it as the creative response to the restructuring of employment, the cruel hours of labour extracted from women are neglected by the state and the male-dominated labour movement alike. André Gorz, in one of the most imaginative socialist responses to a post-industrial capitalism, writes:

Nowhere is the line separating left and right clearer than on the question of time; the politics of time. According to whether it is a politics (and policy) of the right or the left, it may lead either to a society based on unemployment or to one based on free time. Of all the levers available to change the social order and the quality of life, this is one of the most powerful.[4]

This echoes Marx's point about the politics of time and class domination:

In a capitalist society, spare time is acquired for one class by converting the whole life time of the masses into labour time.[5]

Nonetheless because both Gorz and Marx naturalize women's labour, they cannot see the feminist antithesis:

In a patriarchal society, spare time is acquired for one gender by converting the whole life time of the women into labour time.

Indeed, with the recrudescence of market economics by Reaganomics and the retreat from the welfare state represented by Thatcherism, the state is intent on making sure that for the majority of women their time will not be their own.

The Labour of Love

It has been feminism, aided by the crisis in the welfare state, which has not only named and thus brought into visibility the distinctive labour of women, but has also insisted that we understand its double-sidedness both as labour and as love.[6] This combination of menial labour, often involving long hours, boring repetitive housework and very complex emotional work with children, husbands and dependent elderly people, has not been easy to unravel. It has been salutary to read Charlotte Perkin Gilman's classic *Women and Economics* (1898)[7] and note how slowly we have recaptured the clarity of her distinction between the real claims of mothering children and those of servicing men. It was right to insist that women's work be denaturalized, that it was integral to the division of labour and that it was socially and financially undervalued.

According to this ideology, where 'skill' is, women are not. The undervaluation of unpaid labour is of a piece with the under-valuation of women's employment. To use Elson and Pearson's[8] term, women are inferior bearers of labour and their presence in any significant way within an occupation signals that it is a low-status occupation, requiring only modest financial reward. It is still the case that a woman at home with very small children or an elderly relative replies 'No, I don't work; I'm only a housewife', or, at best, 'No, I don't work, I am at home still looking after my children/my elderly father/etc.' The lack of esteem in the domestic sphere is replicated by the lack of status in employment. Childcare work is ranked as lower in the socio-economic hierarchy of occupations than minding cars in a parking lot.

Skills which are acquired by women through practice within the home are both undervalued and systematically denied their social origins. This is so whether they are utilized in paid or unpaid labour. In the new electronics world factories, women's skill at microcircuitry and patience with repetitive tasks tend to be seen as biological attributes.[9] Within public caring labour the relational skills of women, even where acknowledged, as when it is said that a patient needs TLC (Tender Loving Care), still do not rate acknowledgement in terms of status or financial reward. In the domestic context women's nurturative qualities are simultaneously praised and seen as pre-scientific practices awaiting the emancipatory certainty of scientific knowledge.

Experiential knowledge is thus dismissed and trivialized, while an arrogant objectivizing science seeks to instruct women in its own practices. Not for nothing does the woman in the cartoon say, 'Well, if I get my instincts biologically I'm not having you tell me what to do!' The increasing tendency to make caring 'scientific' has eroded women's confidence, delegitimizing the knowledge they have gained individually and inter-generationally from the practice of caring.[10] This elitist conception of science, as knowledge handed down by experts, appoints itself to lead women into emancipation, for when it has succeeded in mapping a definition of mothering, it will be entirely possible for men to carry it out. As with other elitist theories, this one turns on the denigration and disempowering of those it purports to aid. For example, it refuses to understand the emotional complexity and particularity of child rearing; as Carol Gilligan[11] puts it, this 'intuitive ability' is not an innate faculty but one 'that comes only with a certain sort of training'.

Lacking the language to explore the tacit knowledge derived from caring, the practice and the knowledge are treated with even less social esteem than is accorded to the tacit knowledge of manual labour.

Women themselves discussing child rearing emphasize the accumulation of skill – the second baby is easier than the first. At the same time, each infant is unique and requires a special and highly flexible response. The problem for women has been how we share and develop collective knowledge when experiential knowledge has been dismissed as purely subjective. Studies of mothers consistently report that women's sense of self-confidence has been eroded by the medicalization of reproduction. Yet those areas of caring, where the direction is almost entirely in male hands and claims to be guided by the achievements of science, are precisely those where fad and fancy seem to have been most free. The sorry history of medicine, above all psychiatry and gynaecology, provides all too many examples of women as victims of such scientific fads and fancies.

There is evidence that the intervention of scientific 'experts' into areas of domestic work has actually harmed practice. Waerness[12] examined cookery books and showed how those inspired by the latest scientific nutritional thinking led to unsound advice, while the practical guides offered by woman cookery writers still had a good deal going for them. She makes a parallel argument for cooking to that made by Ehrenreich and English,[13] Versluysen[14] and Donnison[15] for the replacement of the female midwife by the – in reality more ignorant – male doctor. The knowledge born of practice was frequently more securely founded than the proposals from a fragile – and often arbitrary – science.

Discipline and Women's Labour

Doing women's work brings little recognition, but 'failure' to do it can cause criticism, anger, even violence on the part of an individual man. If that failure takes place around children, it may result in social care intervention for the mother, ranging from psycho-therapeutic support to psychosurgery, to the forcible removal of her children from her. Unpaid the labour of housewifery and childcare might be, but as a form of unfree labour it is carried out against a backdrop of extraordinarily powerful sanctions. Indeed, where marxists routinely speak of the capitalist state as acting beyond the interests of the individual capitalist and on behalf of the logic of capital, there is an equivalent analysis of the patriarchal state acting beyond the interests of the individual man and on behalf of a logic of patriarchy.

Discussions of women's labour often fail to reflect on the punishments inflicted on women for 'non-compliance'. Yet these often savage punishments (a beating for a burnt meal to murder for infidelity) police the boundaries of women's familial labour as surely as factory fines and overseer beatings police the labour of free labourers and slaves. Yet, unlike the latter, violence against women is routinely seen as rooted in biology, both his and hers, rather than as an integral aspect of the sex-gender division of labour. Its stubborn resistance to being moved out of nature and into culture speaks of the enormous task which remains for feminists and their allies. While it is true that housework and personal caring work are now much more widely seen as 'work' rather than as the natural expression of femininity itself, the savagery of the punishments for inadequate performance or labour refusal are so great that there is a tendency to think of men's violence as a problem of a different kind, to be considered in different terms than the sex-gender division of labour. These 'different terms' invoke a vague biologism, an unarticulated sense that it is natural for men to be violent to those who care for them. Yet the naturalism of the connection between violence and caring only holds when they are between men and women, and, being natural, may be deplored but impossible to oppose. It is only when we look at the juxtaposition of caring and violence in relationships between men, that explanations are sought in culture rather than in nature.

Liberal and radical white opinion learnt, for example, from the writings of the revolutionary and psychiatrist Frantz Fanon[16] about the extent of torture used by the French against the Algerians at the height of their struggle for national liberation. But such opinion also learnt how the colonized colluded and were meant to collude in their own oppression. Fanon describes how the French police officer, who worked as a torturer, sought psychiatric help from him so that the torturer could continue in his work without experiencing personal discomfort. While the reader understands the grotesque nature of the request, at no point is either the white colonialist or the colonized relegated to nature.

The possibility that something very similar goes on every day between men and women is a matter few wish to discuss. Men rely on the emotional support of women to sustain them, even in their violence. Even where individual men play no part in violence, at least at the interpersonal level, the active opposition is for the most part left to women. Thus even non-violent men benefit from the violence of others. The lack of resistance simultaneously denies the existence of violence and colludes with the naturalistic justification of violence. Men's violence is rendered natural and normal, so integral to being a man that it becomes difficult to connect it to other aspects of men's lives, let alone to place violence within a theory of knowledge.

The relationship of men and women to interpersonal violence is very different. Men may be violent to one another, to women and to children. Women are rarely violent to other adult people, whether women or men, but their relations with children and elderly dependent people can be violent. While not wishing to deny this violence, I would see it as stemming from the enforced nature of their caring work, as women are required by both individual men and by the expectations of the state to give care to dependents. Caring labour, above all unpaid caring labour, cannot be straight-forwardly equated with the forms of labour which concern things rather than people. Consequently, compulsory unpaid caring not only diminishes the freedom of the care giver, it also threatens the safety of the cared for. But these reflections on the specificities of the violence of women serve to highlight the contrast with the violence of men. Given that the potentiality of the modern state for collective violence is at an unparalled historic level, then it is more than time that we began to trace the connections between the everyday violence of men's culture and the inbuilt militarism of so much of modern science and technology.

At the very birth of modern science in the seventeenth century, Francis Bacon used rape as his central metaphor, to invoke the process whereby the scientist forced nature and wrested her secrets from her.[17] Except for a minority of scientists, Nature was seen as something separate from humanity, to be 'dominated' or 'exploited' – the possibility that a pacific relationship between humanity and nature could offer the central metaphor was a possibility that until the rise of ecology as both a subject and a social movement could not be seriously considered. Even today scientists use a language soaked in militaristic and aggressive sexual metaphor when they describe their laboratory practice.[18] The central and masculinist values of violence and domination are embedded within science; in science as elsewhere Virginia Woolf's observation illuminates: 'the values of men are different from the values of women . . . it is however the values of men that prevail.' Men's violence and women's caring are locked together, each integral to the ordering of patriarchal society.

Alienated and Non-Alienated Caring

It has been both a theoretical and an empirical problem that even where we tried to separate housework from peoplework, they continually merged. Caring, despite the best efforts of social work and psychotherapy, requires much more than the abstraction of words. We could feel the satisfaction of caring for someone, making someone content, finding all the little pieces of comfort that were important to that small child, that very elderly person – a mixture of words and silences, of favourite food and drink, of hard work in cleaning up a wet or dirty bed, of special ways of doing things. Often tiring but satisfying, you knew you had taken care of someone who needed you. All the senses were involved; the person looked good, felt good, sounded good, smelled sweet. Yet the pleasure did not just belong to the carer; it belonged also to the cared for. Was it all a con? Was this part of the emotionalization of housework? For in an entirely negative way emotion as integral to caring labour has become historically linked through the processes of mass consumption to a degrading emotionalization of housework. At its nadir in television advertisements women are invited to feel that love is super white shirts for their husband, their children. A woman's feminine identity as madonna/whore is beamed out as the sexually attractive, perennially young woman smelling, touching, looking at immaculate laundry. It is important to see that this emotionalized housework, even within industrialized countries, is a relatively new phenomenon associated with the emergence of middle-class houses without servants, together with the new access of working-class males to homes with the new luxury of housework.

But this does not mean that the pleasure of caring for someone is unreal, nor that it does not involve work. Rather, it means that we have to analyse the forms of caring labour. Under what conditions do women freely care and under what conditions is caring extracted from them? For caring, like other forms of labour, exists predominantly in its alienated form but also contains within itself glimpsed moments of an unalienated form. It is important with all forms of labour to insist that the experience of the unalienated form is located – however fleetingly – within the alienated, as otherwise we have no means of conceptualizing the future social relations and labour processes of a society which has overcome alienation. The analysis of caring labour thus offers us a means of understanding why work can on one occasion offer great satisfaction and on another be the site of tremendously hostile and painful feelings, in which the cared for person confronts the carer as a hostile object. The same analysis also speaks of the pleasure and satisfaction we find in the reciprocal care of feminism.

For an account of women's alienated labour it is hard to improve on the reflections of a woman journalist, Diana Eden,[19] writing about her elderly neighbour, Mollie:

> She is tiny, ancient and suffering from senile dementia. During
> the day she is adequately cared for by the social services. She

has a home help, Meals on Wheels and an ambulance takes her to a home for the elderly. But as night falls the social services disappear into the sunset. Darkness heralds most distressed and active hours. . . . She hammers on neighbours' doors, or more specifically on my door.

Now I like to think of myself as a well meaning *Guardian*-reading humanitarian and I am therefore interested to record the venom with which I receive Mollie's attention. Leading her whimpering, freezing frame back to her flat, changing her pee-soaked knickers, tucking her up in her desperate, shit-smelling bedroom overwhelms me with guilt and a fury that I resent having to feel.

Less visibly, at least because it is masked by the ideology of romantic love, husbands and grown sons extract caring labour from wives and mothers. Hartmann[20] estimates that for every grown man in her home a woman has to provide an additional seven hours labour a week. The problem is so deep that some women take care to carry out domestic labour when their husbands are not around, as, understanding the husband's sensitivity to the new demands of gender equality, they don't want him to feel guilty by seeing how much work actually has to be done. Another strategy is for the woman to accept the man's definition of what labour is necessary and what unnecessary, and to join him in prioritizing public labour.

In similar vein Kari Waerness,[21] beginning with a common understanding of caring as 'taking responsibility' and providing nurturance, makes a helpful distinction between three kinds of caring: the mutual caring reciprocally exchanged between equals; enforced caring extracted, above all, from the woman; and caring for dependents – by these she means those who by age or disability need help to care for themselves. She sees mutual caring as offering no problems, only pleasure. Her strongest strictures are directed towards enforced caring in which women are coerced into doing caring work for, typically, male others. Her third category of caring for ('natural') dependants she sees as necessary and hence acceptable labour.

It is above all, as Hilary Graham[22] puts it 'when labour outlasts love' that the recognition of caring as labour is inescapable. The accounts of women caring for husbands who have become totally dependent through accident, stroke and the like (a phenomenon aided by the age imbalance between husbands and wives) describe a world of unrelenting labour in which women, enchained by the social expectation of what the neighbours, health and professional workers think, but also by what they themselves feel as duty, cannot escape. Elizabeth Cady Stanton may have announced at Seneca Falls in 1848 that 'Women's self-development is a higher duty than self-sacrifice', but the ideology of self-sacrifice appears to be remarkably robust. Even if Carol Gilligan[23] is right and women are increasingly trying to balance the claims of personal self-development and the just claims of others, *unless* this balancing takes place in a context of resource – not least income – adequacy, then for many women it will fail, for, while Gilligan may be right for the educated and middle-class women, these choices and that balancing of claims are unlikely to be available for women additionally disadvantaged by class and race.

Alienated or unalienated, freely exchanged in reciprocal caring, given as a labour of love or enforced by an individual man or by the state, internalized by duty or the fear of gossip, women's caring labour is much more than the formation of feminine identity. As a profoundly sensuous activity, women's labour constitutes a material reality which structures a distinctive understanding of the social and natural worlds. Feminism has developed a strong sense of the potentiality of this new epistemology in offering a transformative knowledge of the social. Yet if it is to go beyond being a mere speciality within the social sciences, it has to claim the full strength of a feminist materialism which offers to overcome the old and oppressive dichotomy between the natural and the social.

The Search for Theory

While anger has fuelled the search for explanations of the unequal division of paid and unpaid labour in society, it has also meant that the search is not merely for explanatory but for transformative theory. This requirement means that what was to become a passionate debate, particularly in Britain, over the social origins of domestic labour, was evaluated not only for its own internal theoretical consistency but also as to how it measured up to experience. We remember wonderful aphorisms like Pat Mainardi's[24] 'His resistance is the measure of your oppression' as she analysed all the weird and wonderful ways men have of buckpassing domestic labour; and we know that any theory which shuts out the satirical joke born of experience, has to be reworked. Materialist theory began by locating the social origins of domestic labour in capitalist social relations. Women, argued Selma James and Maria Rosa Dalla Costa,[25] do housework because it benefits capitalism and therefore should be paid. The intense debate which surrounded this writing positively served to accelerate the theoretical struggle against the naturalization of women in both bourgeois and socialist politics. On the other hand, negatively, the theory understood domestic labour as a relationship between women and the capitalist system. The theory failed to grasp that women came into society as 'not-men'. It thus conceptually lost both men, and sex-gender relations, within its analysis. While to Marx's crucial question '*cui bono*'? this theory rightly replied that capital benefited from the unpaid labour of women, by dissolving men as a category it failed to see that men also benefited. But perhaps the most negative by-product was that the power of marxist language to define the problem threatened to erase women's experience. The anger and wit which had sharpened the earlier feminist critique gave way to increasingly Talmudic exchanges.[26] Compared with the exhilaration of the rediscovery of housework as work, these refinements to theory were often experienced and criticized, as an unwanted separation between the theoreticians and the activists. (Some famous cartoons bore witness to the conflict, not least the image of two women cleaners sweeping up polysyllabic words, complaining that if they – the theoreticians – had to clean up they wouldn't use all these long words.)

In response to this theoretical preoccupation with capitalism, Christine Delphy's[27] pamphlet *The Main Enemy* offered a newly dramatic and intensely debated position. Delphy focused on domestic labour in relationship to men, arguing that women's labour can only be understood in the context of two modes of production; she drew attention to what she termed the domestic mode of production in which men benefited from and controlled the labour of women. In this key paper Delphy spoke relatively little about the capitalist mode of production, seeming to take its existence as self-evident. It was for Heidi Hartmann[28] to provide the second half of the equation. Her initial work examined the allocation by sex of occupations within the labour market. She argued that it was within the capitalist mode of production that men were able to exclude and marginalize women, thus forcing them into relations of subordination within the factory and the home. Later,[29] when she examined housework, her position moved subtly, to one in which she saw the household as another locus of struggle.

Hartmann's dualism has been criticized from a number of perspectives. For example, it has been argued that it is not appropriate to speak of more than one mode of production. Yet, third-world studies clearly document the co-existence of different modes of production. A more serious difficulty is contained in Iris

Young's[30] criticism that by setting the problem up in this way the analysis of the sex-gender system becomes *auxiliary* – and subordinate – to the analysis of class relations. Were we to stay with Delphy's position, which restored gender to the centre of the debate, then the criticism has some validity in that it is difficult to see any transformative contradiction within Delphy's formulation of the domestic mode of production. By default, the dynamic of social change is left with the contradiction of classes within the capitalist mode of production; although Delphy makes the antagonistic relation between the genders very clear (stressing that she is totally opposed to any biologistic reductionism), nonetheless there is little sense of how feminists may deepen the contradictions so as to bring about the new society. Delphy thus offers a feminist functionalism which, despite its radical critique, has no theory – or vision – of change. Hartmann's version of dualism is less easily criticized this way. This is partly because there are certain flexibilities in her position; in the first paper she argues that the sex-gender system within a capitalist society is largely determined within the capitalist mode of production; in the second she locates the household as a vital terrain of struggle for both gender and class relations. She is among those who have emphasized the specific character of women's domestic work as embracing both the production and reproduction of human beings and, as such, being *fundamentally different* from labour directed towards the production of things.

The Trouble with Patriarchy

At the centre of the desire to move beyond dualism, which sees capitalism and patriarchy as relatively autonomous systems of domination, lies a deep unease with the concept of patriarchy. The most serious objection concerns its ahistoric character. The concept of patriarchy is seen as having a universal character claiming to suffuse all relations between human males and females. It is always 'History'; 'Herland', by implication, cannot come about. There is force in such criticisms, made most cogently by Sheila Rowbotham, Joan Smith and Iris Young.[31] Thus, Zillah Eisenstein is criticized for her use of the concept of patriarchy which she sees as 'universal in Western society', so that partriarchy 'changes historically, but universal qualities of it are maintained even if they are specifically redefined'. Throughout history men have retained their power by dominating the public realm and relegating women to the private. Hartmann, too, not only speaks of patriarchy as predating capitalism and persisting within it, but also refers to it as 'universal'. Not surprisingly, she is less than optimistic about the prospect of changes in the economic organization of society doing anything other than changing the forms through which sexual hierarchies are organized.

Insofar as the concept of patriarchy does embrace a sense of universality and timelessness, then Joan Smith justly points to the political danger that feminists unwittingly provide support for their clear enemy – sociobiology. The thesis of the 'Inevitability of Patriarchy' gains support if feminists themselves claim it is everywhere, all the time, but simply changing in form. Nonetheless, while there are strong political grounds for considering how we discuss patriarchy, losing the term would also be a political loss, for it has great polemical power. Its absence would invite us back to the earlier analysis in which the question of women's labour was seen as ultimately determined by the capitalist mode of production. Hence the relevance of Smith's[32] agenda for a non-dualist analysis:

> It is hardly anti-feminist to suggest that a woman, in her kitchen, who depends on her husband's wage, and thus his goodwill, is in a situation no less determined by the processes that compose the *world capitalist system* than is an unemployed male Black worker in Detroit, a female Black subsistence farmer in southern Africa, or a white male fully employed computer technician in Menlo Park. *The task is to discover the processes that create these divergent yet ultimately united patterns of labour relations.*
>
> [My emphases] (p. 105)

Smith has thus already discovered the answer to the problem as lying 'in the world capitalist system': the overarching theory has always been there. A materialist theory of knowledge should have anticipated the necessity of the feminist critique to the general critique of capitalism. According to Smith, marxism would have always been a feminist marxism. That it has not, indicates either that we are giving a new meaning to the term capitalism or that we need a new name to describe the new reality.

(Smith's critique of Hartmann's concept of patriarchy and the political danger of its universalism is fascinatingly echoed within Hartmann's piece in her critique of the concept of the family. Hartmann notes that the massive effort into family history which has produced a complex contradictory and diverse understanding in which 'the' family' disappears, at a political level the research interest in family history leads to a belief that there is such a thing as 'the family'. The Mounts of this world understand this very well, arguing that despite all intervention by external powers, 'the subversive family' waits to spring back into existence with all its 'natural' resilience. Given that Ferdinand Mount[33] was part of Mrs Thatcher's Think Tank, Hartmann's anxiety would seem, in the light of the British experience, to be well-founded. Indeed, political parties fall over themselves in their desire to claim that they are 'the party of the family'.)

There are also very substantial problems with an unqualified concept of capitalism. Although the concept was a relatively straightforward matter for Marx, writing as he did at the opening of the capitalist epoch and witnessing the slow unfolding of British capitalism around him, today we have a multiplicity of capitalisms. The Nordic countries are capitalist, but many would speak of them as welfare capitalist. Pinochet's Chile is capitalist – and fascist; Reagan's America and Thatcher's Britain are different from either. And so on. Capitalism as a concept needs grounding in concrete actuality every bit as much as patriarchy. Again, while there is a world capitalist system, there is also a massive state socialism, where the position of women – while not identical to that under capitalism – is not that far apart either.

To sum up the argument so far: first, the development of a pure patriarchal mode of production (Delphy's project) or a pure patriarchal mode of production/reproduction (Hartmann's) serves as an analogue to Marx's pure capitalist mode of production. Marx's abstraction was never intended to correspond even with his laboratory example of Britain, and neither would a pure feminist abstraction necessarily fit any specific historical context. The concept of patriarchy used in this way escapes the theoretical charge of being ahistoric. Nonetheless, we need to be aware of the persistent ingenuity of a dominant masculinist culture in systematically misreading our concepts for their purposes.

A feminist materialism is almost necessarily dualist, but this has the character of a stepping stone, linking the profound restructuring of the socio-economic organization of society and an impressive array of old and new social movements. Our theoretical inability to transcend dualism is, in a materialist analysis, connected to nothing less than our difficulty in actual practice at finding the alliances/new forms of political struggle between the old labour movement and the new social movements of ecology and feminism.

Towards a Feminist Epistemology

Hartsock's paper 'The Feminist Standpoint'[34] represents an un-
equivocal response to the critique of dualism. She uses Marx's
materialist theory of knowledge to grasp what she unflinchingly
speaks of as the 'sexual division of labour'. She is well aware of the
dangers of this strategy, but argues, following Sara Ruddick, that
some features of human life are 'invariant and nearly unchangeable'
while others are 'certainly changeable'. She points to the fact that
women bear children (still) as evidence of the former and that they
rear children as evidence of the latter. Her language represents a
very deliberate attempt 'to keep hold of the bodily aspect of
existence – perhaps to grasp it over-firmly to keep it from floating
away?'

Hartsock's approach carries with it the difficulty that although she
uses Marx's method against his own naturalistic thinking about the
division of labour within the family, the concept of sex pulls her
arguments too strongly back to nature. However, this is a small
point, easily met by the use of the cumbersome if precise notion of
the sex-gender division of labour. What is more exciting is
Hartsock's general approach to a distinctive feminist epistemology
arising from women's experience/activities/labour within the world.
While a main focus of her paper is the United States motherhood
literature, and particularly the work of Nancy Chodorow and Jane
Flax, she also discusses, rather more briefly, but helpfully, women's
unique labour and knowledge. Here she compares the knowledge
available to the (male) capitalist, the (male) proletariat, and to all
women regardless of class background.

> The focus on women's subsistence activities rather than men's
> leads to a model in which the capitalist (male) leads a life
> structured completely by commodity exchange and not at all
> by production, and at the furthest distinction from contact
> with material life. The male worker marks a way-station on the
> path to the other extreme of the constant contact with material
> necessity in women's contribution to subsistence. There are of
> course important differences along the lines of race and class.
> (p. 292)

She tellingly cites Marilyn French's[35] account of Mira reflecting on
the significance of cleaning the loo:

> Washing the toilet used by three males, and the floor and the
> walls round it, is, Mira thought, coming face to face with

necessity. And this is why women are saner than men, did not come up with mad absurd schemes men developed; they were in touch with necessity, they had to wash the toilet bowl and floor. (p. 214)

My own arguments (begun in *Hand, Brain and Heart*[36]) of how a feminist epistemology might be developed for the natural sciences, follow a parallel thread. And my similarly grounded story comes from listening to a radical male sociologist develop a social constructionist account of old age. I was sitting next to one of my feminist students who had a good deal of experience of working with elderly and acutely disabled people, and with other women who also cared for them. She was beside herself with anger: 'you can tell that he has never cleaned up a doubly incontinent old person.' Just so; such sensuous activity would have constrained his insane social constructionism.

Hartsock goes on to discuss women's other work, of the production/reproduction of men and other women.

The activity is far more complex than the instrumental working with others to transform objects. (p. 293)

I will not recapitulate Hartsock's review of the object-relations school of feminist psychoanalysis, although I would note in passing that the United States work is much more securely located in a biosocial perspective, whereas its British sister work, perhaps because of its more literary origins, is much less well integrated. From the differential experience of being mothered, the male infant has to become the boy and man – to learn to abandon the material reality of that early experience. 'Masculinity', she writes, 'must be attained by opposition to daily life, by escaping the female world of the household to the masculine world of public life.'

At this point in Hartsock's analysis she speaks of a distinctive male experience which 'replicates itself in both the hierarchical and dualistic institutions of a class society and in the frameworks of thought generated by this experience.' Here she merges the attack on Western culture and its oppressive dichotomies with her analysis of the male experience, where I would want to hold on to the distinction between manual and mental labour dividing men as a group. Thus, while it may be true that masculinity is closer to the culture of death, it is a particular stratum of men who advance that culture in ever more frightening technological forms. In *Hand, Brain and Heart* I was tracing the connections between the achievements of the radical science movement in struggling to bring about a unity of intellectual and manual labour on the one hand, and their consequent knowledges on the other. I argued that the specific nature of women's labour offers a distinct knowledge of both the social and the natural worlds; thus a transformative science must demand the unity of hand, brain and heart.

The deadly character of contemporary science is locked into its alienated and abstract form. Following Sohn Rethel,[37] I would accept that this abstraction arises from the division of labour between men into manual and intellectual. The Cultural Revolution in China was seen by Sohn Rethel, and indeed many or most of the New Left, as offering a vision of immense historical significance. They saw within it both the possibility of transcending hierarchical and antagonistic social relations, and also a means of creating a new science and technology, which would be neither about the domination of nature nor about the domination of humanity as part of nature. Especially today, when the experience of the Cultural Revolution is problematic to assess, it is important to affirm our need of the project it represented.

Male Lucas aerospace workers in Britain have in their practice come to very similar conclusions to Sohn Rethel. Beginning with their opposition to the threat of redundancy and a moral distaste for being so deeply involved in the manufacture of war technology, these workers went on to design, and in some cases make, what they spoke of as 'socially useful' technologies such as new kidney dialysis machines. In this they have simultaneously contested the division of mental and manual labour in the production of science and technology and, through the unity of 'hand' and 'brain', begun the long struggle to transform the 'commodity' itself.

The home-based kidney dialysis machine, enabling the community care of kidney patients whilst not depriving them of technological help, is a paradigmatic example of the partial progress offered by the unity of brain and hand. It takes for granted, and thus erases, the caring labour needed to enable the patient to use the kidney machine in the home context. It is not simply that research and everyday experience point overwhelmingly to unpaid personal care-giving being the responsibility of women, but that silence about the care-givers' task implies – once again – that care-giving requires no specially learnt skills and demands, only love, not labour. It is left for women to reflect that, while they may welcome the new technology in significantly improving the quality of life of someone they care for, it is they who, in a community care ideology whether of the left or right, will be required to pick up the burden of unpaid caring labour.

A Feminist Epistemology in, of and for the Sciences

By discussing the nature of women's labour I have tried to show how the exclusion both of women, and of women's knowledge, from the practice and cognitive domain of the sciences has come about, and have indicated some dimenions of the price of their exclusion.

A feminist epistemology derived from women's labour in the world must represent a more complete materialism and a truer knowledge. Such an epistemology transcends dichotomies, insists on the scientific validity of the subjective and the need to unite cognitive and affective domains; it emphasizes holism, harmony and complexity rather than reductionism, domination and linearity. In this it builds on traditions in the sciences which have always been present, though submerged within the dominant culture. It joins hands with the critique of actually existing science which has developed within the alternative movements.

Of course, as Elizabeth Fee[38] argues, a *fully* feminist science is not achievable until society itself has been transformed by the feminist project. And yet this pessimism is not exactly justified, because it is always possible to point to other discourses within the sciences which, even if unable to overwhelm the hegemonic discourse, nonetheless continue to offer alternative knowledges. The same circumstances that brought the Second Wave of feminism into history offer feminism the possibility of developing its own here-and-now prefigurative forms and knowledges. The struggle around our own bodies – who is to know about bodies, and who is to control them – are of a piece with the concern about the natural environment. The character of the late-twentieth-century crisis is both social and natural. This crisis has called into being both feminism and its sister the ecology movement, whose agenda in many ways parallels that of feminism, and whose struggles, together with those of feminism, touch the lives of men as well as women. The recognition of the contrast between the ecology movement and masculine science underlies, as a constant theme, the pages of Carolyn Merchant's *The Death of Nature* and Susan Griffiths's *The Roaring Inside Her*.

This paper shares with a number of feminist theoreticians[39] the claim that a feminist materialism offers a 'successor science'. It has better truth claims and as such is capable of generating the transformative knowledge which will enable us to bring about new social relations between human beings and a new relation-ship between humanity and nature. The paper argues that this transformative knowledge stems from our increasingly conscious understanding of women's labour in the world. In similar vein Sandra Harding[40] suggests that the possibility of a successor science arises with the development of historically 'new people'. These derive from 'the conflict between the forms of producing persons (gendered persons) and the resistance by increasing numbers of women and by some men to living out mutilated lives within such sexual politics'. She looks to 'persons whose activities are characteristically womanly and yet who also take on masculine projects in public life' as key producers of the new knowledge.

In a recent paper Harding speaks of the tension between those feminists engaged in the successor science projects and those engaged in the generation of post-modern epistemology. In, for example, the later writings of Jane Flax, and recently in Evelyn Keller's[41] new book, the post-modernist programme is most fully elaborated. Sceptical of the successor science project as merely seeking to develop an alternative hegemony, the post-modernists see the enemy as hegemony itself. Instead of an alternative hegemony, they seek a plurality of discourses in which the very construction of gender is at issue. This view thus offers the most radical alternative to the existing hegemonic construction of epistemology, since it does so by leaving to one side the issue of the political power of a masculinist science. Yet this particular issue cannot be ignored, and the project of the successor science remains critical for feminism's political struggle to transform the sex-gender system. 'What else' writes Harding[42] 'could serve as the epistemological tools for this struggle?'. Yet she moves on to propose that feminism needs both these feminist epistemologies, that it would be intellectually and politically a mistake to seek the domination of either in isolation. It is a measure of the strength and self-confidence of feminist theorizing that feminism no longer feels compelled to accept either/or dichotomies, that we acknowledge the non-linearity of feminist theory and that we draw on metaphors of spinning and quilt-making to serve as images of the distinctive and collective nature of our work. Lastly, a feminist epistemology is grounded in struggle, as Donna Harraway[43] writes:

> A socialist-feminist science will have to be developed in the process of constructing different lives in interaction with the world. Only material struggle can end the logic of domina-tion. . . . I do not know what life science would be like if the historical structure of our lives minimised domination. I do know that the history of biology convinces me that the basic

knowledge would reflect and reproduce the new world, just as it has participated in maintaining our old one.

Notes

1 Nancy Hartsock, 'The Feminist Standpoint', in S. Harding and M. B. Hintikka (eds), *Discovering Reality: Feminist Perspectives in Epistemology, Metaphysics, Methodology and the Philosophy of Science* (Reidel, Dordrecht, 1983).
2 Mao Tse Tung, *Five Philosophical Theses* (Beijing Foreign Languages Pub. House, Beijing 1975).
3 A selection of feminist writings which reclaimed women's labour for history must include: Betty Friedan, *The Feminine Mystique* (W. W. Norton & Co., New York, 1963); Hannah Gavron, *The Captive Wife* (Penguin, Harmondsworth 1966); Ann Oakley, *The Sociology of Housework* (Martin Robertson, London 1974); Lee Comer, *Wedlocked Women* (Feminist Books, London 1974).
4 Andre Gorz, *Farewell to the Working Class* (Pluto Press, London 1982).
5 I want to make it clear that I use marxism in this paper as a philosophical metatheory; marxist categories are sexblind and cannot be simply transferred to become feminist tools of enquiry.
6 Janet Finch and Dulcie Groves (eds.) *A Labour of Love: Women, Work and Caring* (Routledge & Kegan Paul, London 1983).
7 Charlotte Perkins Gilman, *Woman and Economics* 1898.
8 Diane Elson and Ruth Pearson, 'Nimble Fingers make Cheap Workers: An Analysis of World Export Manufacture', *Feminist Review*, No 7, Spring 1981.
9 Hilary Rose, 'Women and the Restructuring of the Welfare State' in E. Oyen, *The Future of the Welfare State* (Gower, London 1986).
10 Barbara Ehrenreich and Deirdre English, *For Her Own Good: 150 years of the Experts' Advice to Women* (Anchor/Doubleday, New York, 1979).
11 Carol Gilligan, *In a Different Voice: Psychological Theory and Women's Development* (Harvard University Press, Cambridge 1982).
12 Kari Waerness, 'On the Rationality of Caring', in H. Holter (ed.), *Patriarchy in a Welfare Society* (University of Bergen Press, Bergen, 1984).
13 Ehrenreich and English, *For Her Own Good*.
14 Margaret Versluysen, 'Old Wives' Tales: Women Healers in English History' in C. Davies (ed.), *Rewriting Nursing History* (Croom Helm, London 1980).
15 Jean Donnison, *Midwives and Medical Men* (Heinemann, London 1977).
16 Frantz Fanon, *The Wretched of the Earth* (McGibbon & Kee, London 1965).
17 Carolyn Merchant, *The Death of Nature: Women, Ecology and the Scientific Revolution* (Harper & Row, New York, 1980).
18 Evelyn Keller, *Reflections on Gender and Science* (Yale University Press, New Haven 1985).

19 Quoted in Hilary Land and Hilary Rose, 'Compulsory Altruism for Some or an Altruistic Society for All' in P. Bean et al., *In Defence of Welfare* (Tavistock, London 1985).
20 Heidi Hartmann, 'The Family as the Locus of Gender, Class and Political Struggle', *Signs: an International Journal of Women in Culture and Society*, Vol 6, 3, Spring 1981.
21 Kari Waerness, 'On the Rationality of Caring'.
22 Hilary Graham, 'The Labour of Love' in Finch and Groves, *A Labour of Love*.
23 Carol Gilligan, *In a Different Voice*.
24 Pat Mainardi, 'The Politics of Housework' in L. Tanner (ed.), *Voices of Women's Liberation*, No. 7, New American Library.
25 Selma James and Maria Rosa dalla Costa, *The Power of Women and the Subversion of Community* (Falling Wall Press, Bristol 1973).
26 Each has their own nadir; mine was Paul Smith, 'Domestic Labour and Marx's Theory of Value', in A. Kuhn and A. M. Wolpe (eds.) *Feminism and Materialism* (Routledge & Kegan Paul, London 1978), which restated pretty much the classical marxist position.
27 Christine Delphy, *The Main Enemy* (Women's Research & Resource Centre, London).
28 Heidi Hartman, 'Capitalism, Patriarchy and Job Separation by Fix' in Z. Eisenstein (ed.), *Capitalist Patriarchy and The Case for Socialist Feminism* (Monthly Review Press, New York, 1979).
29 Heidi Hartman, 'The Family as the Locus of Gender, Class & Political Struggle', *Signs*, Vol 6, 3, Spring 1981.
30 Iris Young, 'Beyond the Unhappy Marriage: A Critique of the Dual Systems Theory' in L. Sargent (ed.), *Women & Revolution* (South End Press, Boston 1981).
31 Sheila Rowbotham, 'The Trouble with Patriarchy' in S. Rowbotham (ed.), *Dreams and Desires* (Virago, London 1983); Joan Smith, 'Feminist Analysis of Gender: a Critique' in M. Lowe and R. Hubbard (eds.), *Women's Nature: Rationalizations of Inequality*, (Athene Pergamon, New York 1983).
32 Ibid., 105.
33 Ferdinand Mount, *The Subversive Family: An Alternative History of Love and Marriage* (Jonathan Cape, London, 1982).
34 Nancy Hartsock, 'The Feminist Standpoint'.
35 Marilyn French, *The Women's Room* (André Deutsch, London 1978), 214.
36 Hilary Rose, 'Hand, Brain & Heart: Towards a Feminist Epistemology the Natural Sciences', *Signs: an International Journal of Women in Culture and Society*, Vol 9, 11 (1983).
37 Alfred Sohn Rethel, *Intellectual and Manual Labour: a Critique of Epistemology* (Macmillan, London 1978).
38 Elizabeth Fee, 'Women's Nature and Scientific Objectivity' in R. Hubbard and M. Lowe (eds.), *Rationalizations of Inequality* (Pergamon, Oxford 1983).
39 In addition to the feminists I have already discussed, I would add the materialist psychologists: Nancy Chordorow, *The Reproduction of Mothering* (University of California, Berkeley 1978); Jane Flax, 'The

Patriarchal Unconscious' in Harding and Hintikka (eds.), *Discovering Reality* (1983); Sara Ruddick, 'Maternal Thinking', *Feminist Studies*, Vol, 6, 2, Summer 1980; Dorothy Smith, 'Women's Perspective as a Radical Critique of Sociology', *Sociological Enquiry*, Vol 44 (1974).

40 Sandra Harding, *The Contradictions and Ambivalences of a Feminist Science*, Philosophy Dept., University of Delaware, 1984 (mimeo).

41 Evelyn Keller, *Reflections on Gender and Science.*

42 Sandra Harding, *Contradictions and Ambivalences of Feminist Science.*

43 Donna Harraway, 'The Biological Enterprise: Sex, Mind and Profit from Human Engineering to Sociobiology' in *Radical History Review*, Vol 20, Spring/Summer 1979, 232.

11   Feminist Visions of Health: an International Perspective

Sheryl Ruzek

Introduction and Background

Over the past 15 years feminists in North America, Europe, and increasingly other parts of the world have directed attention to the quality and quantity of health services available to women, the social control aspects of medicine, and the need for women to assert control over their own bodies and reproductive potential. Women have organized and taken political action, and established alternative services to improve women's health and create a more caring, humane approach to providing health and medical care services.

Feminists do not always agree on definitions of feminism, nor on the most salient problems facing women nor strategies to remedy them. Feminism, in the broadest sense, can be defined as a world view which places women at the centre of analysis and social action. It involves an ideological commitment to fostering the well-being of women both as individuals and as a social group in all spheres of life. But what does this really mean? How shared is the interpretation of the practical implementation of such a commitment? In western industrialized countries, those who view themselves primarily as liberal feminists, radical feminists, and socialist feminists assign quite different meanings and actions to this commitment. Thus, liberal feminists see feminism as a social movement designed to ensure for women 'equal opportunites' in both public and private spheres, and concern themselves with many issues of the safety and efficacy of medical care for women. Radical feminists see the movement as involving more fundamental reordering of both public and private spheres and question many aspects of conventional medical care including the appropriateness of medical professionals providing much of routine care to women. Radical feminists often support the creation of alternative services by and for women which emphasize self-help and minimize professional distinctions. Socialist feminists seek to raise awareness of how the dynamics of industrial capitalism make securing women's health problematic. They also emphasize working to eliminate or at least minimize the consequences of the social class system by extending the benefits of the welfare state to all women. All feminists involved in health activism are concerned with the quality of care and women's experience of health. Questions about how to set priorities for intervention, and what action to take, generate considerable debate. Disagreement over definitions of problems, goals, priorities and strategies is to be expected in any broad-based social movement which attempts to act on behalf of the interests of diverse groups and individuals. Some of the most difficult issues feminists face internally are the inequities which stem from race and class stratification and individual differences in perception of health needs. Externally, the women's health movement faces considerable opposition from organized medicine and other interest groups.

In this chapter I describe some of the historical circumstances and social conditions which have fostered and impeded feminist criticism, analysis and action for health in recent years. I present the values and philosophies underlying common feminist strategies to improve women's health and health care, and note how the dynamics of race, social class, and the political economy of industrialized health care systems make such changes problematic.

Health Issues Concerning Women

While feminists readily agree that the health care systems of most western industrialized countries are unresponsive to the needs of both men and women, they find health care systems particularly problematic for women. In many western countries the organization of health care systems emphasizes women's reproductive roles. In the United States, women are encouraged to use obstetrician-gynaecologists (surgical specialists) as their primary-care physicians. From puberty until well past menopause, many women see no other type of physician regularly. Thus analysis of women's relationships with obstetrician-gynaecologists in the United States has reflected women's use pattern and perception of this experience as shared with other women. The centrality of reproductive rights in the larger contemporary feminist movement has also been a key factor in the shaping of the women's health movement, first in the United States and later in Canada and Europe.

With the resurgence of feminism in the United States in the late 1960s and early 1970s, women rebelled at the control men had over women's bodies and reproductive functions. Doctors, health policy-makers, and bio-medical researchers as well as lawmakers, predominantly male, were viewed as acting in men's rather than women's 'best interests'. Attempts to gain equal rights in education, politics, employment and the family were recognized as impossible unless women could control their reproductive capacity. Arguing for women's right to both contraception and abortion, many feminists assumed that, if women were freed from bearing and rearing unwanted children, the traditional role expectations that subordinate them might lose their strength. Women might then choose not to have children, or not to marry, or they might choose to experience and express their sexuality in ways which are not culturally approved.

The abortion issue was and remains controversial. It is a powerful issue for feminists, because women are socialized to value mother-hood, yet at the same time motherhood oppresses women and limits life chances in the wider society. In virtually every country where there is feminist activity, reproductive control is a central issue and has proven to be a rallying point for educational programmes, alternative services, lobbying, and sometimes underground or illegal provision of abortion. Without this core of reproductive rights and reproductive health issues, there would not be an international women's health movement.

In recent years older health activists have become concerned that young women – women who came of age sexually after the legalization of abortion in most western industrialized countries – fail to understand the critical importance of the availability of abortion to women's well-being. Because they have not experienced the fear of unwanted pregnancy without the possibility of recourse to abortion as a backup to contraceptive failure or sexual risk-taking, younger women are less motivated to work to maintain abortion rights or provide access to abortion services. Abortion is not simply a neutral 'medical service', but one which is or is not available depending on historical political circumstances. Therefore, ensuring every woman's right to abortion (whether she chooses to have one or not) is a central tenet of contemporary western feminism.

Reproductive rights are not the only feminist health issue, however. The safety and efficacy of treatments and the social control aspects of medicine are also central concerns. Over the past fifteen

years, women have learned that, despite physicians' claims about the
safety of oral contraceptives, there is alarming evidence of serious
side effects (Seaman 1980). Diethylstilbestrol (DES) was recognized
as the cause of a rare form of vaginal cancer in young girls, yet
continued to be prescribed as a 'morning after' pill on college
campuses (Seaman and Seaman 1977). Standard hospital childbirth
practices seemed organized more for the convenience of doctors than
for the health and well-being of mothers and babies (Wertz and
Wertz 1977; Rothman 1982; Boston Women's Health Book Collective
1976). Unnecessary hysterectomies were sometimes performed for
profit or to give doctors in training surgical experience (Corea 1977;
Bunker 1970; Lembcke 1956; Scully 1980). Poor women were
sometimes sterilized against their will, or without their informed
consent, because of personal biases of physicians and social policies
reflecting race and class discrimination (Clarke 1984; Petchesky
1979). Even fairly sophisticated critics of the health care system in
the United States were shocked to learn that intra-uterine devices
(IUDs), touted as extremely safe and effective, were never tested by
the Food and Drug Administration (FDA) or any federal regulatory
body before being marketed. The brewing controversy over the
efficacy of radical mastectomy as compared to less mutilating modes
of treatment came to light, and women in the United States could
not understand why physicians remained so attached to this
disfiguring treatment compared to physicians in some European
countries. Ironically, the liberalization of the abortion laws in the
United States, coupled with the rise in demand, subjected women to
some of the most exploitative medical experiences imaginable. In
New York, for example, in 1971 a woman could pay $75 for a first-
trimester abortion at a non-profit clinic or up to $1,500 for the same
service if she fell prey to a profiteering referral service (Ruzek
1978).

Whilst many of these 'facts' about American medicine existed in
the medical and social science literature, it was only with the advent
of a social movement that this information came to be widely
dissseminated. The women's health movement quickly grew into a
separate social movement, largely because of the pre-existing
communication networks in the general feminist movement.
Feminist newspapers, journals and bookstores all served key roles in
letting women know about health issues and organizing them for
action. Over time, there emerged publications and organizations
focussing almost exclusively on health issues, first in North America
and later in Europe.

Feminist Visions of Health

Feminist health activists organized to educate themselves and other women about health issues, provide alternative services, and work to influence public policies affecting women's health. These activities reflect (1) a commitment to self-determination in seeking health and health care, (2) an emphasis on the caring and sharing aspects of health rather than the deployment of technologies alone, (3) a recognition of the multiple definitions and political nature of assessments of 'quality of care', and (4) a concern that medical services be both accessible and affordable in relation to women's actual economic position. After considering these central themes I will go on to explore some strategies for implementing change in different types of health care systems.

Self-Determination in Seeking Health Care

Abortion has already been discussed as an inalienable feminist right to ensure women's self-determination in their medical care more generally. The key to this is shifting the social distribution of medical knowledge (anatomy, physiology, medical procedures, use of simple technologies, treatments) from being the exclusive property of certain health professionals to being the shared property of patients and a widening array of non-physician health providers. This shifting of knowledge includes the right of women to make crucial decisions about where and under what conditions they will give birth, to be involved in decision-making about treatment approaches even for serious diseases such as breast cancer, and to be fully informed about the risks and benefits of all diagnostic and treatment procedures.

Women's control over medical care is increasingly resisted in medical and legal arenas. The grounds for resistance are that women's demands interfere with the rights of others – particularly the right of the unborn child not to be aborted or to receive what are considered to be 'standard medical services' in a hospital during birth. Some conflicts over women's right to self-determination are bitter because they refute the cultural myths that all women want to be mothers or that the interests of mothers and babies are the same. Other conflicts over self-determination raise difficult questions about the responsibility of physicians to provide whatever is considered the 'standard of care' in their communities. In the United States, large medical malpractice lawsuits have made it increasingly

difficult for women to refuse diagnostic and intervention technologies, because physicians believe that they need to have records
of having performed these procedures to protect themselves against a
potential malpractice lawsuit.

Caring and Sharing

Sharing, caring and nurturing characterize women's roles in relation
to others in the family and in women's professional health work –
prototypically nursing and midwifery. These forms of caring and
sharing are seen as inappropriately undervalued in the larger society.
Alternative services are organized to elevate these elements of
medical care to a central place in service delivery. To do this,
however, requires a significant reorientation of health care providers
which has been attempted in feminist self-help groups and clinics.
Although it is often difficult to achieve the ideals set forth by
feminists for caring and sharing, the humanistic philosophy em-
bodied in the ideal contrasts starkly with the approach of conventional western industrialized medicine. The latter is organized
around a narrow bio-medical model in which professionals deliver
medical technologies and lay people are passive receivers.

Feminists involved in clinics conceptualize routine health care as
an ongoing process and seek to minimize distinctions between
providers and receivers of care, experts and lay persons. Group
discussion and care is encouraged in order to give women opportunities to share common health concerns with peers as well as
experts. In group sessions, women have time to think of questions
and relay important diagnostic information, information which is
often lost in hurried three- to five-minute individual medical
consultations – the norm in most highly industrialized medical care
systems. The advantages and disadvantages of contraceptive
methods, childbirth procedures, and treatments for menopausal
symptoms or routine gynaecological disorders can be explained more
thoroughly in a group than individually, and groups offer social-
psychological peer support simply unavailable in the one-to-one
doctor-patient relationship. Physicians, nurses, and other providers
who attempt to work within this model find that they learn a great
deal about how women actually experience health events, drugs, and
devices. This knowledge is unavailable to health professionals
practicing in conventional settings (Ruzek, 1977). There are, of
course, limits to the circumstances under which this new form of
practice is feasible, given the organizational structure of the delivery
of services. While in both North America and Europe there is a

cultural belief that individual 'private' care is superior to group care (which was historically reserved for disadvantaged groups), this belief can be modified, as it has been in the shift from exclusively individual to family and group psychotherapy.

But not all health care is provided by paid providers. Even in countries which have widely accessible medical services, most health care-giving is provided informally in the home and in communities, by women. With women's increasing participation in the paid labour force, the caring and nurturing women traditionally provide in the home are seen as constituting part of the 'double burden' of work women bear in industrialized societies. As self-help, self-care, and social support are increasingly recognized as valuable to the maintenance of health, feminists are concerned that these aspects of the traditional female role will be expected of them either without compensation in the home, or in the form of low-paid para-professional work in the formal health care system. Thus, sharing and caring carry with them the possibility of more humanistic approaches to health care, but also the possibility of women's strengths being used against them.

Quality of Care

Disillusionment with the quality of western medical care involves both the evaluation of the efficacy and risks of many technical diagnostic and therapeutic procedures, and the social and psychological aspects of medical care. Thus, quality of health care involves integrating both 'objective' criteria of safety and efficacy and 'subjective' experiences of medical care.

Western medicine tends to focus on the efficacy of treatment in rational, objective terms such as 'reduction in mortality' or 'reduction in hospital days' and ignores the process and experience of health care. While 'outcome' criteria are appropriate measures for some health problems, they are neither as concrete nor as indicative of 'quality of care' as they seem at first glance. The quality of care and quality of life issues in human, subjective terms, are also more difficult to measure. They do not fit the bio-medical model on which the practice of contemporary medicine is built. In the bio-medical model the patient's own experience of physical, social and psychological disequilibrium receives relatively little attention and is often discounted unless it can be shown to be 'objectively measurable', or simply an obstacle to the receipt of medical care in the first place.

Thus, for example, women's complaints about side-effects of oral contraceptives and IUDs were discounted by most professionals until 'objective' scientific evidence confirmed that they pose serious hazards including death (Seaman 1980; Seaman and Seaman 1977). Women's concerns about overmedicated labour and delivery and separation from their infants after birth were at first largely ignored. Consumer groups' pressure for alternative childbirth approaches came at a time when the birth rate was dropping and hospitals had to compete vigorously to fill their beds to keep up revenues. Thus, some changes were made, but under the rubric of advances in 'scientific knowledge'. Thus more 'natural births' were defined as facilitating mother-infant 'bonding' which could be measured using quantifiable psycho-social indices (Wertz and Wertz 1977; Rothman 1982; De Vries 1985).

Medical historian Stanley Joel Reiser points out that today physicians face such an array of elaborate technology to provide them with 'objective' evidence that they have lost faith in their clinical judgement. Physicians are thus forced into a self-perpetuating and escalating cycle of reliance on diagnostic tests and machines which they themselves do not fully understand, and which often have little utility for guiding clinical decisions (Reiser 1978). Reliance on tests reduces the time practitioners feel they need to spend listening to the patient or making diagnoses. This reliance on tests also reinforces an emphasis on rare medical events and downplays the reality that most medical visits involve rather routine problems easily manageable by less highly specialized practitioners. This creates yet another layer of mystification to reinforce the power and control of physicians, and makes it even more difficult for women themselves to make decisions about their care. How can a woman 'question' a 'scientific' test? How can women maintain confidence in their own judgements about their health?

The 'quality' issue is compounded by the trend in highly industrialized countries to present 'the latest and newest' in diagnostic and therapeutic medical technologies as 'the best'. Societies or health care systems which cannot, or choose not to, provide 'the latest' in medical technologies are often viewed as failing to provide women with 'the best'. Socialized health systems such as the British National Health Service and pre-paid health plans such as Kaiser Foundation Health Plan in the United States are often suspected of failing to 'keep up' and of being stingy. But we must ask if 'the latest' or the most expensive is, indeed, the 'best', considering the record of safety, efficacy, and social consequences of medical inventions.

For women, the potential for suffering the iatrogenic effects of medical drugs, devices, and practices is heightened by the fact that women's biological life-events – menstruation, conception, pregnancy and childbirth, lactation, and menopause – are all medically managed in industrialized societies. Over the life-cycle, women are more often exposed to medical intervention than are men and thus more at risk of suffering iatrogenic effects. In addition to the medical hazards already noted, new childbirth technologies such as electronic fetal monitoring are associated with increased maternal morbidity and mortality and infant morbidity (Banta and Thacker 1979). DES (diethylstilbestrol) given to prevent miscarriage caused vaginal cancer in some exposed females' children and is now suspected of causing sterility in exposed males, and breast cancer in the mothers who took the drug. Estrogen replacement therapy, widely used to alleviate menopausal symptoms, is suspected of increasing the risk of breast and uterine cancer (Seaman and Seaman 1977).

The list of hazards goes on and on. This is not simply an isolated series of unfortunate events but the predictable outcome of laissez-faire medical technology development. Historically, a large proportion of medical technologies ushered in with enthusiasm are shown eventually to be ineffective or even harmful. Furthermore, scientific testing of new technologies is rarely if ever undertaken after a technology is widely disseminated (Reiser 1978; McKinlay 1981). Given the probability that any new technology will eventually be shown to be less safe and less effective than claimed at the outset, and given the fact that the greatest advances in health status are less likely to come from medical interventions than improvements in living and working conditions (McKeown 1979; Cochrane 1971), medical technologies should be used more cautiously and appropriately. Ultimately, the state must take an active role to reorder health care priorites and women must plan a central role in reshaping these priorities to ensure that 'quality' as defined by women in varying life circumstances is taken into account.

Cost of Care

Ideally medical care should be available to women at no cost or at a cost they can afford, given the reality of their economic status in society. The cost of medical care has been a more salient issue in the United States than in Canada or Europe where routine care, including childbirth and gynaecological examinations, are provided either by a national health service or within a near-universal health insurance coverage. In 1981 in the United States, the median income for full-time year-round women workers was $12,000. Many women are the sole support of their families. Close to six million families are maintained by women in the United States (Department of Labor 1983). Women are frequently left without any medical insurance whatsoever. When they become divorced or widowed they usually lose the right to coverage under their husbands' employer-provided policy. Women also lose coverage when they lose their own jobs which provided medical insurance. The National Citizen's Board of Inquiry into Health in America estimated that in 1984, over 33 million Americans were without any medical insurance. Eligibility for public state-paid coverage has been tightened over the past five years to the point that a woman must be nearly destitute (have virtually no savings or property) to receive coverage (The National Citizens' Board of Inquiry into Health in America 1984).

While, theoretically, individuals may purchase individual fee-for-service health insurance coverage from companies such as Blue Cross, or group pre-paid health maintenance plans such as the Kaiser Foundation Health Plan, a woman must pass a screening examination. Women are rejected when they have medical histories of hypertension, back problems, obesity, or cancer. In short, women with health problems who need coverage the most are least likely to be able to purchase it. In addition, premiums are costly. In 1985, an individual Blue Cross plan which pays 80% of covered charges cost $62.00 per month – nearly 6½% of the average working woman's monthly income. The Kaiser Plan, a capitation plan which provides most services for under $5.00 per visit, is more affordable at $57.65 per month, but still costs 6% of a woman's average monthly income.

The lack of insurance coverage and 20% co-payment required by plans such as Blue Cross (either individual or employer provided) means that American women pay a substantial proportion of their personal income for medical services. The dollar amounts can be staggering. For example, in the San Francisco Bay area in 1985, typical charges for routine obstetrical and gynaecological services are shown in Table 1.

Not surprisingly, American families view universal medical care coverage as a basic need. Nonetheless until recently there was little organized advocacy for this. This may reflect in part women's unwillingness to seek 'medical coverage' for what many prefer to define as non-medical life events. It also reflects the class base of the American women's health movement – middle-class white women whose concerns are more often 'quality' than access to services. Economically disadvantaged women for whom access to services is a major concern have not had the time or resources to devote to health activism. The alternative services provided by some groups to low

*Table 1 Typical Costs of Health Care in San Francisco Bay Area,
April 1985*[a]

Routine Gynaecological Appointment (including laboratory fee for Papanicolaou test) mode $95 range $77 – $111	*Cesarean Section without Complications* Physicians Obstetrician mode $1,800 range $1,800 – $2,100 Assistant Surgeon (mandatory) mode $360 range $360 – $525 Total (Obstetrician plus Assistant Surgeon) mode $2,160 range $2,160 – $2,625
Routine First Trimester Abortion mode $190 range $175 – $225	
Normal Childbirth Physician's fee mode $1,500 range $1,200 – $2,500 Hospital fee (for a two-day stay) mode $2,500 range $2,154 – $2,500 Total (Physician plus hospital fees) mode $4,000 range $3,354 – $4,075	Hospital mode $5,000 range $4,000 – $5,000 Total (Physician plus hospital fees) mode $7,160 range $6,160 – $7,625

[a] Telephone survey conducted by Theresa Montini, 4 April 1985.

income women have simply served as stop-gaps to the larger problems of access and equity.

In Canada and Europe where cost is less often a major deterrent to women's access to care, the emergence of alternative services has proceeded quite differently. In Canada, the near universal coverage for fee-for-service reimbursement allowed an organization such as the Vancouver Women's Health Collective to collect standard fees billed by volunteer physicians (Kleiber 1978). In the United Kingdom, feminists have been deterred from establishing alternative services by the example of, and need to support, the National Health Service.

It seems likely that the high cost of medical services in the United States has been a major factor accounting for the strength of the women's health movement there. When one is forced to pay a large proportion of one's income for services which are humiliating, hazardous, and ineffective, resentment is certain to exist. With the availability of a broad based social movement to interpret and channel this discontent, a separate social movement focusing on health could develop fully. Over time, certain features of this movement spread throughout other countries as part of a larger feminist movement.

Strategies for Change

Feminist health activists engage in a wide array of activities which reflect their desire to enhance women's self-determination, promote caring and sharing, improve the quality of medical care, and make medical care more accessible and affordable. They hope that such strategies will alter the quality, quantity, content, and control of medical services on the societal level, institutional level, and in face-to-face interaction with professionals. Activists view all changes at all levels as necessary and interrelated, for what a woman actually experiences in seeking health care is the result of a complex interaction of interlocking values, beliefs, practices and institutional arrangements. How well these mesh with a woman's own identity, and cultural and personal preferences is significantly affected by her race, ethnicity, age, and socioeconomic status. What 'women' want often should be delineated to specify what women in certain life circumstances want. Feminists have gradually come to see the salience of race and class, but only slowly and with some difficulty.

Many health activists believe that it is virtually impossible to create a truly humane health care system for women in a capitalist society. Yet none of the strategies used directly attack the underlying economic organization of society. For example, major efforts are directed toward removing control of obstetrics and gynaecology from male professional dominance and making professionals accountable to consumers, women. This is an example of a strategy many would regard as 'reformist' in that it is designed to persuade or force physicians, hospitals, politicians, the drug industry, and regulatory agencies that it is 'good business' to promote self-determination, freedom of choice, and appropriate definitions of quality care. The major ways in which feminists work to promote women's health include (1) creating new knowledge and educating women, (2) providing alternative services, and (3) influencing public policy.

Creating New Knowledge and Educating Women

Consciousness raising and education on women's health issues is by far the most common feminist strategy for improving women's health. Health activists believe that it is crucial for women to come together and share their personal experiences of health and illness. Unlike conventional health education programs, feminist self-help health groups promote the view that the personal is political by giving women opportunities to discover that many of their experiences are shared by other women. These groups also incorporate a political analysis, pointing out the ways in which interest groups ranging from medical specialities to drug companies cannot be relied upon to act in the best interests of women.

Over time, self-help groups have become more structured and more focused around specific topics. The length and comprehensiveness of groups vary considerably. Some are one day or less; others meet from six to eight weeks or longer. The most common topics for self-help groups include basic anatomy and physiology of women's reproductive system, routine gynaecological problems and treatments, childbirth and menopause experiences, and gynaeological surgery. Individual sessions are sometimes devoted to learning pelvic self-examination – to demystify that part of the body which many women have been taught not to look at or touch. Self-examination skills are also taught to help women to recognize early symptoms of vaginal infections, identify commonly prescribed drugs, and use home remedies for minor problems. Some self-help groups are organized for women at a particular life-cycle stage or a particular sexual orientation; others are mixed. The Black Women's Health Project sponsors over 45 self-help groups by and for black women, many of which focus on diet and exercise for control of hypertension, a condition disproportionately affecting black women in the United States.

Much of the impetus for the spread of self-help and other women's body education came from the Boston Women's Health Book Collective and from the Los Angeles Feminist Women's Health Center, each of which creates and promotes innovative knowledge about women's health by and for women. The Boston Women's Health Book Collective's highly successful *Our Bodies, Ourselves* (1976, 1984) started as mimeographed notes written by women participating in feminist discussion groups and classes. This book has sold over 2½ million copies in the United States alone. In addition there are 14 foreign language editions available – including Spanish, French, Italian, Dutch, Swedish and German. Each of these editions was written in conjunction with women in the countries in which they will be used. They are not simply 'translations' but reflect the needs, concerns and experiences of women throughout the world.

The Los Angeles Feminist Women's Health Center which launched cervical self-examination and has trained feminist health workers from many countries also continues to produce important women's health material. *A New View of a Woman's Body*, for example, includes colour photographs of women's cervixes at different stages of the menstrual cycle – an important contribution to women's self-knowledge (Federation of Feminist Women's Health Centers 1981). The Black Women's Health Project is producing health information focusing on special concerns of black women in the United States – hypertension, lupus, obesity, stress, high perinatal mortality, violence and the social and psychological effects of internalized oppression in black women (Spelman College 1984; National Black Women's Health Project 1985).

Feminist health groups in Canada and Europe also produce important educational material by and for women and offer self-help and body courses modelled after those started by the Boston and Los Angeles women. For example, Feministischcs Frauen Gesundheits Zentrum, a West Berlin self-help centre, offers self-help health courses and publicizes information on hazardous drug and other medical issues. Gruppo Feminista per la Salute della Donna in Rome carries on similar activities and publishes health booklets. The most extensive description of worldwide feminist health education materials and programmes is the Women and Health Resource Guide produced jointly by the Boston Women's Health Book Collective and ISIS, the Women's International Information and Communication Service which has offices in Geneva and Rome.

Feminist educational activities differ significantly from more conventional health education in several ways. The educational material itself is highly personal, written in women's own voices and from their own experiences. Considerable attention is given to the fact that there is great diversity among women in terms of what is 'normal'. Feminist health education and self-care also emphasizes the right and responsibility of the individual woman to make decisions about her health care – and provides the basic information which helps women to do so. Women's clinics often maintain lists of local physicians and hospitals recommended by other women. Some of these attempt to evaluate services systematically in large metro-politan areas. The Vancouver Women's Health . Collective, for example, carried out a detailed study of maternity services in local hospitals and also started a physician evaluation service (A Woman's Place 1972). In addition to aiding individual women seeking services, surveys and pamphlets raise awareness in the community about discrepancies in what is available – an important step in organizing for improvements in services.

Alternative Services

One important debate concerns the long-term consequences of providing women's health services in alternative clinics rather than pressing mainstream health providers to improve services. Proponents of alternative services cite women's immediate need for routine gynaecological care, contraceptive counselling, abortion, and childbirth in supportive, woman-controlled settings. Some argue as well that the participatory care provided in women's clinics could serve as a model for reorganizing conventional services. For instance, in some communities in the United States the competition from women's clinics has brought down fees for abortion in local hospitals. Conversely, other health activists, while supportive of alternative services, feel that the presence of these services may simply take pressure off doctors to improve the quality of care, since women who might be most assertive and active in pressing for change have removed themselves from conventional settings. In the United Kingdom, alternative services have not been much promoted by health activists because of the danger that such a development could undermine the National Health Service. It is argued that the NHS provides greater equity and access to women from all socio-economic groups than private medicine ever could. In addition, women in the United Kingdom are unaccustomed to paying for health services and may be unwilling to pay for alternative services (Doyal 1983).

Many alternative services are popular and heavily used. The Lyon-Martin Clinic in San Francisco which started as a small alternative service for lesbians expanded rapidly and now serves over 300 women each month. About 70 per cent of Lyon-Martin's clients identify themselves as lesbians (personal communication 1985). In Geneva, Dispensaires de Femmes, the oldest feminist women's health care group in Europe, cannot serve all the clients who wish to receive basic gynaecological and pediatric health care there. Priority is given to women in the surrounding geographical area, relatives of regular clients, and women who have had serious problems with the medical care system or who are stigmatized in some way in conventional settings (Gramoni and Chipier 1983). The Feminist Women's

Health Centers (FWHC) which started in Los Angeles have expanded into a federation of clinics in the United States offering gynaecological and abortion services (personal communication July 1985; see International Women and Health Resource Guide 1980 for information on women's clinics throughout the world).

Influencing Public Policy

Feminist health groups in the United States, Europe and in other countries make efforts to influence public policy on matters affecting women's health in ways which fit their own health care systems. As Erica Bates points out, consumers have very different leverage points in different health care systems (Bates 1984).

Because health groups have been in existence for over a decade in the United States, the policy 'successes' are quite extensive and impressive. The National Women's Health Network is the only national membership organization in the United States working exclusively on women's health and influencing health policy at the local, national and international level. With a membership of over 20,000 (including several hundred organizations which represent a constituency of half a million people) the Network can speak on behalf of a sizeable interest group. With headquarters in Washington, DC, Network committees work on reproductive health, occupational and environmental health; alcohol, smoking, drugs; health law, regulations and planning; health needs of women with special needs and backgrounds; and diseases such as breast cancer affecting women. Expert witnesses from the Network have testified at numerous United States Senate and House hearings on birth control, drugs and devices, contraceptive research priorities, nurse-midwifery and hospital childbirth practices, sterilization abuse, and abortion. The Network has also filed class action suits against companies whose products have injured women and has pressured drug companies into publishing patient information on the risks of contraceptive and menopausal estrogen drugs (Boston Women's Health Book Collective 1984).

Many other groups work on the local and regional level to influence policy. In Oakland, California, the Coalition to Fight Infant Mortality (CFIM) conducted a community investigation of the problem of infant mortality in poor and minority neighbourhoods. Their study showed 26.3 infant deaths per thousand live births in 1976 in their community, compared to 3.5 per thousand in a nearby affluent white neighbourhood. The local public hospital finally recognized the problem and made some needed changes, including hiring obstetricians with a commitment to community-based health care. Working with other groups, the CFIM got legislation passed to fund comprehensive perinatal services for low-income women (Boston Women's Health Book Collective 1984).

Other groups organize nationally around a single issue. For example, in the United States, the Committee to End Sterilization Abuse (CESA) testified first in New York and then in Washington to get federal regulations to ensure informed consent and impose a waiting period before sterilization can be performed in order to prevent coercive sterilization of poor and non-English speaking women. Initially, some feminist health groups with largely white, middle-class constituencies testifed against these regulations on grounds that they wanted no state interference in a woman's right to obtain medical services. Over time, however, coalitions were formed between largely minority health activist groups and white middle-class organizations which came to recognize that at times the needs of women with fewer resources and greater vulnerabilities had to be protected by the state – even though the state can, and has, used such authority to prevent some women from exercising what are viewed by feminists as their inalienable right to control their reproduction in any way they see appropriate (Shapiro 1985). In England the campaign against the injectable contraceptive Depo-Provera involves similar issues about social control and the lack of informed consent, as well as necessary concerns about safety (Rakusen 1981).

In many countries women attempt to influence policies by direct action intended to draw attention to problems. Public demonstrations and informational campaigns are common. For example, women in Turin, Italy, occupied a hospital ward to protest at poor service and to negotiate better abortion and maternity care (International Women & Health Resource Guide 1980). Gathering data and evaluating the quality of care is another common approach. The Association of Radical Midwives in London presented an evaluation of maternity policies in the National Health Service to the Subcommittee on Perinatal and Neonatal Mortality of the Expenditure Committee of the House of Commons (International Women & Health Resource Guide 1980).

The very existence of feminist health activity and alternative services can influence policy indirectly. Health professionals working within conventional institutions are able to study the alternative models and approaches pioneered by alternative groups and find ways to incorporate key ideas into these conventional settings. The persistence of alternative services can also provide policy-makers with the awareness that not everyone is satisfied with conventional care. When the dissatisfaction is both widespread and persistent, as in the case of maternity care, studies sponsored by organizations such as the World Health Organization which document the pervasiveness of alternative approaches are potentially important levers for social change (see e.g. Houd and Oakley 1983).

Conflicts and Contradictions

While there is considerable agreement on the need for making health care more responsive to women's needs, just what that actually means often involves conflict and disagreement. As in the case of the need for sterilization regulations in the United States, the perceived interests of white, middle-class women and poor and ethnic minority women came into direct conflict. Similarly, when white feminist health activists complained about the use of an experimental 'super-coil' abortion on poor, black women in Philadelphia on grounds that it wasn't safe and the women hadn't had an opportunity to give 'informed consent', some of the black women objected. From their viewpoint, options were limited and even an experimental abortion was better than none at all. Under such circumstances, 'informed consent', and 'freedom of choice' are phrases that have a very hollow ring (Ruzek 1978).

There are also disagreements between health activists and generally sympathetic health professionals, who often see the world only from a professional perspective. Thus, for example, at the WHO Conference in Edinburgh in 1983, the split between professional and community definitions of appropriate strategies for improving women's heath care erupted repeatedly. In the sessions on childbirth, some physicians and policy-makers resisted the idea that lower-technology approaches and midwives could provide the 'quality of care' that high-technology medicine offers. Many activists disagreed, arguing that family-centred midwifery care is in fact more appropriate as well as more cost-effective. At the same conference there was a decided split in the sessions on training and education of health professionals, between those who favoured educational pro-grammes to teach professionals how to communicate more effectively with patients and those who wanted to see a more fundamental reordering of the health care system to minimize the control and hegemony of health professionals. There was, however, greater consensus in sessions focusing on the need to control the sale of pharmaceuticals, to research important under-researched topics such as menstruation and menopause, and to encourage breast feeding.

A topic which aroused considerable controversy at the WHO Conference and elsewhere is the emphasis increasingly placed on self-help and self-care by WHO, governments and health delivery systems worldwide. The concern is that women are the ones who will end up providing much of this care, adding to their double burden of work in the home and workplace. An expanded role for women as health care providers should not be sanctioned if it simply institutionalizes women's disadvantaged economic status, either in the home or as poorly paid health workers (or both).

This controversy is made more complex because of the conceptual confusion between lay-controlled 'self-help' and medicalized 'self-care'. Self-help groups are controlled by lay persons who share a common problem or condition, and professionals are not usually sought for leadership roles. These groups emphasize the experiential base of expertise rather than the need for formal training, are critical of many conventional theories and practices, and seek to demystify common physical and mental health conditions by sharing information. With the growing fiscal crisis of the welfare state, policy-makers and physicians look for ways to cut overall costs. Recognizing both the popularity and demonstrable benefits of self-help care and self-care programmes, professionals now hope to foster lay participation in an ever widening scope of activities. What are promoted are highly professionalized forms of lay involvement, officially designated as 'self-care'. Rather than questioning or challenging medical practices as self-help groups often do, professionally organized self-care programmes teach people to follow prevailing medical dogma more effectively (Swenson 1978).

At the policy-making level, the concept of 'self-care' is translated into policies of 'deinstitutionalization' and 'community care' for the elderly, patients discharged early from hospital, and mental patients. In the United States, there are indications that public agencies are backing away from their previous responsibility for the sick, reverting to the model of private health care provision in the home, given by women. Most care of the sick has always taken place in the home and been carried out by women, but these new developments mean that the home is fast becoming an official part – an extension – of the health care delivery system. While this extension may sometimes take the form of voluntary activity, it can also be institutionalized into the state's definition of the female role. This has already happened in the Federal Republic of Germany under the 1977 sickness insurance cost control law. Patients are now released from hospital much earlier than in the past, and private nursing care must be provided at home. Insurance will reimburse the cost of professional nursing care only if no one in the family is able to care for the patient. In practice, women not employed full-time outside the home are defined as 'available' and may be called on to care not only for immediate family members (spouse, child, parent, parent-in-law) but for more distant relatives (i.e., cousins and siblings of in-laws). Such relatives are not reimbursed for their services, and if they are officially declared 'available', insurance will not provide reimbursement for any other person to provide the care (Rodenstein 1980). Official endorsement of self-care may thus add to women's domestic responsibilities and reduce employment opportunities for women workers who would otherwise be paid to provide services. In addition, the failure of families to care for their members can be blamed for escalating health care costs, masking other factors contributing to the problem.

In short, self-care is not a panacea for the ills of western industrialized health care systems. It can be useful if it empowers women to take control of their bodies and enables them to care for themselves more effectively on their own terms. It will not, however, solve the fiscal or the moral crisis which capital-intensive speciality medicine has engendered. Indeed, excessive focus on self-care may deflect attention from the problematic underlying social, political and economic conditions. Questions must also be raised about why some forms of home care – particularly home childbirth – are so strongly resisted, while others, such as care for the elderly or patients released early from hospital, are encouraged.

Some Features of Western, Industrialized Health Systems

All western industrialized health care systems reflect the personal-professional priorities of those dominant interest groups who are in positions to make decisions about what is really needed and what is expendable, what people will be able to obtain and what will be forbidden, or at least discouraged. Medical systems in western industrial nations are shaped by professional values which themselves reflect the class and gender interests of their members. Thus, largely male professional interests emphasize health care based on an industrial mode of production in which a privileged professional elite controls and directs the work of the large and relatively poorly paid direct caregivers. Because of the pervasive sex-segregation of occupations and patterns of gender roles in the family and the workplace, men occupy the elite positions while women carry out the bulk of the day-to-day health work, either without pay or poorly paid.

At the policy-making level, too few women have the power and authority to determine how scarce resources will be allocated for various types of services offered by the health care systems. Too few women are in positions in which they can judge if services or technologies are safe and effective by feminist standards. In no society are adequate numbers of women in positions of leadership in the institutions which make these decisions – the state, private or public medical organizations, labour unions, insurance companies, or international health agencies. Women are rarely physicians in policy-level positions, top health administrators, planners, researchers, economists or members of legislative bodies that determine what medical services will be offered by whom, for whom and at what cost. Those few women who presently occupy upper-level positions are typically socialized to conform to conventional professional values, ideologies, and behaviours, some of which may conflict with the actual needs of women as receivers of care. Until the entire structure of medical education and research reflects different priorities, including values defending access and equity, it is unrealistic to expect most women in such positions to behave very differently from their male colleagues. This means that women have access primarily to the type of health care that men deem appropriate to allocate to women. Changing this will take much effort and many years.

While making change will be difficult because of the vested interests of professional groups and producers of medical technologies, there are some reasons for optimism. All industrialized societies are becoming increasingly concerned about the marginal utility of many advanced, capital-intensive technologies. National governments, the World Health Organization, and an increasing number of consumer health groups throughout the world are committed to rethinking how we provide medical care. In this period of reassessment, in a world environment where increased attention to primary care and health promotion is mandated, many of the issues and concerns of feminists may be more easily heard. Certainly the increasing involvement of women at all levels of research, policy, and education as well as service provides, opportunities for forging new alliances and coalitions. Such alliances will move us closer to feminist visions of health care in which women exercise self-determination, caring and sharing are valued and extended, 'quality of care' is defined in more human terms, and safe and effective primary care is more accessible and affordable in relation to women's economic status in society.

References

The author wishes to thank Theresa Montini for research assistance and Kristin Hill and Sally Maeth for typing the manuscript. This chapter draws on two papers prepared by the author for the WHO Regional Office for Europe, Health Education Unit: 'Whose Needs Do Industrialized Health Systems Meet?' Background Paper, Conference on Women & Health, Edinburgh, Scotland, May 1983, and 'Positive Approaches to Promoting Women's Health', a working paper co-authored with Jessica Hill, 1984.

Banta, H. D. and S. B. Thacker, *Costs and Benefits of Electronic Fetal Monitoring: A Review of the Literature* (DHEW Publication No. PHS 79–3245). National Center for Health Services Research. Washington, D.C.: Government Printing Office, April 1979.

Bates, Erica, *Health Systems & Public Scrutiny: Australia, Britain & the USA* (St. Martin's Press, New York, 1984).

Boston Women's Health Book Collective, *Our Bodies, Ourselves – A Book by and for Women*. Second edition, revised (Simon and Schuster, New York, 1976).

Boston Women's Health Book Collective, *The New Our Bodies, Ourselves* (Simon and Schuster, New York, 1984).

Bunker, John, 'Surgical Manpower: A Comparison of Operations and Surgeons in the United States and in England and Wales', *New England Journal of Medicine* 282 (1970), 135–44.

Clarke, Adele, 'Subtle Forms of Sterilization Abuse: A Reproductive Rights Analysis' in R.Arditti, R. D. Klein and S. Minden (eds), *Test-Tube Women: What Future for Motherhood?* (Pandora Press, London, 1984).

Cochrane, A., *Effectiveness and Efficiency: Random Reflections on Health Services* (Nuffield Provincial Hospitals Trust, London, 1971).

Corea, Gena, *The Hidden Malpractice: How American Medicine Treats Women as Patients and Professionals* (William Morrow, New York, 1977).

De Vries, Raymond, *Regulating Birth. Midwives, Medicine and the Law* (Temple University Press, Philadelphia, 1985).

Doyal, Leslie, 'Women, Health and the Sexual Division of Labour: A Case Study of the Women's Health Movement in Britain', *Critical Social Policy* 7 (1983), 21–33.

Federation of Feminist Women's Health Centers, *A New View of a Woman's Body: A Fully Illustrated Guide* (Simon and Schuster, New York, 1981).

Freeman, Rena, *Women and Health – The Lay Component* (World Health Organisation Regional Office for Europe, Copenhagen: September 1982).

Gramoni, Rosangela and Françoise Chipier, 'The Geneva Women's Health Clinic: Promoting Demedicalization and Self-Reliance in Health' (WHO/ Euro. Health Education Unit, Copenhagen, 1983).

Houd, Susanne and Ann Oakley, 'Alternative Perinatal Services in the European Region and North America: A Pilot Survey.' (WHO/Euro., Maternal and Child Health Unit, Copenhagen, 1983).

International Women & Health Resource Guide. A Joint Project of ISIS, Women's International Information and Communication Service, Geneva, Switzerland, and the Boston Women's Health Book Collective, Boston, MA, USA, 1980.

Kleiber, Nancy and Linda Light, *Caring for Ourselves: An Alternative Structure for Health Care.* Vancouver, B.C.: School of Nursing, University of British Columbia. National Health Research and Development Project No. 610-1020A of Health and Welfare, Canada, 1978.

Lembcke, P. A., 'Medical Auditing by Scientific Methods, Illustrated by Major Female Pelvic Surgery', *Journal of the American Medical Association* 162 (1956), 646-55.

McKeown, Thomas, *The Role of Medicine, Dream, Mirage, or Nemesis?* (Princeton University Press, Princeton, NJ, 1979).

McKinlay, John, 'From "Promising Report" to "Standard Procedure": Seven Stages in the Career of a Medical Innovation', *Milbank Memorial Fund Quarterly* Vol. 59, 3, 1981.

National Black Women's Health Project, 450 Auburn Avenue, N.E., Suite 134, Atlanta, GA 30306.

The National Citizens' Board of Inquiry into Health in America. Health Care USA: 1984. Vol. 1, *National Report.* Washington, D.C.: The National Council on Aging, 1984.

Personal communication, June 1985. Lyon-Martin Clinic, 2480 Mission Street, Suite 214, San Francisco, CA 94110.

Personal communication, July 1985. Federation of Feminist Women's Health Centers, 330 Flume Street, Chicago, CA 95928.

Petchesky, Rosalind, 'Reproduction, Ethics, and Public Policy: The Federal Sterilization Regulations', *Hastings Center Report* Vol. 5, 29–41, 9 October 1979.

Rakusen, Jill, 'Depo-Provera: The Extent of the Problem. A Case Study in the Politics of Birth Control', in Helen Roberts, ed., *Women, Health and Reproduction* (Routledge & Kegan Paul, London, 1981).

Reiser, Stanley Joel, *Medicine and the Reign of Technology* (Cambridge University Press, Cambridge, 1978).

Rodenstein, Marianne, 'Fraueninteressen in Gesundheitspolitik undfor-schung', *Soziale Welt* Sonderdruck aus Jahrgang 31, 1980, Heft 2.

Rothman, Barbara Katz, *In Labour: Women and Power in the Birthplace* (W. W. Norton & Company, New York, 1982).

Ruzek, Sheryl Burt, *The Women's Health Movement: Feminist Alternatives to Medical Control* (Praeger, New York, 1978).

Scully, Diana, *Men Who Control Women's Health: The Miseducation of Obstetrician-Gynecologists* (Houghton-Mifflin, Boston, 1980).

Seaman, Barbara, *The Doctors' Case Against the Pill.* Revised edition (Doubleday & Company, Garden City, NY, 1980).

Seaman, Barbara and Gideon Seaman, *Women and the Crisis in Sex Hormones* (Rawson Associates, New York, 1977).

Shapiro, Thomas, *Population Control Politics. Women, Sterilization, and Reproductive Choice* (Temple University Press, Philadephia, 1985).

Spelman College, Atlanta, Georgia. *Spelman Messenger* Vol. 100, 1, Spring 1984.

Swenson, Norma, 'Review of *Self-Care: Lay Initiatives in Health,* by Lowell

S. Levin, Alfred H. Katz and Erik Holst', *Social Science & Medicine* 12, May 1978.

U.S. Department of Labor, Women's Bureau *Time of Change: 1983 Handbook on Women Workers*. Bulletin 298. Washington, D.C.: Government Printing Office, 1983.

Wertz, Richard W. and Dorothy C. Wertz, *Lying-in: a History of Childbirth in America* (The Free Press, New York, 1977).

A Woman's Place, A Vancouver Women's Health Booklet (Press Gang Publishers, Vancouver, 1972).

12 What is Feminism?
A Personal Answer

Dale Spender

My *choice* of feminism was a logical one, a deliberate decision on my part to improve the quality of my life. I selected feminism as a way of life, as a value system and a means of explaining the world and my place within it; while my account of this process may have some cultural peculiarities I suspect that it is not an uncommon one in the white Western world. Many women have a similar story to tell.

I was reared in Australia in not atypical circumstances for my generation. My parents were products of 'The Depression'. They married with very little money and much good will – particularly towards each other. In some respects my mother was never intimidated by convention: partly because of her height and physical prowess she had never attempted the role of the 'fluffily feminine' so there were layers of socialization that she had evaded.

Three years after my parents' marriage I was born. My mother had also defied convention in her use of contraception (the much lauded 'recent' discovery of the sponge); in my mother's case it was knowledge passed on by her mother-in-law, who was a midwife. Having said that she had no sex preference for her first child, the fact that I was a girl then led my mother to desire another daughter. She had never had a sister and always felt this to be an acute loss – so she wanted two girls who could be 'sisters' and she was delighted when my sister, Lynne, was born three years after me. For both my sister and myself there was thus the deep conviction that we were all that was required. And from the day of my sister's arrival mother intentionally set out to structure our 'sisterhood' by impressing on us that we were privileged to have each other, and that our main responsibility was to each other. Neither Lynne nor I has any recollection of ever being 'divided': it was always 'us' versus mother or 'them'. Of course we had disagreements as children (there is a rumour that I would scratch and Lynne would bite), but mother's intention was realized for we were, and are, each other's best friend. This early experience of sisterhood was an important precursor of my later commitment to the 'political' sisterhood of feminism.

However, the early equilibrium was threatened when I was almost fifteen and my brother was born. Suddenly we no longer had mother's undivided attention and we were aware that father had undergone some subtle change with the birth of a son. Underlying this change was the fact that from the age of about thirteen I had started on a collision course with my father. 'Absent' for so much of my life, he began to exercise his authority as I started to shed my childish pursuits and take on the business of being an adolescent. He and his peers defined their duty to daughters as the preservation of virginity – they saw danger lurking behind everything from lipstick to bras, and thirty seconds of one's life unaccounted for. It wasn't exactly what you would call freedom to grow, or even be curious.

I was very insecure emotionally during adolescence. I was too fat; my hair was too straight and too thin; my parents lived too far out of town for me to have a social life after school. I attended a mixed-sex secondary school where I had learnt the new lesson that popularity was not the prize for girls who excelled at their school work – particularly mathematics and science. Unlike the problem of my weight, hair and place of residence, I was readily able to solve the problem of competent performance in mathematics and science, so that by my third year in secondary school I was considered absolutely hopeless – and was therefore a candidate for sexual conquest. I worked – and I fought – to reduce my liabilities. I worked so hard on my hair – washing, rinsing, bleaching, curling, setting – that it was an exhausting routine. I worked on my weight and in retrospect see it as a flirtation with anorexia as I began to vomit regularly after meals. In my effort to find an approved place in the world, I worked to be pleasing, accommodating and ego-enhancing to boys.

Why was my brother treated differently from me? Why did girls have to be virgins? Why was sexual intercourse on the way to the wedding ceremony immoral and evil – but beautiful and honourable on the way home? Why did my father have to appear to be the 'head' of the house? Whereas my father had given little when I challenged his authority in practical terms, it was frequently he who used to give vent to rage when I challenged it in intellectual terms. So I used it – repeatedly. It was probably the only intellectual exercise I had at the time.

Predictably I failed my 'certificate' at fifteen. I was not unduly perturbed by this. To me it seemed like a good excuse to become a hairdresser – after all, I had had plenty of practice. But my parents would not allow me to leave school without a qualification. So we moved – into Sydney – and I found myself at a girls' school. If I had to put a date on my next step towards feminism it would assuredly be my enrolment at Burwood Girls' High School. When I left the school two years later – to go to Sydney University – I had acquired a very different way of viewing the world. Firstly there were no boys in the school and the ordered serenity of the classroom was like science fiction to me. There were women teachers whom I liked, whose lessons I enjoyed and who gently and generously encouraged, criticized, challenged – and in a multitude of ways opened up doors which I had not known even existed. (It is a regret of mine that I did not find the opportunity to go back and thank some of those women teachers – Miss Downie, Miss Benson, Mrs Ryce.) And there was the fact that I was virtually friendless outside school hours in a new neighbourhood, and so, with the sanction and support of my teachers, spent most of my life 'curled up with a book'.

When I finished university in the early sixties I began teaching – in a boys' school. I didn't like it and I wasn't very good at it – and I blamed myself. I also began to listen to the seductive myth that women probably weren't made for paid work anyway. The pattern of my progress through life was all laid out before me and I had few means of resisting it. By the age of 24 I found myself explaining my failure to wed to numerous protestingly happy wives. I did not feel completely convinced by the argument that fulfilment was a fitted kitchen but couldn't yet supply alternative possibilities. Reasoning that I had little to lose, I decided to give marriage a try. Perhaps my body resisted where my mind led, for I was seriously ill for six months before my wedding; and when I later discovered that Crystal Eastman and Charlotte Perkins Gilman – my two heroines – along with Olive Schreiner and many more, had been ill for six months before their marriages. I began to attach significance to this event.

My marriage did not, however, turn out to be the standard journey along the path of women's progress – to children and part-time work. There were two factors which prevented this formula being realized.

Firstly, I moved cities when I married and by an odd quirk of fate my sister Lynne and I were both appointed as English teachers to the same school. The second factor was my marriage. I had never prided myself on my home-making skills and I was resolved from the outset that housework would be shared. But I had bargained without the insidious pressures that would make resolve irrelevant. He worked longer hours at the workplace so it was only natural that I should do the shopping, wasn't it? After all, the shops were still open when I finished school. And if I did the shopping it followed that I should do the cooking. Anyway – he didn't know how to cook (or to wash or iron or clean or mend). I didn't know how to do them either, but there was no question that I was the one with the 'natural' disposition for acquiring these skills and that I would learn.

One of the greatest shocks to my system came with the cooking. Prior to my marriage I had not cooked. When asked what was for supper, I would blithely reply that were were apples, oranges and bananas or chocolate biscuits – a free choice – and my behaviour was usually considered amusing. After my marriage when I continued to refrain from cooking – and to give my customary reply – I found that my behaviour was considered far from amusing. I was the same person, but social codes had transformed me from a defiant individual into a selfish bitch. This, not surprisingly, led me to ask many (silent) questions about the desired characteristics of wives. Mimicking these same desired characteristics I was reluctant to engage in open hostilities with my husband. Publicly much of my energy went into projecting an image of wedded bliss. Privately I would occasionally drop my defences and admit to disappointment. I did try to warn Lynne about the disadvantages of married life – but she didn't listen. She got married and moved into a house around the corner. So, years before we heard the term consciousness-raising, we daily compared notes and 'spoke bitterness', confirming each other's reality to and from school.

How can I explain those years now? They no longer fit with what I know, and I feel impatience with that woman who continued to live her daily life burdened by a sense of constant anxiety and resentment. I was economically independent; theoretically I could have walked away at any time – but practically it was not so simple. The limits of my world were such that I had no idea where to go: it was beyond my understanding that a woman could make a life of her own. The world was solid and set. My trouble was that I couldn't fit in. I was convinced that there was something truly wrong with me – that I was mentally disturbed, neurotic, psychotic – and my emotional state was not improved by constant injunctions to be cheerful and happy because I was, after all, a very lucky girl.

During the first years of my marriage in the late 1960s my efforts to change my life for the better were superbly misdirected, based as they were on the premise that the fault was wholly mine. I may not have been much good at the cooking, but I did try twice weekly visits to the hairdresser (a permanent beehive coiffure never touched by *my* human hand), a rigid regimen of diets and a determination to sew everything from cushion covers to lampshades. These strategies were no help at all: on the contrary they added to my anguish – for it seemed that I had tried everything – and failed. Where I did *not* feel failure was at work. But such were the ironies of the age that the pleasure I gained from my work became just another entry in my list of liabilities. The 'career woman' was among the most reviled and ridiculed of human beings, and I was warned that I was in grave danger of becoming one of these dreaded creatures. Only by a baby could I supply proof that I was really out of danger. I am still not sure how or why I resisted this temptation. It would have been so easy to have created my credentials. Perhaps it was because I had witnessed the changes in my mother's life when my brother was born that I had few romantic illusions about motherhood. Perhaps I was frightened. Perhaps I was reluctant to let go of my work and the one area of my life where I felt at ease. It was not that I ever openly declared that I would not have children – why be so provocative? – but that if I did have them it would be at some distant date in the future. It's possible that I even believed my own rationale.

So instead of the baby stakes I chose the promotion stakes – and became head of the English department. It was the first time that I had ever been in a position of authority and the change fascinated me. On the social scene I would argue with men and be cruelly dismissed, but it was a different matter at work. I remember one occasion when some of the male members of staff descended upon the predominatly female English department with a tape measure. They were amused that the women should protest at their 'little bit of fun' – it was just an innocent bet that they had had and wanted to settle. They were not amused when I made it quite clear that the first one to lay a hand on any woman would himself be taped – and measured.

For my part I was unthinkingly intolerant of men at that stage of my life, despite the fact that I rated myself according to their values. Mostly I just found them silly – with their silly games, their silly jokes, their silly drinking habits, their silly sense of superiority which demanded that their egos be unceasingly soothed. I knew few men for whom I had any respect although I could be desperately hurt – outside work – by the disapproval of the meanest of men. It was an unfair world.

Another nail was driven into the coffin of my femininity when I decided – with Lynne – to go back to university and do a master's degree. A first degree might be overlooked in a woman, but a woman who enrolled for a second degree – and a married woman at that! –

was surely advertising her abnormality. Both Lynne and I were extremely busy with homes to run, students to teach, plays to be produced, magazines to be managed and associations to be attended. Yet while the pace of our lives was hectic we each felt that they were also empty. Life was a purposeless scramble punctuated by self–doubt and the uneasy sense that surely there must be something more.

Today I am embarrassed when I re–examine that life style of the past. In comparison with so many women in the world I led a privileged existence. My egocentricity and ethnocentrism were staggering. Why did *I* not fit in – find my niche, live a satisfying, stimulating, sensible life? I never asked, what sort of life is this, what do I know and how do I know it, and what purpose does it serve? I never queried how the life I led as a white Australian woman might compare with other life-styles. I asked only superficial questions about the values, ideologies and mores surrounding me, and then they were questions designed more to confound others than to open doors for myself.

Since that time I have come across Florence Nightingale's description of women's fate: 'death by intellectual starvation'. She was convinced that the only way women would be made in the shape that men desired was when they were 'locked out' of knowledge. I have since discovered that there is more than one way of locking women out of knowledge. We don't have to be deprived of entry to institutions of learning: we can attend, year after year (I have been twelve years a university student) and learn little or nothing that matches with our lives, meets with our understandings, affirms our existence, connects us to asking relevant questions about the world. In my own case, the more I learnt, the more convinced I was that the world was incomprehensible, and that it was because I had not the capacity to understand. (Determination I did have – twelve years is a long time to keep trying!)

That was probably the lowest point in my life, the time when I was closest to despair. I had tried everything and nothing worked. There were no other options left, I remember the distinct feeling that if I 'let go' – even for a second – I would have a 'nervous breakdown' (thus appropriately fulfilling the expectations of some around me).

My sister and I talked, endlessly. But we saw no way out. I cannot speak for Lynne but for myself I can say that my paranoia was my strength. 'Don't let the bastards get you' was a phrase that was the common currency of my life. It applied just as much at the university as it did outside it. Again, the scene at university was male dominated, which is putting it politely. If ever I had thought that women's place could be in the world of letters, I experienced a rude awakening, being made to feel stupid by so many 'superior', 'scholarly' men. While the whispers of 'women's liberation' had not reached us at that stage, we were more than ready for them. We had both become explicitly critical of the 'male ego' and my first, and rejected, dissertation for my MA was a critique of male domination in the Australian novel.

At this point Germaine Greer entered my life. She gave me my mental health. Initially, reading *The Female Eunuch* was like reading a horror story: all those clues that I had ignored, all those awful connections I'd never dared make, all that evidence I had not been brave enough to examine; all put together, and pushed at me with great force. Some of it I wanted to deny, declare it exaggerated and yet I knew it was authentic. I have never forgotten my reaction to the chapter 'Loathing and Disgust' which begins with the sentence 'Women have very little idea how much men hate them'. Recognition came with that line – but so too did some resistance.

The easiest way to describe my response is to say that I started laughing. It was a mixed laugh – joy, relief, hysteria, satisfaction, suppressed anger, curiosity? I am sure that I was suddenly years younger. I know – from looking at photographs – my whole body posture changed. Without conscious effort I also became healthier, more active – and lost weight. I could say much about what I learned from Germaine Greer – about women being 'oppressed' (I had never used that word before), about the extent to which we were confined, distorted, used and abused. Women, I had been instructed directly and indirectly from my cradle, were passive; they wanted and needed to look up to men; they were only content when dominated and domesticated. And I had believed this, and had spent almost thirty years trying to hide my deformity, to conceal my assertiveness, my lack of respect for most of the men I knew, to conceal my discontent with domination and domestication so that I would not be found out and branded as a female failure. What Germaine Greer was asking me to see was that to be a true female in these terms was to be a *human* failure. The world turned on its head!

What I also came to understand is that much of human existence is intellectual existence. As human beings we create symbols, the systems of symbols which provide us with the explanations and meanings of our daily life and world: we *invent* our reality without consciouness. Prior to 1970 I lived in a world where belief in the inferiority of women was woven into the fabric of existence. Many a time I was confronted with crude claims that women were 'good for one thing only' and that if I stepped out of line what I needed was 'a good fuck'. Instead of being seen as *the* value system of society, however, such 'slips' were more often excused as the excesses of a few men, and the ideological gloss according to which women are used in the name of love remained intact.

In other words, prior to 1970 I agonized over my failure to live constructively in the world: after 1970 I was outraged that I had ever been called upon to practice such a peculiar set of customs. I had retrieved my sanity and was set for survival – as a feminist. I have sometimes compared this transition with the experience of anthropologists who in studying other cultures, as outsiders, may be anything from mystified to amused, from intrigued to contemptuous, noting the operation of a belief system they do not share, and attempting to 'crack the code' of the culture so that previously inexplicable practices become meaningful. Feminists are like anthropologists, studying a foreign culture, adopting the role of outsider as they document the working of a belief system (the centrality and superiority of the male) which they do not share. When feminists said SEXISM, loudly and clearly, they cracked the code of the culture of male domination. But feminism is a flexible world view. There is not one part of me that would subscribe to the view that feminism is true, and all other ways of viewing the world are false. If feminism, then, is no more true than patriarchy, what is feminism? Feminism is a set of explanations which make the most sense of my experience, and my life and the lives and experiences of many other women I know. But I also choose to be a feminist for reasons far removed from my own personal convenience and peace of mind. I am a feminist because I think that feminism is based on a 'better' set of assumptions than any other world view I have encountered. I think it is a fairer way of viewing and organizing the world. I assume that human beings are equal, that we can learn to live in harmony with each other – and the planet – and that there is no necessity for violence, exploitation, persecution, war. These assumptions underlie feminist philosophy: they do not underlie patriarchal philosophy.

A premise of patriarchy is domination – the domination of women by men, of black by white, of poor by rich; it is domination glossed over by rationales of competition and meritocracy ('May the best man win') but it is still domination. And domination has another side – the reality of those who are dominated. What I learnt from my entry to feminism is that most of what we know has come from the perspective of those who do the dominating. They have described and decreed what the world looks like from where they stand and their words are the accumulated heritage of our culture. Those who are *dominated* have a very different view. But rarely has their view been given expression and, if expressed, even more rarely has it been granted recognition or validity. The one who gives orders has a very different experience from the one who must obey them, and the one who does the violating must make use of a very different frame of reference from the one who is violated, but those who are ordered and those who are violated are the silenced members of our society, by definition: if they had a voice they would not be subjected to ordering and violation.

So what I have done as a feminist is to try and break some of those silences – to try and show the way the humanity of the silenced is denied and defiled by the very structure of domination.

What I must avoid at all costs is the perpetuation of structures of dominance: an 'outsider' I may be in some respects, but I am still a product of a culture in which dominance frequently goes unchallenged and 'makes sense'. I fall short of my own standards of feminism if I dismiss the view that is different from my own, if I devalue the explanation of an experience I do not share. The challenge for feminism is to be able to include the diversity of human experience: feminism would fail if it imposed a set of explanations which demanded conformity. That would be but another expression of dominance.

I do not want to suggest that this is all feminism is. I do not want to deny or minimize the impact of the physical world, and I am conscious of the immense privilege I enjoy when I can state the importance of the intellectual dimension. When one's stomach is empty, the intellect is directed towards finding food; when one is under fire, the intellect is concentrated on the need to survive. There are many women for whom these are the primary necessities – and no amount of 'thinking differently' will put food in the bowl or stop the guns. But I do want to suggest that there will be little changed in this social order – where poverty, starvation, war are endemic – unless we all begin to think differently.

Looking back, it is not too much to claim that in 1970 I also *discovered* women. I had always assumed that the relationship I had with my sister Lynne was wholly biological: it had not occurred to me that the structure of the relationship could be carried over into my relationships with other women, who were not my biological sisters.

But my entry to feminism was marked by more than my discovery that I liked women. It also had implications for my relationship with a man. I was still married. It was difficult; I had changed – he had not. I was increasingly criticized for my associations with crazy women who were giving me all the wrong ideas and daily making me more of a disaster. The day we separated we had the same argument that we had the day we were married: why should I be responsible for his washing, ironing, cooking, cleaning? I was backed up by Pat Mainardi's article 'The Politics of Housework'; he was backed up by a whole society. I have never needed an explanation of the statement THE PERSONAL IS POLITICAL.

Men! An issue over which feminists agonize – how to relate to men – and one which I have been instructed not to evade here. I stand by my former statement that I affirm the equality of *all* human beings and I would not have feminist ideology do to men what patriarchal ideology has done to women. But I have to admit that I have a problem with men, the problem of their power and what it has done to them. I do not for one minute believe that men are born with the value system that they generally manifest but that having acquired it, I have met few men who are willing or able to discard it.

Currently, I live with a man: the 'other side' of that statement is that apart from my brother and my father, he is the only man I know. This is because there are few other men with whom I feel comfortable or who contribute to the improved quality of my life. I stand exposed as an 'Oh, but my guy is different' feminist. My work, most of my social life and much of my intellectual and emotional sustenance come from my women friends, and the recognition that this should be so is one of the reasons that the man I live with *is* different. We are not a conventional couple. (After ten years without meeting him, my friend Diana Leonard decided he is only a myth.) We are two (Australian) human beings with our own lives and work (he is an academic) and we live under one roof in mutual concern and co-operation. Some aspects of our lives we share (Australian red wine, for instance) and some we do not. Each is able to provide the other with strength and support.

For more than a decade feminism has been for me a way of living and working in the world in order that it might become a better place for all human beings. Feminism has been for me the entry to a more worthwhile life, and it has opened up new vistas where co–operation, diversity and dignity are possible. In this world view I have a place and a responsibility. There is nothing else more important than feminism. My sanity and survival have depended on it: the sanity and survival of the species depend upon it.

References

Chesler, Phyllis, *Women and Madness* (Allen Lane, London, 1972).
Friedan, Betty, *The Feminine Mystique* (W. W. Norton, New York, 1963; Penguin, London, 1965).

218 *What is Feminism? A Personal Answer*

Greer, Germaine, *The Female Eunuch* (McGibbon & Kee, London, 1970).
Mainardi, Pat, 'The Politics of Housework' in Robin Morgan (ed.),
  *Sisterhood is Powerful: An Anthology of Writings from the Women's
  Liberation Movement* (Vintage Books, New York, 1970), 501–9.
Nightingale, Florence, 'Cassandra' in Ray Strachey, *The Cause: A Short
  History of the Women's Movement in Great Britain* (1928; reprinted Virago,
  London, 1978), 394–418.

13 Are Feminists Afraid to Leave Home? The Challenge of Conservative Pro-family Feminism

Judith Stacey

Feminism today is afflicted by a crisis of confidence. First the rise of the New Right, an organized antifeminist social movement with legions of devoted female activists, forced feminists to the painful recognition that we could not speak for or to all the women we hoped to represent. Then the collapse of liberalism sealed a profound rightward shift in the social and political climate that made attacks on feminist ideology and politics attractive vocations, not only for neoconservatives, but, more disturbingly, for prominent leftists as well.[1] Soon the media was welcoming the appearance of a 'post-feminist' era whose arrival it celebrated with tales of the accomplished young women who had rejected feminist ideology.[2] And now a feminist backlash has emerged. Mounted by notable, self-identified feminists, this backlash represents an attack on the core beliefs and politics of the women's liberation movement and gives chastening evidence that the New Right and the collapse of liberalism have taken their toll. Responding to a widespread crisis in personal life and to perceived inadequacies in the ways feminism has addressed this crisis, the backlash poses a serious challenge to the women's movement. Indeed, it initiates a new and conservative terrain of struggle over what feminism will mean in the next historical period.

This internal backlash was foreshadowed in 1977 by Alice Rossi's 'A Biosocial Perspective on Parenting', a then startling rejection of feminist cultural analysis by an eminent feminist scholar.[3] The backlash has become far more explicit and strident in recent literature by Betty Friedan, Jean Bethke Elshtain, and Germaine

Greer, the three most significant voices of what I am labelling conservative pro-family feminism.[4] Recent writing by Friedan and Greer, on the one hand, and by Elshtain, on the other, commands feminist attention for nearly opposite reasons. Friedan's pivotal, highly public role in the founding of contemporary feminism makes any new statement of hers newsworthy and politically significant. She is an important sculptor and barometer of mainstream feminist consciousness as well as of popular perceptions about what feminism is. Thus when her new book, *The Second Stage*, accuses the women's liberation movement of developing a 'feminist mystique' that is more problem than solution, feminists are compelled to take notice. Similarly any statement by Greer commands a wide audience because she was a major media star of early Second Wave feminism, portrayed most often as that rare feminist who possessed (hereto-)sex appeal.

Elshtain's work, on the other hand, presents a more elite, a more strictly theoretical formulation of conservative profamily feminist thought, but it is a formulation that has received an extraordinary amount of circulation. The central themes of her book, *Public Man, Private Woman*, have been reproduced and elaborated in countless essays published in an unusually wide array of left-wing scholarly and political journals.[5] The prestige of her publishers, particularly Princeton University Press, and the classical nature of the Western theoretical tradition within which she situates her projects, have brought Elshtain instantaneous recognition within the academy where she is exerting considerable influence as a feminist scholar.[6] What is more, she is a self-identified feminist whose perspective on women, the family, and politics is held by a growing number of nonfeminists and even antifeminist intellectuals who have been gaining increasing legitimacy within progressive discourse in the United States.[7] Perhaps the most blatantly reactionary formulation of this perspective appears in Carol McMillan's *Women, Reason, and Nature*, another Princeton publication that Elshtain endorses on the dust jacket and in public lectures.[8] By pursuing the logic of central themes in new conservative feminist thought to its extremity, McMillan's book alerts us to their most troubling political implications.

Conservative feminist thought is both complex and contradictory. Friedan and Elshtain, for example, directly attack each other for the profound theoretical and political differences that characterize their perspectives, and the differences are indeed significant. Greer largely ignores direct discussion of feminist theory or politics. But the unacknowledged commonalities in all three views of feminism and the family are equally striking and greater cause for feminist concern. The first purpose of this essay, therefore, is to provide a preliminary characterization of the basic parameters of conservative pro-family feminist thought that justifies observing such diverse specimens as members of the same species. A second purpose is to criticize the substance and implications of this literature. Here I will argue that theoretically and politically this new conservative tendency represents a great leap backwards for feminists and other progressives. Friedan, Elshtain, and Greer reflect and fuel broader antifeminists and politically reactionary developments in their writings. Finally, I think it is important to go beyond simple condemnation and engage seriously with some of the issues raised by the pro-family feminists. Feminists should not simply dismiss this new conservative thought, for there is radical feminist ancestry to several of the themes that conservatives develop. More importantly, conservative profamily feminists play on some of the weaknesses in feminist response to the contemporary crisis of personal life – weaknesses in our conception of personal politics and our understanding of childhood, heterosexuality, and female subjectivity. Indeed, backlash feminists help to identify a challenging agenda for the development of feminist theory and politics for those unwilling to capitulate to the conservatism of the period.

Retreat from Sexual Politics

The central definitive characteristic of conservative pro-family feminism is a repudiation of sexual politics, the distinctively radical core of the women's liberation movement of the 1960s and 1970s.[9] The germinal insight of feminist thought was the discovery that 'women' is a *social* category, one that has subordination at its core. Sexual politics was a form of direct struggle against this social construction, a form of struggle against the systemic, structural subordination of women. Reflecting the ambiguous, dual meaning of the word 'sexual', feminist sexual politics has included efforts to transform gender and sexuality both in the public sphere and individually in the 'privacy' of our kitchens and bedrooms. For many, this politicization of intimate relationships, particularly of female-male relations, was the most explosive and threatening aspect of feminist sexual politics, and it is this form of sexual politics in particular that conservative pro-family feminists reject in an attempt to avoid all forms of direct struggle against male domination.

This repudiation of sexual politics is linked to three additional characteristics of conservative feminist thought. First, it promotes a 'pro-family' stance that views sexual politics, and particularly the politicization of personal relationships, as threatening to 'the family'. Second, it affirms gender differentiation and celebrates traditionally feminine qualities, particularly those associated with mothering. Finally, the new conservatives believe that struggle against male domination detracts from political agendas they consider more important. Let us look at the ways this hostility to sexual politics shapes Friedan's, Elshtain's and Greer's very different versions of conservative pro-family feminism.

The second stage of Friedan's book title refers quite directly to her attempt to transcend sexual politics. Although the temporal referents are ambiguous, Friedan uses 'first stage' to designate the women's liberation movement of the 1960s and 1970s and its fight for sexual equality through a sexual politics that often pitted women against men. Thus, the second stage (which Friedan alternately exhorts us to enter or claims is an evolutionary necessity already under way) is one in which women join with men to complete the 'sex role revolution' begun by the women's movement. The central objective of this revolution appears to be that of making the world safe and more livable in, for dual-career, coparenting couples. According to Friedan, the primary ideological project of first-stage feminism was to shatter the debilitating hold that the feminine mystique has on popular consciousness. This was the task most necessary to the first-stage goal of attaining full access for women to mainstream institutions, resources, and power. Although Friedan does not pretend that this goal has been achieved, she believes the feminine mystique is no longer the problem. It has been replaced, she argues, by a 'feminist mystique' which is now a (perhaps *the*) major barrier to the realization of stage-two liberation. The goal of second-stage liberation is to transcend female/male polarization, 'to achieve the new human wholeness that is the promise of feminism,'[10] and this goal is to be achieved by transforming public values and leadership styles from their outdated 'Alpha' to the needed 'Beta' mode. (Alpha designates traditionally 'Western male' models of hierarchical, authoritarian, strictly task-oriented leadership based on instrumental, technological rationality. Beta, 'the new mode', emphasizes fluidity, flexibility, interpersonal sensitivity, all of which are supposedly 'feminine' in origin.)

The 'feminist mystique', which Friedan believes now stands in the way of this revolution, is the rigid, increasingly dogmatic ideology of first-stage feminism, an ideology, as Friedan describes it, that adopts a male model of careerism and public achievement as female goals, thereby denying women's needs for intimacy, family, and children. This mystique, which Friedan herself did so much to shape, is based on a 'serious ideological error' and has egregious political consequences. First-stage feminists allowed antimale rage and excessive reaction against a family identified as oppressive to women to lead them falsely to pose family and career and family and equality as either/or choices for women. Not only did this deny feminists' own deep needs for family security, but it also played into the hands of antifeminist political reactionaries by perpetuating 'the myth that equality means death to the family',[11] a myth that terrified most Americans, who depend on the family for their security and emotional sustenance, and who see in the family the last bastion of intimacy in an alienating world.

Friedan calls upon feminists to transcend the immature errors of our movement's youth and to make the family our 'new frontier'. The primary failure of the first stage, 'was our blind spot about the family.' We antagonized too many women, and men, by our extreme reaction against the role of wife and mother. Our new goal should be to avoid polarization between women and men and between feminists and antifeminists, and we can do so if we centre our struggle on the right to *choose* to *have* children. Thus we should avoid 'incendiary sexual issues' like lesbianism and calls for abortion on demand. Abortion rights should be placed in the context of a struggle to choose to have children rather than be seen as a part of a program for sexual liberation. It is time for feminists to elevate the fight for a multifaceted approach to childcare above sexual issues. Such a shift in priorities and ideology will enable feminists to retrieve the pro-life, pro-family moral principles from the political Right.

Avoiding political polarization is not simply a strategic manoeuvre for Friedan. Rather, she believes that polarization is actually false: 'There are *not* two kinds of women in America.'[12] Nor are the needs of women and men incompatible. The appearance of irreconcilability is a false impression that has been created and manipulated by political extremists on both sides. Almost all women, and men, need and want family *and* equality. 'Polarizing rhetoric' is the real problem. It should not be surprising to learn, therefore, that Friedan believes the 'cutting edge' of second-stage liberation may prove to be the 'quiet movement among American men.' Men, now in the process of involvement, have begun, according to Friedan, a quiet, but revolutionary shift in public values, leadership styles, and institutional structures. Thus women and men, who have been following opposite evolutionary trajectories, may now meet both in the family and outside. In this mutual quest for second-stage liberation women and men will not retreat to the family, but will embrace it 'in terms of equality and diversity,'[13] and will apply the 'generating mode', a mode rooted in women's traditional familial experience, and expressed in the structures of the women's movement, to broader problems of national and social survival.[14] By this Friedan seems to mean that as women and men share familial and public responsibilities and values they will be able to humanize capitalist corporations and the armed services.[15]

Friedan offers two basic political strategies for achieving stage-two liberation. Men and women in the evolutionary vanguard should take advantage of the flexibility of the capitalist system and restructure it to meet their new needs. Here she recommends adoption of more flexible architectural and housing arrangements, zoning laws, mortgage financing, and social services. Second, and more importantly, she calls for a massive self-help effort that builds upon the American tradition of self-reliance and the existing foundation of voluntary organizations. New-mode activists cannot rely upon, and do not need, the 'tired welfare state', which in any case is alienating. Instead of antagonizing conservatives by making claims upon the state, 'we' should join with them to bridge the liberal/conservative and the volunteer/professional chasms. Thus Friedan concludes with her own version of an 'end of ideology' plea for pragmatism.

In short, *The Second Stage* represents a liberal's response to the failure of liberalism and a feminist's response to the setbacks of feminism. Friedan calls for a retreat from what Zillah Eisenstein optimistically labelled the 'radical future of liberal feminism.'[16] While maintaining sexual equality as a vague, futuristic goal, Friedan seeks to curtail explicitly feminist struggles to achieve it, and she collaborates with the neoconservative program to dismantle the welfare state. Ironically, the only area in which Friedan remains staunchly liberal is in her definition of the family she wishes to protect: 'The family is who you come home to.'[17] Facing squarely the reality that there is no going back to the 'classical family of Western nostalgia', and indeed indicating scant desire to do so, Friedan's definition proclaims her tolerance for a broad array of contemporary forms of family life and of purposeful efforts to establish voluntary communities on the basis of shared interests and needs.

Tolerance for diverse family and community structures is what distinguishes Friedan most dramatically from Jean Bethke Elshtain, the more theoretical conservative feminist, with whom she otherwise shares a great deal. Elshtain affirms a far more traditional definition of family and community: 'By "family" I mean the widely accepted, popular understanding of the term as having its basis in marriage and kinship.' Elshtain explicitly derides Friedan's definition of the family as 'insulting to family men and women'[18] and takes Friedan's critique of feminist family politics further down a reactionary political trail.

Public Man, Private Woman is Elshtain's two-part discourse on political theory. Part 1 applies what she terms a 'self-reflective feminist consciousness' to the images of public and private as they appear in classical Western political theory from the Greeks, through the early Christian theologians and major Enlightenment figures, up to Hegel and Marx.[19] Part 2 then inverts the lens to criticize contemporary feminist theory and politics from the vantage point of the way in which Western political theory has treated the public and the private. The most ambitious goal of this portion of the book is to develop 'a critical theory of women and politics'. In her effort to construct such a theory, Elshtain divides feminist thinking into four categories – radical, liberal, Marxist, and psychoanalytic. Her highly selective, often unfair, choice of representative theorists and her distorted presentation of their works is partially offset by the rather compelling criticisms she offers of epistemological and political failings characteristic of contemporary feminist thought.[20] Perhaps her most effective and original contribution here is her analysis of the inadequacies in feminist theorizing about citizenship and polity.

Public Man, Private Woman, however, also has a polemic mission, a mission which has been more directly explicated in a series of Elshtain's political essays. The most imporant of these are 'Feminism, Family, and Community', an article that provoked a rather nasty exchange between Elshtain and Barbara Ehrenreich, and 'Homosexual Politics: The Paradox of Gay Liberation.'[21] The now-clichéd epigram of sexual politics, 'the personal is political' is Elshtain's primary polemical target because she believes it represents the collapsing of all boundaries between public and private life and thereby leads to the erosion of both realms. Politicizing personal life, Elshtain warns, heralds an end to privacy and an end to politics, the ultimate consequence of which is totalitarian control over personal and civic life. Because Elshtain equates the private with the family, and the family with personal life, her antipathy to personal politics is essentially a rejection of struggles that politicize family relationships. Following Christopher Lasch and certain analyses of family and capitalism first developed by Max Horkheimer, Elshtain identifies the family as the last haven in a bureaucratic capitalist and totalitarian socialist world, a world she sometimes identifies as 'modernity'. She views the family as the source of values necessary for resistance to corporate power and to antidemocratic tendencies in the modern world.[22] Thus, like Friedan, Elshtain criticizes feminists for an attack on the family which she considers irresponsible, distorted, and fueled by politics of rage. Feminists, she charges, have celebrated family breakdown and denigrated mothering, all of which, she agrees with Friedan, has served to alienate 'ordinary citizens'.[23]

Elshtain, however, carries her critique of the feminist politicization of family relations and the search for alternatives to traditional family forms in a far more conservative direction than Friedan. She excoriates the search for alternative families and communities, for example, as inauthentic, individualistic, and irresponsible. The search is unauthentic because 'there is no way to create real communities out of an aggregate of "freely" choosing adults';[24] it is individualistic (rather than maturely individuated) because it smacks of the selfish bad faith of the me-generation, human potential, self-actualization enthusiasts; and it is irresponsible towards children, the victims of such experiments, who, Elshtain argues, should be at the very centre of feminist theory.[25] Elshtain goes pretty far here. She attempts to rescue Selma Fraiberg's celebration of 'every child's birthright', full-time mothering, from feminist opprobrium and expresses considerable hostility to collective forms of childrearing.[26] She also takes assorted potshots at feminist support for female labour force participation, feminist criticism of the morality and motives of Right To Life women, and feminist disregard for the profound significance of biological differences between the sexes.

Thus, in her own version of second-stage politics, Elshtain calls for 'social feminism', a perspective she never defines too precisely, but which involves placing children at the centre of feminist concern, preserving traditional families and communities, maintaining a clear boundary between public and private life, and sustaining those aspects of gender differentiation that are necessary to social life.[27] Distinctly reminiscent of the 'domestic feminism' of the late nineteenth century whose self-defeating sentimentality she criticizes, Elshtain's 'social feminism' attempts both to preserve traditionally feminine values of nurturance rooted in the private sphere, and to infuse these into 'ethical polity', her term for the ideal public sphere.

Pursuing one logic of Frankfurt School analysis to an anti-modernist conclusion, Elshtain criticizes feminists for capitulating to market imperatives, succumbing to instrumental rationality, and seeking technocratic solutions to moral and political problems. In so doing, she indicts an image of feminism that fuses Shulamith Firestone's test-tube babies with the new corporate executive woman. Feminists, through these sins, have contributed to the domination of nature, and it is time, she believes, for them to adopt a 'politics of limits', a politics that avoids utopian efforts to change that which cannot be changed without dire human consequences.

The limits which concern her most are those having to do with biology, gender, family, and sexual morality, just those areas in which feminists have tried, through the politicization of the personal, to intervene. Here Elshtain tends to mistake her own, often moralistic, preferences and judgements for more universalistic moral principles. She justifies her hostility to collective child-rearing, for example, by employing an indefensibly idiosyncratic selection of evidence to show that children reared collectively are dangerously vulnerable to conformist pressures. But the most significant political limitation Elshtain advocates is resistance to state intervention in private life. Her opposition to, indeed her profound disdain for, the liberal welfare state, is far more extreme than Friedan's. But, unlike Friedan, she does not accept the responsibility of offering an alternative politics other than a rather lofty celebration of the ideal of active citizen participation in a democratic 'ethical polity'. In summary, Elshtain provides a nominally feminist variation of Lasch's analysis of family and capitalism. She repudiates the politicization of personal relationships as threatening to the social institutions that nurture the individual and the intimate ties crucial to the generation of democratic resistance. What she adds to this is a celebration of traditional female values, which, she believes, also are threatened by sexual politics.

The differences between Friedan's second stage and Elshtain's social feminism are not minor. They maintain nearly contrary views of capitalism and modernity and incompatible definitions of the family and community that reflect the very different intellectual and political traditions within which they work. Friedan is one of the many disenchanted liberals who retain a progressivist faith in capitalist development and individual initiative despite their serious loss of confidence in the prospects for, or the efficacy of, federally sponsored social reforms.[28] Elshtain is one of those disenchanted democratic socialists whose profound loss of confidence in the prospects for, or the efficacy of, democratic socialist politics has turned a critique of capitalism into a romantic antimodernism.[29] The irony of this perspective is that its hostility to modernity extends to many modern movements for anticapitalist social change, such as the new Left and the radical wing of the women's movement.

228 Are Feminists Afraid to Leave Home?

But Friedan and Elshtain offer a vision of feminism with far more unity than they realize. The central affinity in their feminism is their rejection of sexual politics, a rejection motivated by three views they hold in common. First, both believe that sexual politics, and especially the critique of personal and heterosexual relations, threaten the family, by which Elshtain means the conventional families of 'ordinary people', and Friedan, a more pluralist conception that favors the families of dual-career, coparenting couples. They agree that this form of sexual politics is immature and dangerous, a politics of rage, of reaction, of displacement – in short, a denial by feminists of our own needs for intimacy and security and of our own vulnerability. Similarly, both Friedan and Elshtain are particularly hostile to the antimale sentiment embedded in the feminist critique of personal relations, especially where it contributes to the denigration of heterosexual love.

Second, at the same time that Friedan and Elshtain criticize the antimale sentiment of sexual politics, they claim that it is actually antiwoman. Both interpret the feminist critique of a gendered division of labour as a phallocentric privileging of public life, careers, and male rationality, which contributes to the denigration of motherhood, the major source of value, esteem, and identity for most women. Elshtain is more consistent and coherent on this score. It is rather difficult to swallow this criticism from Friedan, one of the most influential architects of the careerist ideology of liberal feminism. Similarly, both Friedan and Elshtain affirm the value of gender-based traits over and against the early feminist goal of androgyny. Again, Friedan is somewhat inconsistent, because her ideal of dual-career, coparenting, self-actualized humans still appears rather androgynous. Yet she applauds the first female graduates of West Point for learning 'to master the male skills and play the male game, without losing their own identity as women, without trying to turn themselves into men.'[30] Elshtain, however, locates gender in the body, 'the irreducible bedrock of whom I am,'[31] and approvingly cites Peter Winch's observation 'that masculinity and femininity are not simply *components* of a life but its *mode*.'[32] Thus she finds the critique of gender difference to be antinatural, and one of those 'assaults on a given order [that] sweep along in their trail much that makes life liveable, diverse, and charming as well as that which makes it exploitative and unjust.'[33] Elshtain employs a similar logic in her opposition to the gay liberation movement, which threatens, she fears, to eliminate the (charming?) differences between heterosexuality and homosexuality.[34]

Third, both authors regard sexual politics, the struggle against women's subordination in general, as diversionary from, or even antagonistic to, an arena of politics they consider more important. Friedan worries that sexual politics is impeding a necessary evolutionary shift to 'Beta' style leadership and institutional forms that demand the transcendence of false polarizations. Elshtain, on the other hand, sees the 'ethical polity' jeopardized by a politics that erodes the family, the source of individuals' capacity to resist market imperatives and totalitarian tendencies. Finally, it is crucial to underscore that in rejecting sexual politics, both Friedan and Elshtain identify contemporary feminism itself as a serious problem that must be solved by its replacement, in the one case by the 'second-stage sex role revolution', and in the other by 'social feminism'.

This analysis applies readily to the recently published *Sex and Destiny* by Germaine Greer.[35] Greer, too, has views that distinguish her sharply from either Friedan or Elshtain, but given her reputation as a sexual radical, it is more startling to discover that *Sex and Destiny* also represents a retreat from sexual politics and, many would say, a retreat from sex itself. *Sex and Destiny*, subtitled 'The Politics of Human Fertility,' is a passionate, undisciplined book riddled with inconsistencies and contradictions, but it has an emotional core. Its centre is a heartfelt diatribe (much of it as legitimate as it is familiar) against interventions by Western population planners into fertility behaviour in the 'Third World'. Thus most of the book, unlike those by Friedan and Elshtain, is not written explicitly about, or to, feminists. What is pertinent is the ideology with which Greer attacks the population planners and the Western culture, including feminist culture, she takes them to represent: a romantic anti-technocratic celebration of fertility, children, and the traditional extended – that is, the classic patriarchal–family.

Greer draws a sharp distinction between the nuclear family, an anathema to her, and the capital letter Family she celebrates. She defines the former as a unit in which the relationship of the procreating couple takes precedence over all others, 'all other relations of blood and affinity having virtually withered away,'[36] and views it as the desiccated product and agent of technocratic, consumer society. The 'notion of the Family with a capital F', on the other hand, strives to describe 'an organic structure which can be shown in law, in genetic examination, in patterns of land ownership and parish records, but has its realm principally in hearts and minds.'[37] It is an extended family in which emotional and social priorities are invested in blood relationships, particularly those between women and children.

The model from which Greer has drawn this notion of Family appears to be the peasant community, particularly those she has travelled and lived among in India and southern Italy. Although these are paradigmatically patriarchal orders, Greer admires, indeed she envies, the matriarchal opportunities they offer women. Most desirable of all is the opportunity to share the pleasures and burdens of rearing communally desired children with one's female relatives. Thus Marisa, a poor Italian woman whose dearest wish was 'that her mother would die in her arms', is 'one of the most unequivocally successful women' Greer has ever met because 'her sons-in-law and her grandchildren are firmly bound to her household rather than to her in-laws.'[38]

The modern nuclear family and the Family are, in Greer's view, antithetical. The impoverished nucleated couples in the former turn to a technocratic search for orgasms to compensate the emotional, spiritual, and sensual losses the decline of Family brings. And if the (literally) barren futility of this search weren't sad enough in the cheerless consumer societies of the West, it is downright genocidal of us to impose our antinatalist, anti-child, anti-Family values on the third world through imperialist population interventions.

What is distinctive about Greer's profamily feminism is the explicitly backward nature of the home she is afraid to have us abandon. Greer is uncompromisingly hostile to the conjugally-rooted family that Elshtain and Rossi wish to save, let alone to the pluralistic variety of families Friedan is willing to accept. Quite unlike these other voices of conservative profamily feminism, Greer refuses to forfeit the earlier feminist critique of the isolated nuclear family as the primary site of the oppression of women and children. She longs instead for the matriarchal moments of classical patriarchy.

There are instances in *Sex and Destiny* when Greer makes the irony of her new pro-family perspective explicit:

> It may seem strange for a twentieth-century feminist to be among the few champions of the Family as larger organization than the suburban dyad, for most Families are headed by men and men play the decisive roles in them or at any rate usually appear to, but there are reasons for such a paradoxical attitude.[39]

The reasons Greer offers fail to confront the feminist paradox, but they do provide important clues to some of the emotions that may be driving diverse forms of pro-family feminism.

First, Greer extols the opportunities for sisterhood possible in the Family, but denied the family:

> The Family offers the paradigm for the female collectivity: it shows us women cooperating to dignify their lives, to lighten each other's labour, and growing in real love . . . sisterhood, a word we use constantly without any idea of what it is.[40]

This female collectivity is better for women than their isolation in the suburban dyad, and, Greer believes, it is a far better environment for children. Family women, moreover, 'are not at the mercy of their husbands; indeed, their relationships with the other women in the Family . . . may well be more important.'[41] They also are spared the competitive heartache of the beauty and popularity contests that govern the marriage sweepstakes in the romantic love-based family of consumer society:

> There is no dating game, there is no most popular girl, there is no campus queen. Cross-eyed, pockmarked, flat-chested, good-natured hardworking girls have happier lives than Southern belles, which could strike other, plain, industrious women as fair enough. The most valuable commodity in the Family is a loving heart whose happiness consists in seeing others happy.[42]

Beneath this sentimental romanticization of arranged marriage and the extended Family, one senses despair of the alternatives – a flight from the burdens of constructing intimate relationships on a voluntarist basis: 'I would insist that if you love your Family and honour its achievements, you will love your Family's natural choice. Sexual love is much less hard to arrange than we have all been led to believe.'[43] Greer's ode to arranged marriage is an extreme response to this despair, but the experiences and emotions that prompt it have considerable resonance, I believe, among many contemporary feminists. The pain and difficulties experienced by a generation of feminists who self-consciously attempted to construct alternatives to the family are a major social psychological source of the emergence of pro-family feminism, and one, as I will elaborate later, that may fuel the pro-family retreat from sexual politics.

Certainly most of the attention *Sex and Destiny* has attracted has centred on Greer's apparent retreat from sexual radicalism, particularly her defence of chastity as a form of eroticism and birth control. While there are profoundly idiosyncratic aspects to Greer's new views, critics have overlooked their most important resemblance to the views of other contemporary pro-family feminists. The retreat from sexual radicalism is part of a retreat from sexual politics that Greer shares with Rossi, Friedan, and Elshtain. The only power relations that receive extended attention in *Sex and Destiny* are those that govern relations between rich and poor nations, particularly as these are mediated by population planners and the medical establishment. But for an occasional aside, Greer ignores the systemic, and often brutal, forms of male domination that characterize the Families she romanticizes.

The Great Leap Backwards

An attack on sexual politics is an attack on the radical core of feminist thought and practice – the recognition that the subordination of women to men is systemic and structural. Friedan, Elshtain, and Greer seek to avoid direct struggles to end this subordination. Despite a few rather vague affirmations of sexual equality, none identify male domination as a problem requiring political, or any other, attention. Friedan wants us to shift to a concern for 'human' problems; Elshtain asks us to evaluate female-identified virtues. Greer's new preoccupation with the imperialism of global population planners totally displaces concern for women's subordination. None of them support direct efforts to confront the domination of women by men.

In Friedan's case, this reticence may be partly strategic. She thinks we cannot win sexual equality if we antagonize men, or other women, for that matter. Elshtain, however, appears uninterested in, even hostile to, the subject of male domination. That is why her often cogent criticisms of feminist theory and politics appear arrogant and mean-spirited. She rarely seems to comprehend what all the feminist fuss is about.[44] Elshtain is far less interested in achieving gender equality than in preserving female moral and social sensibilities that have been linked historically with the social subordination of women. But preserving female values, particularly in a gendered sphere, will not threaten male domination. Nor, I believe, will it threaten the economic or political structures of capitalist or state socialist societies, evils of greater concern to Elshtain. On the contrary, as feminist scholars have taken pains to demonstrate, female domesticity can be readily adapted to play crucial roles in sustaining various systems of social domination.[45] Elshtain fails to grapple with questions about the extent to which female virtue is tied to female subordination or to the separate spheres her book title, *Public Man, Private Woman*, underscores, and its text fails to challenge. This failure leads her to overlook the negative components of 'maternal thinking', a concept she borrows enthusiastically from Sara Ruddick.[46] Elshtain also fails to make concrete the role of female citizenship and male familial responsibilities in her 'ethical polity'. Instead she makes a suprapolitical appeal from an infusion of maternal values into the public arena, an appeal which is not an adequate substitute for political analysis.

The repudiation of sexual politics leads to the major theoretical failing of conservative feminist thought – the loss of a conceptual framework for analysis of the sex/gender system. To my mind this loss represents a forfeit of the single most significant theoretical advance of contemporary feminist theory – the capacity to analyse the *social* processes through which individuals, cultural forms, and social systems are engendered. On the one hand, the retreat from sex/gender analysis is merely implicit in the political analyses offered by Friedan and Greer, who do not present their works as contributions to feminist theory. Elshtain, on the other hand, is a self-identified feminist theorist who criticizes all varieties of contemporary feminist theory. Although the individual criticisms she provides are often cogent, they do not emanate from the perspective of a putatively better theory of gender or a better theory about the liberation of women. Indeed, Elshtain grounds herself in a rather abstracted, ahistorical reading of western political theory, from which stance she provides no gender theory at all.[47] This tendency represents a potentially grave loss not only for feminism, but also for social theory in general, for gender theory illuminates the analysis not only of women, or of gender, nor even of the family (although these have been the major objects of its analysis so far), but also of many of the broadest epistemological and theoretical concerns of western scholarship.[48]

The loss of a sex/gender theory is the most serious theoretical consequence of the conservative feminist retreat from sexual politics, but it is not the only one. Closely associated is the disappearance of a feminist critique of the family. One of the more valuable achievements of feminist theory has been its effort 'to deconstruct the family as a natural unit, and to reconstruct it as a social unit' – as ideology, as institutional nexus of social relationships and cultural meaning.[49] The new conservative attempt to fortify the family (which Friedan, Elshtain, and Greer mistakenly equate with 'the natural') exempts it from analysis and returns it to its prefeminist status as an ahistorical essence. Both Friedan and Elshtain explicitly condemn feminist analysis of the family as distorted, but neither attempts to offer a more faithful view. Friedan's thoroughly pluralist, and rather content-free, definition of family allows her to evade the issue entirely, while Elshtain simply renders the family universal: 'The family's status as a moral imperative derives from its universal, pancultural existence in all known societies.'[50] In a similar way Elshtain romanticizes the nuclear family, and in so doing obscures its internal authority structure by portraying it as the source of authentic community ties and the source of resistance to the dehumanizing logic of 'modernity'.

On the basis of equally compelling logic, however, and on the basis of no less sufficient evidence, one could argue that the breakdown of the conventional nuclear family has the capacity to generate communitarian behaviours and oppositional attitudes. This would be a reasonable interpretation of the matrifocal 'domestic networks' of the poor, black, urban ghetto analyzed by Carol Stack,[51] and Nancie Gonzalez, reflecting on the meaning of her personal experience and her fieldwork in the Dominican Republic reaches similar conclusions: 'Unlike the nuclear family which tends to turn inward, tries to be affectively and economically self-sufficient and draws its strength from a strong bond between husband and wife, the female-headed household can only survive if the woman maximizes her extended kin, neighbourhood and friendship relations. In a sense, the Dominican Republic was my testing ground as an independent head of household and I was even stronger upon our return.'[52]

Moreover, refinements in analyses of the 'gender gap' in recent United States voting patterns suggest the existence of a more profound 'marriage gap'. During recent national elections, un-married voters of both sexes have revealed themselves to be significantly more hostile to Reagonomic politics and right-wing political candidates than their married counterparts.[53] The rebels and refugees from the nuclear family may be more sensitive to social needs than the 'authentically' familied.[54] Thus Greer's despair of, and Elshtain's hostility to, creating real communities out of 'freely' choosing adults may be misguided. Here Elshtain is inconsistent as well in ignoring the fact that the traditional marriages she champions are also based on the free choice of adults as are the political movements she praises, such as those against militarism or the rights of the handicapped.

Critiques of sexuality, particularly of heterosexuality, by feminists and gay liberationists have also centred on establishing its social and historical construction, but conservative pro-family feminists represent a retreat to essentialism here as well. Indeed, their treatment of sexuality makes one begin to suspect that one strong personal motivation in framing their position may be anger towards the denigration of heterosexuality by many radical feminists. Elshtain's writings, in particular, are laced with romantic affirmations of heterosexual union as 'the tantalizing prospect of a coming together of differences, of some fructifying collaboration.' Indeed she constructs her political vision in this very imagery: 'a unifying myth of a body politic, the coming together of separate elements in order to "give birth" to a social world that links past and future and makes history possible.'[55] The very logic of her metaphor grants heterosexuals a privileged relationship to the ethical polity.

As all this might suggest, the conservative pro-family feminists give no attention to the internal dynamics of family and sexual systems nor to the agency of familial and sexual subjects. Thus Friedan presumes that family and sexual liberation will take care of themselves once extremists of all stripes allow technological and biological advances to take their evolutionary course, and from within such a framework she sees sexual politics or the struggle against male-dominated personal relations as a distraction. 'Sexual politics has been a red herring, an acting-out of feminist reaction, a diversionary tool with which the forces of political, economic and religious reaction . . . seek not only to beat women back but also to distract people generally from their economic-political exploitation and divert them from their autonomy.'[56] Elshtain, in contrast, has no sympathy for those who seek to liberate individuals from present familial and sexual arrangements, and she portrays the limitations of these arrangements as the result purely of broader economic and political forces.[57]

Thus the new feminist conservatism discards the most significant contributions of feminist theory and, more alarmingly, provides in their place a feminism that turns quite readily into its opposite. Perhaps the easiest way to illustrate this inversion is to take even a cursory glance at *Women, Reason, and Nature*, by Carol McMillan. Unlike Friedan or Elshtain, McMillan does not present herself as a feminist. Instead, she adopts the supposedly neutral stance of an analytical philosopher in order to examine epistemological 'errors' shared, she believes, by feminists and sexists alike. The book's argument, however, is a logical extension of Elshtain's *Public Man, Private Woman*, and it leads McMillan to several startlingly anti-feminist conclusions.

Women, Reason, and Nature begins tamely, if not originally, with a critique of western rationalist logic and values, whose central flaw is a false dichotomy and hierarchy between reason and emotion, culture and nature. According to McMillan, the failure of rationalism to recognize the cognitive aspects of emotion or to see the rationality and agency required by the seemingly emotional work of the domestic realm has resulted in an unfortunate privileging of technology, manipulative skills, and the control of the natural environment, on the one side, and the denigration of women, mothering, and domesticity, on the other. McMillan believes that feminists and sexists both have bought into this 'male' rationalist mistake and that this lamentable purchase has led feminists to the 'misguided' goals of equality and androgyny.[58] The goal McMillan prefers is a revision of the original value system and a society that better prepares women for our 'natural' relationship to children.[59] These priorities lead her, like Greer, to oppose all interference with 'natural' female reproduction and female mothering. Heterosexist appeals to the 'natural' relationship between sexuality and procreation accompany her rejection of almost all forms of birth control as well as of abortion. She is opposed to unisex education, daycare, and even coparenting. And she pursues the antimaterialistic logic of Elshtain's critique of female labour force participation to a defence of female economic dependence upon men![60]

Women, Reason, and Nature is important because it demonstrates the logical progression of basic tenets of conservative pro-family feminist thought, thereby illuminating inconsistencies and, perhaps, bad faith in the latter. Elshtain waffles on questions of abortion, coparenting, and daycare, and attempts to accommodate a closeted space for homosexuality; Greer is contradictory on abortion and evades the other questions; Friedan ignores the contradictions between her support for these practices and her rejection of sexual politics. But McMillan is unabashedly anti-feminist on all counts. She extends to its logical terminus the new conservative celebration of nature over technology, of female domestic values, of a clear public/private boundary, and of biologically rooted gender differences as well as rejection by backlash feminists of feminist conceptions of women's oppression. The logical terminus proves to be classical patriarchy.

The Challenge of Conservative Feminism

It would be reassuring if the only challenge posed by this literature lay in exposing the antifeminist implications of conservative pro-family feminist thought, for that would locate the problem entirely outside the feminist camp and would allow me to end this essay right here. Unfortunately, however, not all the roots of conservative feminist thought lie outside the realm of feminist theory and politics. Thus, conservative pro-family feminism represents a more serious challenge than that of contending with one more alien antagonist. It is possible to identify radical feminist ancestry in elements of conservative feminist thought. And it is important to recognize that backlash feminists are responding, however poorly, to genuine social problems as well as to problems in feminist theory. Contrary to Friedan's, Elshtain's, and McMillan's portrayal of feminist ideas as monolithically antimaternal, contemporary feminist visions are actually characterized by unresolved tension between advocating androgyny and celebrating traditionally female, and especially maternal, values. Much radical feminist writing in particular foreshadows the emphasis that Elshtain, Greer, and McMillan place upon female biological processes and the affirmation they give to the nurturant qualities associated with mothering.[61] The new conservatives' development of this maternal goddess theme, a theme implicit in a good deal of contemporary feminist writing, suggests the political dangers of such formulations. Feminist historians have also elaborated these pitfalls in their analyses of the 'old conservative feminism' of nineteenth-century domestic feminists.[62] Instead of celebrating the feminine, we need to retain a vital tension between androgynous and female-centred visions. We need to recognize contradiction and to apply a critical perspective that distinguishes between giving value to traditionally female qualities and celebrating the female in a universalistic and essentialist manner.

The new conservative ideology has social psychological sources as well, for it is a reactionary response to a broad social crisis in family and personal life. The work of Friedan, Elshtain, and Greer speaks from and to a reservoir of unmet needs for intimacy, nurturance, and security that feminists experience as much as other women and men. Before elaborating on this collective experience, I would like to place it in a broad social structural framework.

The history and fate of feminism are intimately tied to the history of the family. A profound crisis in the modern nuclear family system in the West, which incubated throughout the twentieth century and erupted in the 1960s, helped to generate Second Wave feminism and its (our) focus on a 'personal politics' that would reconstruct gender and family relationships. The massive increase of female participation in higher education and the labour force are both cause and effect of this family crisis; they both facilitate and are made necessary by family change. Thus the feminist critique of the modern nuclear family was mounted precisely when that family system had begun its irreversible decline. This is not a paradox. Effective criticism requires alternative visions which are most accessible when change is underway. Second Wave feminism became identified as antifamily and antinatalist because we assumed as one of our appropriate historic tasks an attempt to speed the pace and influence the direction of family and gender change. A great deal of our theoretical efforts centred on the negative social and psychological effects of the housewife/mother role.

But as I suggested, the housewife/mother role was already in decline, and not all of the consequences were beneficial for many women. Indeed, as the data indicating the feminization of poverty and of the working class suggest, women have borne a disproportionate share of the burdens of gender and family change. Many have had reason to partake of 'The Fear', as Deirdre English describes it, 'That Feminism Will Free Men First.'[63] It isn't remarkable, therefore, that an antifeminist backlash emerged and found a pro-family ideology to be an effective strategy for organizing women as well as men to oppose sexual equality and women's rights; not remarkable, but the active participation of women in successful struggles to defeat the ERA and curtail abortion rights has been a bitter pill for feminists. It shattered the invigorating illusion that feminism could speak for and to all women, an illusion that underlay the ideology of sisterhood.

The emergence of pro-family feminism must be analyzed in this context. It is fueled, in part, by the thoroughly laudable desire to understand and speak to women who have ignored or rejected a feminism perceived, half accurately, as antifamily. But I believe it has even more powerful personal roots in the collective biographical experiences of a particular generation of feminists.

The preoccupation of many feminists who, in the late 1960s and early 1970s, were in their twenties and early thirties, was with finding ways to escape from or avoid the traps of wife and motherhood in the nuclear family. Feminists of the New Left student generation left and refused marriages, delayed childbearing decisions, and experimented with sexuality and collective households. Those who were already parents struggled to share mothering with men and to establish more collective forms of responsibility for children. Feminists challenged the deeply held cultural belief that woman's nature or cultural tradition were sufficient justification for family organization, particularly for women's exclusive responsibility for children. Our response to family crisis was to craft nonsexist voluntary relationships as a step towards liberating women and children. (It is interesting, in this regard, to recall the vision of family Germaine Greer herself sketched out in her book of that period, *The Female Eunuch* – an entirely voluntary rural community in which children would be reared by a mobile core of 'parents of both sexes and a multitude of roles to choose from.'[64])

Avoiding marriage and motherhood proved far easier, of course, than attaining gender equaliy, let alone liberation. The social structural and cultural changes necessary for the latter remain far from view, while many feminists, who have served as the shock troops of family change, have been the special victims of the failures of voluntarism. Three sorts of personal traumas seem to be particularly widespread among those who shunned traditional marriage and childrearing arrangements: 'involuntary' singlehood, involuntary childlessness, and single parenthood.

I place 'involuntary' singlehood in quotes to indicate its ambiguous roots. It has proven to be the status of a great many heterosexual feminists who have refused inegalitarian relationships and found the pool of eligible feminist men to be painfully inadequate. A great longing for intimacy, and a measure of bitterness, is not an uncommon reaction. Nor have lesbians been spared the loneliness of 'involuntary' singleness, as voluntarism has proven to be weak grounding for longterm committed relationships of any sexual variety.

Involuntary childlessness is one of the cruellest, unanticipated traumas afflicting many feminists in the 1980s, and the one that has most to do with the passions fueling Greer's new book. Few among those of us who deferred childbearing decisions until the biological limits considered the possibility that an affirmative decision might be impossible to implement. Yet problems of infertility, miscarriage, foetal genetic defects, and stillbirth have prevented startling numbers of feminists from bearing the children they delayed for so long. Many others have mourned the passing of their reproductive years before they were able to establish the personal or economic stability they considered prerequisite to intentional mothering.

Finally, for many of those feminists who chose mothering outside the conjugal dyad, or who left those dyads with their children, single parenting has proven to be particularly difficult. The widespread failure of communal households both reflects and aggravates this difficulty. The arrival of children was a precipitating factor in the collapse of many communes, while single mothers suffer most from the withdrawal of collective responsibility for children. Greer's idealization of Family represents an effort to ground the communal responsibility for children that she always desired in the more enduring bonds of blood and kinship.

Aging, in the rightwing and 'postfeminist' climate of the 1980s, has been a traumatic experience for many Second Wave feminists, and we lack convenient scapegoats for our distress. Analyses of capitalism and patriarchy, however astute, are small solace for whatever collective sense of responsibility we feel for the failures of alternative gender and family forms. Perhaps this accounts for the strident and unmodulated quality of recantation in the new pro-family feminism. (Although a scapegoating element also is evident in the tendency of several conservative feminists to blame *other* feminists for ideological and political errors.) But this is quite unfortunate, because a nondogmatic atmosphere in which feminists can engage in collective reflection on our experience and ideology is precisely what we need right now.

Drawing on experience to modify earlier views is the sign of a vital social movement. It would be cause for concern if feminists were inalterably opposed to reassessing the antifamilism of the late sixties and early seventies. This is quite a different thing, however, from the overreaction of a backlash which, I believe, most of the new pro-family feminism represents. We must confront the challenge of the problems inherent in voluntarist family forms by giving even greater analytical and political attention to questions of intimacy, child rearing, childlessness, and sexuality.

The need for intimacy is real, and it is not convincing to presume that all relational problems will disappear with patriarchy, capitalism, and racism. I perceive three central issues feminist theory must address in order to develop a more viable approach to family politics. First, there is the rather thorny question of whether it is possible to reconcile fully egalitarian relationships with long-term commitment. Friedan claims that equality strengthens the family, but I am unconvinced. I am troubled by the possibility that there are more than 'transitional' contradictions between the goals of emotional intimacy and security and equality in relationships.

Efforts to secure lovers equal access to individual fulfillment appear to place considerable strain on couples' long-term relationships. For heterosexuals, part of the difficulty may derive from the need to struggle for such equality against the profound psychological effects of early childhood socialization for gender asymmetry. But there is some evidence that maintaining long-term commitments within egalitarian relationships is a serious problem for lesbians as well,[65] and I am not convinced that this difficulty would disappear with the last generation of 'patriarchically' socialized individuals. It seems possible that another part of the instability in contemporary primary relationships stems from blurring of clearly demarcated roles and spheres, and this too appears to be at least as significant a problem for lesbians as for heterosexual couples.[66] None of this of course, is reason to abandon the struggle for egalitarian relationships, but it does suggest the need to begin an extensive and probing discussion of our vision. With what, beyond tolerance of instability and diversity, do feminists propose to replace the failing 'modern nuclear family' system? Few of us have faced this issue squarely, and I believe we are paying quite a costly political and personal price for not doing so.[67]

The second, and related, problem that conservative pro-family feminism helps to locate is the need for more developed feminist theories of child development. Resenting the transhistoric female responsibility for unilateral nurturance of children, and perhaps fearing, and thus denying a bit too hastily, the possibility that the needs and interests of contemporary women and children may not be fully compatible, feminist theorists have tended to neglect the question of what children need. But this is an issue that feminists should not, indeed cannot, avoid. Our silence creates a vacuum too readily and inappropriately filled by the likes of Fraiberg, Elshtain, and McMillan, all of whom have contributed to a category of literature that has recently mushroomed in an alarming manner.[68]

Third, feminist theory is vulnerable in its treatment of heterosexuality. We have done a better job of criticizing heterosexuality as institution and practice (and thereby briefly driving analysis of it underground for many feminists) than studying its history or appreciating its complexity and continued vitality, even for feminists.[69] In part this reflects an issue raised at the Tenth Barnard Conference on the Feminist and the Scholar, the idea that, within the movement, heterosexuality among other forms of sexuality has been considered 'politically incorrect'. But the inadequacy of feminist analysis of heterosexuality relates as well to two deeper problems in feminist theory and politics.

The first of these is the matter of 'false consciousness'. Female heterosexuality as well as female antifeminism often are presumed by feminists to be signifiers of false consciousness, the successful products of patriarchal hegemony.[70] But this concept won't do. It is tied to a model of socialization as conditioning that Elshtain and others criticize correctly for portraying women only as victims, robots, or fools. Historically, this perspective on consciousness has fostered arrogance on the part of political theorists toward many among their intended constituencies. Moreover, such a formulation of female consciousness leaves unresolved the contradiction of accounting for feminism itself. How and why does 'true' feminist consciousness arise in the face of 'patriarchal' socialization? Psychoanalytic feminist theory offers an advance over the cruder model of socialization implicit in the 'false consciousness' stance, but thus far few of its practitioners have turned much attention to questions of sexual or political identity. Psychoanalytic theory by itself is not sufficiently grounded in culture and history to develop the sort of theory of consciousness and ideology that we need to counter the conservative retreat.

The second problem conerns the 'subject' of feminism. Is it woman or gender justice? Most, including Elshtain, seem to presume that it is the former, or that the two are indistinguishable. Thus many feminists have adopted a woman-identified stance as the best strategy toward the goal of equality between women and men. But for a good many feminists, woman identification has become an end-in-itself, and one that can lead, as Elshtain argues, to a retreat from politics, or that can evolve into a simple affirmation of femaleness that turns readily into a variation on Elshtain's 'social feminism'. The latter approach tends to ignore, or even to thwart, the goal of gender justice. I believe that those who share my strong preference for the latter goal, and who continue to identify it with the ultimate transcendence of gender as a rigid social tracking system, will have to discard the once-invigorating illusion that feminism speaks for all women. We must accept the likelihood that many women will remain antagonistic to the goal of gender justice no matter what consciousness-raising effort feminists expend. For, contrary to Friedan, I believe there are *at least* two kinds of women (and men) in the United States. Not merely rhetoric, but genuine differences in social values and political interests divide feminists from our opponents.

Conservative pro-family feminist thought makes clear that similar lines of fissure threaten to fracture contemporary feminism from within. Conservative pro-family feminism, having already shifted the terrain of feminist discourse in a more defensive direction, represents an attempt to redefine feminism in a way that undermines its radical potential. I believe that 'old' unreconstructed feminists must forge a political theory and programme that comes to grips with the difficult issues that the new conservative feminism helps to identify, and that only in so doing can we hope to prevail in this important struggle over what feminism will mean in the not-yet-post-feminist period.

Notes

This is an expanded version of 'The New Conservative Feminism', which appeared in *Feminist Studies* 9, No. 3 (Fall 1985).

I am grateful to Donna Haraway for encouraging me to develop the ideas in this article and to the following friends and colleagues for their challenging and helpful reactions to my efforts to do so: Wini Breines, Barbara Epstein, Jane Flax, Arlie Hochschild, Joyce Lindenbaum, Lyn Lofland, Claire Moses, David Plotke, Debbie Rosenfelt, Mary Ryan, Barrie Thorne, and Kay Trimberger. Most of all, I wish to thank Judith Newton for her extraordinarily intelligent and thorough editorial work on the original article.

1 Midge Decter was one of the earliest neoconservatives to attack feminism in *The New Chastity and Other Arguments against Women's Liberation* (Coward McCann, New York, 1972). More recently, a neoconservative 'pro-family' literature has emerged that identifies feminists as major villians in the breakdown of the family. See, for example, Rita Kramer, *In Defense of the Family: Raising Children in America Today* (Basic Books, New York, 1983); and Peter Berger and Brigitte Berger, *The War Over the Family: Capturing the Middle Ground* (Anchor, New York, 1983). Similar themes have appeared on the left. See, for example, Christopher Lasch, *Haven in a Heartless World: The Family Besieged* (Basic Books, New York, 1977); Ivan Illich, *Gender* (Pantheon, New York, 1983); Michael Lerner, Laurie Zoloth, and Wilson Riles, Jr., 'Bringing It All Back Home' (Friends of Families, Insitute for Labor and Mental Health, Oakland, California); and Michael Lerner, 'Mass Psychology and Family Life: A Response to Epstein and Philipson', *Socialist Review* 69 (May-June 1983): 103–10. For a witty response to the Left literature, see the review of Jean Elshtain's books by Arlie Hochschild, 'Is the Left Sick of Feminism?' *Mother Jones*, June 1983, 56–8.

2 Susan Bolotin, 'Voices from the Post-Feminist Generation', *New York Times Magazine*, 17 October 1982, 28–31, 103ff.

3 Alice Rossi, 'A Biosocial Perspective on Parenting', in a special issue on the family in *Daedalus* 106 (Spring 1977). For a critical review of its place in the early stages of the backlash, see Wini Breines, Margaret Cerullo and Judith Stacey, 'Social Biology, Family Studies, and Antifeminist Backlash', *Feminist Studies* 4 (February 1978), 43–67.

4 It is quite difficult to assign a fully satisfactory label to this genre of literature. Zillah Eisenstein calls it 'revisionist feminism' and divides the authors treated here into neoconservative and 'Left Feminist' revisionists. Barbara Ehrenreich has used the *New York Times* epigram 'postfeminist'. My first impulse was to brand this thought 'antifeminist feminism'. There are problems with each of these formulations, however, that lead me to settle for now on 'conservative pro-family feminism'. Revisionist and antifeminist feminism imply the existence of a feminist orthodoxy from which a self-identified feminist can be judged 'objectively' to have departed. Instead I believe that conservative feminism represents a struggle over what feminism will mean in the next

political period. 'Postfeminism', on the other hand, is too broad for my purposes. It includes explicitly antifeminist as well as nonfeminist varieties of backlash thought. The new conservative feminists, I believe, echo 'old' conservative themes present in the domestic feminism of the nineteenth century.

5 See her *Public Man, Private Woman: Woman in Social and Political Thought* (Princeton University Press, Princeton, 1981). Elshtain has also published articles in *The Nation, Dissent, Progressive, Democracy, Telos, Polity, Politics and Society, Salmagundi,* and *Humanities in Society.* Moreover, an article of hers appeared in the feminist theory issue of *Signs,* and she has presented papers as a feminist theorist at conferences such as the Berkshire Conference on the History of Women.

6 Several readers of an earlier draft on this article objected to my including Elshtain within the boundaries of feminism on the grounds that my own critique of her work makes a convincing case for denying her the label. Tempting as I find this stance, I do not think it is adequate. Elshtain is actively contesting for the meaning of the label and has succeeded already in attaining a public identity as a feminist theorist. Moreover, several years ago she published articles with an explicit sympathy for socialist feminism. See, for example, 'The Feminist Movement and the Question of Equality', *Polity* (Summer 1975), 452–77.

7 See, for example, the writings by Lasch, Illich, and Lerner cited in note 1.

8 An acerbic review by Barbara Ehrenreich of Carol McMillan's *Women, Reason, and Nature* (Princeton University Press, Princeton, 1982) provided one of two hostile exchanges between Ehrenreich and Elshtain. See Ehrenreich's 'Are Feminists Sexist?' *The Nation,* 12 February 1983, 180–2; and the exchange of letters, 'Feminists and Sexism' and 'Ehrenreich Responds', *The Nation,* 12 March 1983, 290. Elshtain also endorsed McMillan's book in a lecture she delivered in the Department of Sociology at the University of California, Berkeley, in February 1983.

9 Recently, a number of people have suggested that feminism has lost the dual meaning of the sexual and become a movement strictly for the liberation of gender while the gay liberation movement, particularly the gay male liberation movement, is the contemporary home of a politics for the liberation of sexuality. For variations of this view see Deirdre English, Amber Hollibaugh, and Gayle Rubin, 'Talking Sex: A Conversation on Sexuality and Feminism', *Socialist Review* 58 (July-August 1981), 43–62; Dennis Altman, 'Sex: The New Front Line for Gay Politics', *Socialist Review* 65 (September-October 1982), 75–84; and Edmund White, 'Paradise Found', *Mother Jones,* June 1983, 10–14. I do not think it is quite accurate to separate gender from sexual liberation in this way, however. Feminists have not abandoned the goal of sexual liberation, but are deeply divided over the definition of this goal. For a historical perspective on this division, see Linda Gordon and Ellen Carol DuBois, 'Seeking Ecstasy on the Battlefield: Danger and Pleasure in Nineteenth-Century Feminist Sexual Thought', *Feminist Studies,* 9 (Spring 1983), 7–25.

10 Betty Friedan, *The Second Stage* (Summit Books, New York, 1981), 41.

11 Ibid., 52.
12 Ibid., 228.
13 Ibid., 260–1.
14 Readers may note an apparent contradiction between this positive characterisation of the women's liberation movement and the book's portrait of that movement as propelled by rage and reaction. The contradiction can be reconciled by recognizing Friedan's consistent view of herself as the representative of the mature, responsible, sensible wing of feminism beleaguered by extremists.
15 Thus Friedan has considerable praise for enlightened leadership training being offered to corporate executives and future military leaders at Harvard and Stanford business schools, at West Point, and the Air Force Academy. See Friedan, 243.
16 Zillah Eisenstein, *The Radical Future of Liberal Feminism* (Longman, New York, 1981). As Eisenstein points out, Friedan has resisted the radical implications of feminism from the start. For an analysis of Friedan's development as a neoconservative feminist, see Eistenstein's *Feminism and Sexual Equality* (Monthly Review Press, New York, 1984).
17 Friedan, 319.
18 Jean Bethke Elshtain, 'Feminism, Family, and Community', *Dissent*, Fall 1982, 447.
19 For a book review that discusses some of the contributions and problems in Elshtain's treatment of this theoretical tradition, see Ann M. Lane, 'Public Woman', *Democracy*, July 1982, 107–15.
20 For example, Shulamith Firestone's *The Dialectic of Sex: The Case for Feminist Revolution* is taken to be a significant representative of radical feminist thought. As for distortion, Elshtain interprets Nancy Chodorow's, *The Reproduction of Mothering: Psychoanalysis and the Society of Gender* (University of California Press, Berkeley, 1978) as a brief for collectivized childcare.
21 The exchange between Ehrenreich and Elshtain, 'On Feminism, Family, and Community', appeared in *Dissent*, Winter 1983, 103–9. An additional exchange between Marshall Berman and Elshtain, 'Feminism, Community, Freedom', appeared in *Dissent*, Spring 1983, 247–55. Elshtain's 'Homosexual Politics: The Paradox of Gay Liberation', was published in *On Homosexuality*, a special issue of *Salmagundi* 58–9 (Fall 1982-Winter 1983), 252–80.
22 Christopher Lasch, *Haven in a Heartless World*; Lasch, *The Culture of Narcissism: American Life in an Age of Dimishing Expectations* (W. W. Norton, New York, 1979); Max Horkheimer, 'Authority and the Family', in his *Critical Theory* (Herder & Herder, New York, 1972).
23 As Ehrenreich and Berman both point out, Elshtain does not include feminists or political people in this category.
24 Elshtain, 'Feminism, Family, Community', 442.
25 Elshtain, *Public Man, Private Woman*, 333.
26 Although Elshtain claims she is not opposed to daycare, she never supports it and worries ambiguously about pushing children 'prematurely into a group context'. See *Public Man, Private Woman*, 330.
27 Elshtain never specifies the distinction she draws between the necessary and destructive aspects of gender differentiation.

28 For fuller information on this theme, see Eisenstein, *Radical Future of Liberal Feminism*, and her *Feminism and Sexual Equality*.

29 In fact Elshtain was one of the more conservative frequent contributors to *Democracy*, a journal that articulated the politics of this antisocialist and anticapitalist perspective. For an astute, illuminating evaluation of the first two volumes of *Democracy*, see David Plotke, '*Democracy* on Democracy', *Socialist Review* 74 (March–April 1984).

30 Friedan, 195.

31 Elshtain, *Public Man, Private Woman*, 38.

32 Ibid., 38, n. 42.

33 Ibid., 307.

34 Elshtain, 'Homosexual Politics'.

35 Germaine Greer, *Sex and Destiny: The Politics of Human Fetility* (Harper and Row, New York, 1984).

36 Ibid., 264.

37 Ibid., 265.

38 Ibid., 268.

39 Ibid., 286.

40 Ibid., 286.

41 Ibid., 288.

42 Ibid., 289.

43 Ibid., 294.

44 For example, Elshtain provides an intelligent critique of the feminist anti-pornography and anti-rape movements, but one that exhibits little sympathy for feminist concern with these issues. See 'The Victim Syndrome', *The Progressive*, June 1982, 42–7.

45 On capitalist society, see, for example, Heidi Hartmann, 'Capitalism, Patriarchy, and Job Segregation by Sex', in *Capitalist Patriarchy and the Case for Socialist Feminism* (ed.), Zillah Eisenstein (Monthly Review Press, New York, 1979), 206–47; *The Family in Oneida County, 1790–1865* (Cambridge University Press, New York, 1981). On socialist societies, see Judith Stacey, *Patriarchy and Socialist Revolution in China* (Berkeley and Los Angeles, University of California Press, 1983); Natalie Sokoloff, 'Cuban Women: Strengths and Weaknesses of the Cuban Revolution for Women' paper presented at the American Political Science Association/New Political Caucus annual meeting, New York, September 1981).

46 Sara Ruddick, 'Maternal Thinking', *Feminist Studies* 6 (Summer 1980), 342–67. Ruddick employed this concept in a dialectical effort to develop a female epistemology rooted in the practice of mothering. Elshtain ignores such negative effects of the practice as parochialism, obsessiveness, and conformity.

47 Lane's 'Public Woman' illustrates some of the difficulties with Elshtain's approach to theory.

48 For a sampling of feminist contributions to epistemology, see Julia Sherman and Evelyn T. Beck (eds.), *The Prism of Sex: Essays in the Sociology of Knowledge* (University of Wisconsin Press, Madison, 1979); and Sandra Harding and Merrill B. Hintikka (eds.), *Discovering Reality* (D. Reidel Publishing Co., Hingham, MA, 1983).

49 The quote is from Rayna Rapp, 'Household and Family', in Rayna

Rapp, Ellen Ross, and Renate Bridenthal, 'Examining Family History', *Feminist Studies* 5 (Spring 1979), 181. For a sampling of feminist family deconstruction, see Barrie Thorne (ed.), *Rethinking the Family: Some Feminist Questions* (Longman, New York, 1982); Michele Barrett and Mary McIntosh, *The Anti-Social Family* (Verso, London, 1983); and Sherry Ortner and Harriet Whitehead (eds), *Sexual Meanings: The Cultural Construction of Gender and Sexuality* (Cambridge University Press, Cambridge, 1981). But feminists are not the only scholars involved in this effort. See also Jacques Donzelot, *The Policing of Families* (Pantheon, New York, 1979); Mark Poster, *Critical Theory of the Family* (Seabury, New York, 1978); and Jean-Louis Flandrin, *Families in Former Times: Kinship, Household, and Sexuality* (Cambridge University Press, Cambridge, 1979).

50 Elshtain, *Public Man, Private Woman*, 327. Elshtain's use of evidence in support of this claim borders on the absurd. Archaeological remains of flowers placed in a prehistoric grave indicate, to her, the universality of familial love, while the wild boy of Aveyron and Charles Manson demonstrate the dangers of weak family ties.

51 Carol Stack, *All Our Kin: Strategies for Survival in a Black Community* (Harper and Row, New York, 1974).

52 Nancie Gonzalez, 'The Anthropologist as Female Head of Household', *Feminist Studies* 10, No. 1 (Spring 1984), 97–114.

53 Adam Clymer, 'Poll Shows a Married-Single Gap in Last Election', *New York Times*, 6 January 1983, 10; Maureen Dowd, 'Single Voters Viewed as Supporting Reagan Less', *New York Times*, 16 December 1984, 31.

54 For an uncompromising critique of the family that rests on these grounds, see Barrett and McIntosh. I review this book in 'Should the Family be Saved?' *Socialist Review*, 74 (March-April 1984).

55 Elshtain, 'Homosexual Politics', 265.

56 Friedan, 313. Friedan is unable to identify the source or nature of 'economic-political exploitation', however.

57 This seems incongruent with her sympathy for psychoanalytic thought. However, Elshtain reserves analysis of the internal dynamics of the family for the family as a passive structure. She appears to recognize little human agency in the breakdown of the traditional family, nor does she seem to understand human desires to restructure families or sexuality.

58 Note that McMillan collapses equality and identity. More troubling, she ignores feminist criticisms of 'male' rationalism and Western dualism that are quite similar to her own. See, for example, Susan Griffin, *Woman and Nature: The Roaring Inside Her* (Harper and Row, New York, 1978); Nancy Hartsock, 'The Feminist Standpoint: Developing the Ground for a Specifically Feminist Historical Materialism', in Harding and Hintikka (eds), *Discovering Reality*, 283–310. Moreover, she ignores feminist work that specifically analyzes the rationality and morality of 'female' epistemology such as Ruddick's 'Maternal Thinking' and Carol Gilligan's *In a Different Voice: Psychological Theory and Women's Development* (Harvard University Press, Cambridge, 1982). In fact, McMillan's book is shockingly ignorant of feminist work.

Shulamith Firestone is made to serve as the principal representative of feminist thought.

59 To be sure, McMillan has a more nuanced view of the concept 'natural' than does Elshtain. She views it not as a strictly biological category, but as a culturally mediated one that carries equally imperative social consequences.

60 Feminists, she argues, are wrong to accept the social equation of money and value. Economic dependence, McMillan claims, is not the same as economic weakness. See *Women, Reason, and Nature*, 79.

61 This is a particularly important theme in such literature as Griffin's *Woman and Nature* and Adrienne Rich's *Of Woman Born: Motherhood as Experience and Institution* (W. W. Norton, New York, 1976). It was the impulse behind Rossi's 'Biosocial Perspective'. It also characterizes a good deal of feminist art, such as Judy Chicago's 'The Dinner Party' and Emily Culpepper's film, *Period Piece*.

62 See, for example, Barbara Leslie Epstein, *The Politics of Domesticity: Women, Evangelism, and Temperance in Nineteenth-Century America* (Wesleyan University Press, Middletown, Conn., 1981); Kathryn Kish Sklar, *Catherine Beecher: A Study in American Domesticity* (Yale University Press, New Haven, 1973); and Ellen Carol DuBois, *Feminism and Suffrage: The Emergence of an Independent Women's Movement in America, 1848–1869* (Cornell University Press, Ithaca, 1978).

63 Deidre English, 'The Fear That Feminism Will Free Men First', in *Powers of Desire: The Politics of Sexuality* (eds), Ann Snitow, Christine Stansell and Sharon Thompson (Monthly Review Press, New York, 1984).

64 Germaine Greer, *The Female Eunuch* (McGraw-Hill, New York, 1971), 232.

65 See for example, Joyce Lindenbaum, 'Competition in Lesbian Relationships', *Feminist Studies* (1985, in press).

66 Lindenbaum discusses problems with merging. I wonder too whether recent positive re-evaluations by lesbians of butch-femme role-playing in lesbian relationships might not be fueled partly by an attraction to more clearly demarcated boundaries. See Joan Nestle, 'Butch-Fem Relationships: Sexual Courage in the 1950s', *Heresies* 12 (1981), 21–4.

67 Barrett and McIntosh's *The Anti-Social Family* is an important exception. They directly argue that we should replace the family with nothing. I discuss my reservations about this stance in 'Should the Family Perish?'

68 See, for example, Kramer; Berger and Berger; Valerie Polakow Suransky, *The Erosion of Childhood* (University of Chicago Press, Chicago, 1982); and Marie Winn, 'The Loss of Childhood', *The New York Times Magazine*, 8 May 1983.

69 This has begun to change a bit recently. See Jane Lazarre, *On Loving Men* (Dial Press, New York, 1980); and Ellen Kay Trimberger, 'Feminism, Men, and Modern Love: Greenwich Village 1900–1925', in *Powers of Desire*.

70 This is the analysis of female heterosexuality, for example, in Adrienne Rich's extremely popular essay, 'Compulsory Heterosexuality and Lesbian Existence', *Signs* 5 (Spring 1980), 631–60.

Index